CW01583620

Handbook of FORENSIC TOXICOLOGY for MEDICAL EXAMINERS

D. K. Molina, M.D.

CRC Press
Taylor & Francis Group
Boca Raton London New York

CRC Press is an imprint of the
Taylor & Francis Group, an **informa** business

CRC SERIES IN
PRACTICAL ASPECTS OF CRIMINAL AND FORENSIC INVESTIGATIONS

VERNON J. GEBERTH, BBA, MPS, FBINA *Series Editor*

Practical Homicide Investigation: Tactics, Procedures, and Forensic Techniques, Fourth Edition
Vernon J. Geberth

The Counterterrorism Handbook: Tactics, Procedures, and Techniques, Third Edition
Frank Bolz, Jr., Kenneth J. Dudonis, and David P. Schulz

Forensic Pathology, Second Edition
Dominick J. Di Maio and Vincent J. M. Di Maio

Interpretation of Bloodstain Evidence at Crime Scenes, Second Edition
William G. Eckert and Stuart H. James

Tire Imprint Evidence
Peter McDonald

Practical Drug Enforcement, Third Edition
Michael D. Lyman

Practical Aspects of Rape Investigation: A Multidisciplinary Approach, Third Edition
Robert R. Hazelwood and Ann Wolbert Burgess

The Sexual Exploitation of Children: A Practical Guide to Assessment, Investigation, and Intervention, Second Edition
Seth L. Goldstein

Gunshot Wounds: Practical Aspects of Firearms, Ballistics, and Forensic Techniques, Second Edition
Vincent J. M. Di Maio

Friction Ridge Skin: Comparison and Identification of Fingerprints
James F. Cowger

Footwear Impression Evidence, Second Edition
William J. Bodziak

Principles of Kinesic Interview and Interrogation, Second Edition
Stan Walters

Practical Fire and Arson Investigation, Second Edition
David R. Redsicker and John J. O'Connor

The Practical Methodology of Forensic Photography, Second Edition
David R. Redsicker

Practical Aspects of Interview and Interrogation, Second Edition
David E. Zulawski and Douglas E. Wicklander

Investigating Computer Crime
Franklin Clark and Ken Diliberto

Practical Homicide Investigation Checklist and Field Guide
Vernon J. Geberth

Bloodstain Pattern Analysis: With an Introduction to Crime Scene Reconstruction, Second Edition
Tom Bevel and Ross M. Gardner

Practical Aspects of Munchausen by Proxy and Munchausen Syndrome Investigation
Kathryn Artingstall

Quantitative-Qualitative Friction Ridge Analysis: An Introduction to Basic and Advanced Ridgeology
David R. Ashbaugh

Practical Criminal Investigations in Correctional Facilities
William R. Bell

Officer-Involved Shootings and Use of Force: Practical Investigative Techniques
David E. Hatch

Sex-Related Homicide and Death Investigation: Practical and Clinical Perspectives
Vernon J. Geberth

Global Drug Enforcement: Practical Investigative Techniques
Gregory D. Lee

Practical Investigation of Sex Crimes: A Strategic and Operational Approach
Thomas P. Carney

Principles of Bloodstain Pattern Analysis: Theory and Practice
Stuart James, Paul Kish, and T. Paulette Sutton

Cold Case Homicides: Practical Investigative Techniques
Richard H. Walton

Practical Crime Scene Processing and Investigation
Ross M. Gardner

Practical Bomb Scene Investigation
James T. Thurman

Practical Analysis and Reconstruction of Shooting Incidents
Edward E. Hueske

CRC Press
Taylor & Francis Group
6000 Broken Sound Parkway NW, Suite 300
Boca Raton, FL 33487-2742

Printed in the United States of America on acid-free paper
10 9 8 7 6 5 4 3 2 1

International Standard Book Number: 978-1-4200-7641-7 (Hardback)

Library of Congress Cataloging-in-Publication Data

Molina, D. K.
Handbook of forensic toxicology for medical examiners / D.K. Molina.
p. ; cm. -- (CRC series in practical aspects of criminal and forensic investigations)
Includes bibliographical references and index.
ISBN 978-1-4200-7641-7 (hardcover : alk. paper)
1. Forensic toxicology--Handbooks, manuals, etc. 2. Medical examiners (Law)--Handbooks, manuals, etc. I. Title. II. Series: CRC series in practical aspects of criminal and forensic investigations.
[DNLM: 1. Forensic Toxicology--methods. 2. Pharmacokinetics. W 750 M722h 2010]

RA1228.M65 2010
614'.13--dc22 2009021589

Visit the Taylor & Francis Web site at
http://www.taylorandfrancis.com

and the CRC Press Web site at
http://www.crcpress.com

Table of Contents

Series Editor's Note

This book is part of a series entitled *Practical Aspects of Criminal and Forensic Investigation.* This series was created by Vernon J. Geberth, New York City Police Department Lieutenant Commander (Retired), who is an author, educator, and consultant on homicide and forensic investigations. This series, written by authors who are nationally recognized experts in their respective fields, has been designed to provide contemporary, comprehensive, and pragmatic information to the practitioner involved in criminal and forensic investigations.

Acknowledgment

The author would like to thank Dr. Vincent J. DiMaio, for his support, teaching, and inspiration, and Sherron Tucker for her assistance with manuscript preparation.

Contributor

Veronica M. Hargrove assisted Dr. Molina with a great deal of the background research and review necessary to complete this book. She has a Masters of Science degree in toxicology from the University of Texas Health Science Center in San Antonio and is certified as a Forensic Toxicology Specialist by the American Board of Forensic Toxicology. She is currently employed as a toxicology chemist at the Bexar County Medical Examiner's Office in San Antonio, Texas.

Author's Note

It is important to note that the purpose of this book is to assist forensic professionals in the interpretation of common toxicology results. Forensic toxicology not only encompasses the identification and quantification of drugs, but also the meaning of those drugs in the setting of death: Did the drug cause death? Contribute to death? Is it unrelated? This book is in no way meant to substitute for a thorough death investigation and complete autopsy, as toxicology results should never be interpreted in a vacuum. Interpretation of toxicology results depends on a multitude of factors including the time since death/intoxication, the possibility of tolerance, and the presence or absence of other drugs that may lead to interactions and toxicity even if all of the drugs present are within the "therapeutic range."

The concentrations given in this book are a compilation of the data in the literature, mostly coming from case reports. Articles were chosen based on scientific merit and the lack of confounding factors in causing the death or toxicity; thus, some sources listed in other texts are not considered here. The lethal and toxic cases listed represent pure, single drug intoxications unless otherwise noted. The therapeutic/nontoxic concentrations given were usually determined in the healthy living population during pharmacokinetic studies, although some concentrations reflect postmortem data from individuals dying of unrelated causes who were known to be taking therapeutic doses of the medication.

The half-life and volume of distribution are given, when known, as this data may assist in the interpretation of the values obtained. Pounder* argues that drugs with a volume of distribution greater than 3 L/kg may show significant postmortem redistribution, and samples from sites other than peripheral blood may require more scrutiny.

The book includes common drugs of abuse, poisons, and prescription and over-the-counter medications. It is not meant to be comprehensive; it is meant, as the title suggests, as a quick reference. Should you desire a more comprehensive approach, there are several in-depth toxicology texts available, but this book serves a different purpose.

* Pounder DJ (1994), The nightmare of postmortem drug changes, in CH Wecht (Ed.) *Legal Medicine*. Lexis Law, Albany, NY, pp. 163–93.

List of Abbreviations Used

ABFT: American Board of Forensic Toxicology
aceta: acetaminophen
ASA: aspirin
BAC: blood alcohol (ethanol) content
bid: twice a day
d: day
g: gram
gtts: drops
hrs: hours
im: intramuscular
iv: intravenous
kg: kilogram
L: liter
λ: half-life
mEq: milli-equivalent
mg: milligram
min: minute
mL: milliliter
mos: months
μg: microgram
NAME: National Association of Medical Examiners
ng: nanogram
NRI: norepinephrine reuptake inhibitor
NSAID: non-steroidal anti-inflammatory
OTC: over the counter
po: by mouth (per os)
pr: per rectum
prn: as needed
q: every
qam: in the morning
qd: once a day
qHS: at bedtime
qid: four times a day
sc: subcutaneous
SNRI: serotonin and norepinephrine reuptake inhibitor

SSRI: selective serotonin reuptake inhibitor
supp: suppository
susp: suspension
TCA: tricyclic antidepressant
tid: three times a day
V_d: volume of distribution
w/: with
wk: week
yr: year

Collection and Selection of Toxicologic Specimens 1

> The proper selection, collection, and submission of specimens for toxicological analysis is of paramount importance if analytical results are to be accurate and their subsequent interpretation is to be scientifically sound and therefore useful in the adjudication of forensic cases.
>
> **Forensic Toxicology Laboratory Guidelines (2006)**

Most postmortem cases contain a plethora of specimens available for toxicologic analysis, but it is important to know which specimens are most useful for yielding drug concentrations that are practical for interpretation. Not all specimens may be available in all cases. For instance, decomposed bodies may no longer have blood, yet may have vitreous, urine, and tissue. Victims of high-velocity trauma (i.e., plane crashes, explosions) may have very limited specimen selection as only muscle or other tissue may be obtainable. The purpose of this chapter is to give a brief overview of the types of specimens available, the utility of the each specimen, and the collection criteria.

Types of Specimens and Utility

Blood

Blood is the most common and preferable sample to use, when possible. The majority of data reported regarding the therapeutic and toxic concentrations of drugs was obtained from blood specimens. Blood is a relatively easy sample to obtain and store. For postmortem studies, peripheral blood is more desirable than central blood as it is less affected by postmortem redistribution. It is usually recommended that femoral blood be obtained preferentially, followed by subclavian, heart and, lastly, cavity blood. Unfortunately, in cases of severe trauma or decomposition, blood may not be available.

Urine

Urine, when present, is also relatively easy to obtain and store. Urine is good as a screening sample, especially with immunoassays, as it tends to have less interfering substances. Drug concentrations in urine do not accurately reflect the corresponding blood concentrations or intoxication level as the concentration may reflect a drug that was ingested many hours, and sometimes days, prior to death. Urine can be used as a second sample for confirmation of a drug's presence.

Vitreous

Vitreous is an excellent specimen to use in the absence of blood. It is isolated, which prevents contamination and allows for greater resistance to the changes of decomposition. It also demonstrates good stability. The main limitation of its routine use is that it is available only in a limited quantity, usually less than 5 mL, and is the most useful specimen for postmortem chemistries. Drug concentrations in vitreous usually reflect the blood levels at about 1–2 hrs prior to death. Metabolites with short half-lives, which are eliminated from the blood quickly, can often be found in the vitreous due to the isolation and lack of metabolic enzymes. For example, 6-monoacetylmorphine (6-MAM) can be found in heroin overdoses even after the 6-MAM has been metabolized from the blood. Vitreous is an excellent specimen for water-soluble substances including ethanol (for which it is often used as the confirmatory specimen), barbiturates, and carbamates.

Bile

Bile is usually not a first-line specimen but can be useful in certain circumstances. With the commonality of cholecystectomies, bile is not always present, and when it is available, it is usually in limited quantities, typically less than 10 mL. Certain drugs are concentrated in the bile, for example, narcotics and benzodiazepines, which can be helpful but can also make interpretation of elevated concentrations difficult.

Tissue Specimens

Tissue samples are usually readily available in large quantities; however, interpretation of drug concentration can be difficult since data is not often available for comparison. Tissue concentrations may also be elevated in oral overdoses and chronically administered drugs.

Muscle

Muscle is a preferred tissue sample as research has shown very good correlation between drug concentrations found in muscle with those found in blood. Unfortunately, published reports on muscle drug levels for comparison are not in abundance as yet.

Liver

Liver has long been used as a secondary sample when blood is not available. Among published studies, liver probably has the most data available for comparison of postmortem drug concentrations. Some drugs, such as tricyclic antidepressants, are sequestered in the liver, resulting in higher levels than in the blood. Liver concentrations may also be higher if the drug was taken orally or if it undergoes hepatic metabolism. In cases of hepatic metabolism, higher concentrations of the metabolites will often be seen in comparison to lower concentrations of the parent drug, which may indicate chronic use versus an acute overdose.

Kidney

Kidney specimens may be used as any other tissue specimens, although the utility of the kidney specimens is mainly in heavy-metal testing as metals often accumulate in the kidney.

Brain

Brain is an alternative tissue specimen for which some, though limited, data is available.

Lung

Lung is a useful tissue specimen for inhaled toxins such as volatile compounds including the halogenated hydrocarbons.

Spleen

Spleen is often utilized as an alternative source for blood in cases of carbon monoxide poisoning.

Adipose Tissue

Fat is an excellent specimen for pesticide poisonings and volatile analysis.

Stomach Contents

Stomach contents are often collected in cases where an oral drug overdose is suspected. Concentrations of drugs in the stomach, however, do not accurately represent the concentration of the drug in the body. The presence of a drug in gastric material, even at elevated concentrations, may not indicate that the drug contributed to death. Stomach contents may be useful in specifying that the blood should be analyzed for a particular drug, which may have been overlooked or not seen without special testing.

Hair

Hair is an excellent screening source for arsenic poisoning and is becoming more commonly used to screen for the chronic use of illicit drugs, including morphine, cocaine, and amphetamines. Hair samples are not routinely used in the postmortem setting as medical examiners are often interested in the drug concentration at the time of death; though hair is often used in the setting of forensic drug testing/performance testing. Drugs can be deposited in hair as it grows, allowing hair samples to yield information about drug intake over a period of months to years, depending on the length of hair sampled (as a general rule, hair grows approximately 10–15 mm per month).

Specimen Collection

Blood

Blood samples should be collected with a new syringe and clean needle. If blood is collected blindly from the femoral or subclavian vessels, it is recommended that a short (1½ inch), large bore needle be used to limit possible contamination from the esophagus or chest cavities, as can occur with use of a longer needle. A minimum of 60 mL of blood should be collected into various tubes for processing. It is recommended that the following amounts be collected into the indicated glass tubes, as drugs can bind to the polymers of plastic tubes:

- One 20 mL red top tube (no preservative) for serology testing.
- Two 10 mL gray top tubes (sodium fluoride as a preservative and potassium oxalate as an anticoagulant) for toxicology testing. The fluoride inhibits *in vitro* metabolism of drugs, especially cocaine.
- Two 10 mL purple top tubes (EDTA preservative) for DNA analysis or genetic studies.

If volatile intoxication is suspected, a 10 ml glass tube with a Teflon-lined screw top is necessary to prevent diffusion of the volatile compounds through a rubber stopper.

Urine

A new syringe and clean needle should be used to collect 10–20 mL of urine, if present, into a red top tube.

Bile

A new syringe and clean needle should be used to collect all the available bile—usually 2–10 mL, when present—into a red top tube.

Vitreous

A new syringe and clean needle should be used to collect all the available vitreous—usually 2–4 mL—into a red top tube.

Tissue

Tissue specimens should be collected with a clean blade and placed in a new, unused specimen container. At least 50 g of tissue is necessary. Muscle samples should preferentially be obtained from an extremity to limit contamination. The quadricep muscle is often used due to its size and accessible location. It is recommended that when the liver is used, the sample be obtained from the deep right lobe to limit contamination from the stomach and intestines. Lung samples should be taken from the apex.

Hair

A clean, unused razor should be used to shave at least 100–200 mg of hair from the body. The hair can then be placed in a new, unused, dry specimen container.

Labeling and Storage

Per the National Association of Medical Examiner accreditation guidelines, it is recommended that samples be labeled with: the type of specimen (i.e., blood, urine); the site of collection (i.e., femoral, subclavian); the case number; the time and date of collection; the name of deceased; and the names of the medical examiner and person collecting the sample (if different). Samples should be immediately refrigerated or frozen until ready for transport to the toxicology laboratory.

Selected Sources

DiMaio VJ and DiMaio D (2001), Chapter 23, Interpretive toxicology: Drug abuse and drug deaths, in *Forensic Pathology Second Edition*, CRC Press, New York.

Forensic Toxicology Laboratory Guidelines 2006 Version, American Board of Forensic Toxicology and Society of Forensic Toxicologists, available at http://www.soft-tox.org/?pn=publications&sp=Laboratory_Guidelines.

Garriott JC (1994), Forensic toxicology for the general pathologist, in Weinstein RS and Gram AR, *Advances in Pathology and Laboratory Medicine,* Vol. 7, Mosby Year Book, St. Louis, MO, pp. 313–339.

Levine B (Ed.) (2002), *Principles of Forensic Toxicology*, American Association for Clinical Chemistry, Washington, DC, USA.

NAME Accreditation Checklist, National Association of Medical Examiners, available at http://thename.org.

Methodology 2

In forensic toxicology, there are two types of tests: screening tests and confirmatory tests. Samples are usually first screened for the presence of medications and/or intoxicating substances, then a more specific, confirmatory test is performed to determine the exact substance and, often, concentration. A confirmatory test should be a different methodology from the screening test and should be run on a different sample/specimen, if possible.

Prior to testing of any sort, the first step is preparation. For many methodologies, the drugs must be separated from the organic matrix in which they are suspended. This can be accomplished by heat, protein precipitation, liquid–liquid extraction, or solid phase extraction. In the postmortem setting, protein precipitation and liquid–liquid extractions are the most commonly used techniques.

Screening Tests

Immunoassay

Use: Can be used to screen for a large number of drugs; can be qualitative or semiquantitative.

Basic Principle: An antibody is designed to react against a particular drug or drug class. The specimen to be tested is combined with the antibody; the antibody binds to the drug in question, yielding a positive screen if the drug is present. If the sample is combined with a known amount of labeled antigen, competitive binding can occur between the antibody, the known amount of labeled antigen, and the unknown amount of drug. The antibody–antigen reaction is then measured, allowing for a semiquantitative determination of the amount of drug present.

Types:

- Radioimmunoassay (RIA).
- Enzyme multiplied immunoassay (EMIT).
- Fluorescent polarization immunoassays (FPIA).
- Kinetic interaction of microparticles in solution (KIMS).
- Enzyme linked immunosorbent assay (ELISA).

Advantages: Relatively easy to use and to perform; requires minimal, if any, sample preparation; good sensitivity even at low concentrations; can be performed using very small sample amounts.

Disadvantages: Limited specificity as can have cross-reactivity between drug(s) and structurally similar compounds; interfering substances may be present within the biological matrix, yielding either false positive or false negative results; requires that an assay has been developed and is available for the desired drug. Urine is the preferred matrix as it has less interfering substances than blood.

Spectrophotometry

Use: Not commonly used except for the determination of carboxyhemoglobin; historically also used for barbiturates and salicylates.

Basic Principle: Molecules will absorb/distort light of different wavelengths in particular ways. A spectrophotometer can measure the changes in the wavelength of light passing through a substance to determine the presence or absence of certain molecules within the matrix.

Types:

- Ultraviolet (UV).
- Visible spectra.
- Infrared (IR).

Advantages: Ease of use.

Disadvantages: Lack of sensitivity and specificity.

Chromatography

Use: When combined with a detector, can be used as a screening test for a large number of drugs.

Basic Principle: Drugs are dissolved into a mobile phase (gas or liquid), which is then passed through a stationary phase (i.e., a column) allowing for separation and isolation of the constituents of the sample. The time taken to traverse the stationary phase is recorded by a paired detector and compared to an internal standard, allowing for detection of each component within the sample.

Types:

- Gas (GC): Uses time to traverse a packed column in a gas matrix; usually paired with a flame ionization detector or nitrogen phosphorous detector for identification.
- Liquid (LC): Uses migration distance in a liquid matrix; can be used on a solid media (Thin Layer) or liquid (HPLC); most commonly paired with ultraviolet detector but can also be paired

with fluorescence or electrochemical refractive detectors for identification.

Advantages: Can vary packing material, temperature, mobile phase components, and flow rate to adjust sensitivity and specificity; can be paired with a detector to increase specificity; HPLC is run at normal temperatures (unlike GC which is run at elevated temperatures), and may preserve heat-labile components.

Disadvantages: Time consuming; requires significant sample preparation; equipment expensive.

Confirmatory Tests

Confirmatory tests are performed when a drug has been identified by one of the screening tests. Confirmatory tests should be performed by a different methodology than the screening test and on a different sample, if possible, or, at least, a different extract of the same sample. The confirmatory test should also be more specific than the screening test. The gold standard for confirmatory testing in forensic toxicology is GC or LC paired with mass spectrometry. This paired method allows for mass spectral analysis of analytes after they have been separated and isolated by chromatography. Mass spectrometry is accomplished by fragmenting a molecule by a barrage of electrons and then analyzing the relative abundance of the fragments (electron ionization) or by ionizing molecules and analyzing the charge transference (chemical ionization).

If mass spectrometry is not available, the American Board of Forensic Toxicology (ABFT) allows for confirmation by the same system as identification as long as a different chemical derivatization and column and, thus, retention time is used. However, this is not recommended by the ABFT and may face scrutiny in a court of law. Confirmation of an immunoassay with another immunoassay is never acceptable.

Testing Panels

Most forensic toxicology laboratories offer five basic screening tests to determine the presence or absence of the majority of forensically significant drugs. These panels include (listed with examples of the drugs/drug types found):

Lower alcohols: methanol, isopropanol, acetone, ethanol

Acid/neutral: barbiturates; meprobamate/carisoprodol; NSAIDs (ibuprofen, naproxen), salicylic acid, acetaminophen; valproic acid and phenytoin

Basic (alkaline): psychoactive medications (antidepressants, antipsychotics); methamphetamine/amphetamine/MDMA; benzodiazepines; antihistamines
Cocaine: cocaine, benzoylecgonine, ecgonine methyl ester
Narcotics: morphine, monoacetylmorphine, hydrocodone, codeine

Additional Testing

Additional testing may be available for THC or other specific drugs. Some substances require special testing procedures for identification. For example, digoxin is detected by RIA and carbon monoxide by UV spectrophotometry or Conway diffusion (semiquantitative). Screens for heavy metals are not uncommonly performed in postmortem cases and can be accomplished by multiple methods, including special atomic absorption, inductively coupled plasma mass spectroscopy (ICP-MS), and neutron activation. The Reinsch test can also be used to determine the presence of arsenic, antimony, bismuth, and mercury. It is recommended that the particular forensic laboratory be contacted regarding any specific requirements.

Selected Sources

Levine B (Ed.) (2002), *Principles of Forensic Toxicology*, American Association for Clinical Chemistry, Washington, DC, USA.
DiMaio VJ and DiMaio D (2001), Chapter 23, Interpretive toxicology: Drug abuse and drug deaths, in *Forensic Pathology Second Edition,* CRC Press. New York.
Garriott JC (1994), Forensic toxicology for the general pathologist, in Weinstein RS and Gram AR, *Advances in Pathology and Laboratory Medicine*, Vol. 7. Mosby Year Book, St. Louis, MO, USA, pp. 313–339.

3 Alphabetical Listing of Drugs

Acetaminophen

Brand names: Tylenol
Classification: analgesic
λ: 1.2–3 hrs
V_d: 0.83–1.1 L/kg
Usual dosage: 500–1000 mg q 4–6 hrs

Source	Therapeutic/ Nontoxic	Toxic	Lethal
Blood	5–26 mg/L	30–300 mg/L	160–1280 mg/L
Vitreous			779–878 mg/L
Urine			180–1780 mg/L
Bile			180–900 mg/L
Liver			220–3260 mg/kg
Kidney			93–188 mg/kg
Brain			220 mg/kg
Skeletal muscle			179 mg/kg
Stomach contents			105–11500 mg

Comments

- Metabolized by CYP 1A2 and 2E1
- Overdoses treated with acetylcysteine
- Causes hepatic necrosis; death usually occurs 3–5 days after ingestion

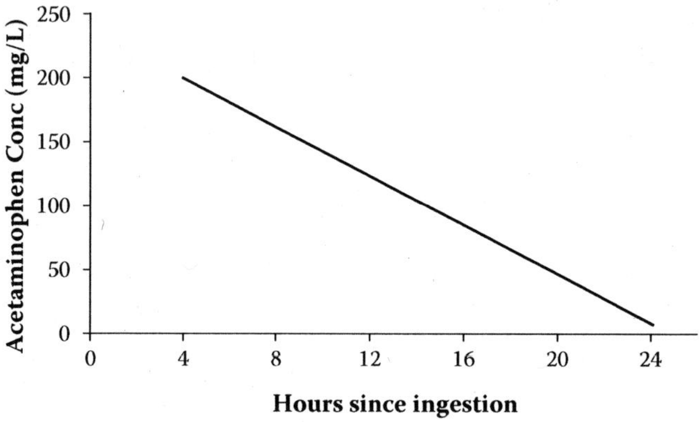

Figure 3.1

- Concentration is interpreted based on time since ingestion
  - Concentrations above the line are indicative of probable hepatotoxicity
  - Concentrations below the line indicate a low risk for hepatotoxicity

Selected Sources

Bexar County Medical Examiner's Office data 1996–2007.

Holzbecher M, Perry RA, and Ellenberger HS (1984), Acetaminophen fatality—A case report, *Can Soc For Sci J*, 17: 32–3.

Jackson CH, MacDonald NC, and Cornett JW (1984), Acetaminophen: A practical pharmacologic overview, *Can Med Assoc J*, 131(1): 25–32.

Robinson AE, Sattar H, McDowall RD, Holder AT, and Powell R (1977), Forensic toxicology of some deaths associated with the combined use of propoxyphene and acetaminophen (paracetamol), *J For Sci*, 22(4): 708–17.

Rumack BH and Matthew H (1975), Acetaminophen poisoning and toxicity, *Pediatrics*, 55(6): 871–6.

Singer PP, Jones GR, Bannach BG, and Denmark L (2007), Acute fatal acetaminophen overdose without liver necrosis, *J For Sci*, 52(4): 992–4.

Acetone

Brand names: component of nail polish remover and industrial solvents
Classification: solvent
λ: 3–6 hrs
V_d: 0.45–0.64 L/kg
Usual dosage: not applicable

Source	Therapeutic/ Nontoxic	Toxic	Lethal
Blood	0.84–20 mg/L	100–400 mg/L	550 mg/L
Urine	0.84 mg/L		

Comments

- Metabolite of isopropanol
- Can be used as an inhalant
- Can be increased in diabetic/fasting states, ranging from:
  - 60–94 mg/L blood
  - 60–90 mg/L urine
  - 60–166 mg/L vitreous
  - Can be as high as 700 mg/L in diabetic ketoacidosis

Selected Sources

Ashley DL, Bonin MA, Cardinali FL, McCraw JM, and Wooten JV (1994), Blood concentrations of volatile compounds in a nonoccupationally exposed US population and in groups with suspected exposure, *Clin Chem*, 40(7 Pt 2): 1401–4.

Bexar County Medical Examiner's Office data 1996–2007.

DiMaio VJ and DiMaio D (2001), *Forensic Pathology Second Edition*, CRC Press. Boca Raton, FL, p. 536.

Ernstgard L, Sjogren B, Warholm M, and Johanson G (2003), Sex differences in the toxicokinetics of inhaled solvent vapors in humans 2. 2-propanol, *Toxicol Appl Pharmacol.* 193(2):158–67.

Kostusiak V, Bekkal R, and Mateu P (2003), Survival after drinking lethal doses of acetone, *Intensive Care Med*, 29(2): 339.

Schulz M and Schmoldt A (2003), Therapeutic and toxic blood concentrations of more than 800 drugs and other xenobiotics, *Pharmazie*, 58(7): 447–74.

Wang G, Mannelli G, Perbellini L, Rainier E, and Brugnane F (1994), Blood acetone concentration in "normal people" and in exposed workers 16 hours after the end of the workshift, *Intl Arch Occupational and Environmental Health*, 65(5): 285–9.

Acetylmethadol

Brand names: Orlaam, LAAM, LAM
Classification: narcotic
λ: 35–100 hrs
V_d: unknown
Usual dosage: 20–120 mg q 48–72 hrs

Source	Therapeutic/ Nontoxic	Toxic	Lethal
Blood	0.05–0.13 mg/L	No data available	

Comments

- Reacts with antiretroviral medications increasing risk for toxicity

Selected Sources

Finkle BS, Jennison TA, Chinn DM, Ling W, and Holmes ED (1982), Plasma and urine disposition of 1-alpha-acetylemathadol and its principal metabolites in man, *J Anal Tox*, 6(2): 100–5.

Hendersaon GL, Wilson BK, and Lau DH (1977), Plasma 1-alpha-acetylemathadol (LAMM) after acute and chronic administration, *Clin Pharmacol Ther*, 21(1): 16–25.

Acetylsalicylic Acid

Brand names: Aspirin (Bayer, Ecotrin)
Classification: NSAID
λ: 15–20 min
V_d: 0.15–0.2 L/kg
Usual dosage: 325–650 mg q 4–6 hrs

Source	Therapeutic/ Nontoxic[a]	Toxic[a]	Lethal[a]
Blood	45–300 mg/L	300–1100 mg/L	400–7320 mg/L
Vitreous	93 mg/L		228 mg/L
Urine			380–1350 mg/L
Liver			258–1000 mg/kg
Kidney			300–1200 mg/kg
Brain			131–700 mg/kg
Skeletal muscle	28–260 mg/kg		663 mg/kg
Stomach contents			140227 mg/L

[a] All concentrations given are for salicylic acid.

Comments

- Rapidly metabolized to salicylic acid (λ 2–19 hrs; V_d 0.1–0.2 L/kg)
- May cause sudden death in asthmatics, regardless of concentration
- May cause Reye's syndrome in children

Selected Sources

Bexar County Medical Examiner's Office data 1996–2007.

Caplan YH, Ottinger WE, and Crooks CR (1983), Therapeutic and toxic drug concentrations in post mortem blood: A six year study in the State of Maryland, *J Anal Tox*, 7(5): 225–30.

Irey NS and Froede RC (1974), Evaluation of deaths from drug overdose: A clinicopathologic study, *Am J Clin Path*, 61(6): 778–84.

Paterson SC (1985), Drug levels found in cases of fatal self-poisoning, *For Sci Intl*, 27(2):129–33.

Levy G (1978), Clinical pharmacokinetics of aspirin, *Pediatrics*, 62(5: 2 Suppl): 867–72.

Rainsford KD (1984), *Aspirin and the Salicylates*, Butterworths, Boston.

Rehling CJ (1967), Poison residues in human tissues in *Progress in Chemical Toxicology*, *Vol 3*, Stolman A (Ed.), Academic Press, London, pp. 363–86.

Rumble RH, Brooks PM, and Roberts MS (1980), Metabolism of salicylate during chronic aspirin therapy, *Br J Clin Pharm*, 9(1): 41–5.

Acrivastine

Brand names: Benadryl Plus, Benadryl Allergy, Semprex D (with pseudoephedrine)
Classification: antihistamine
λ: 2–4 hrs
V_d: 0.6 L/kg
Usual dosage: 2–32 mg tid

Source	Therapeutic/ Nontoxic	Toxic	Lethal
Blood	0.07–0.19 mg/L	No data available	

Selected Sources

Balasubramanian R, Klein KB, Pittman AW, Liao SH, Findlay JW, and Frosolono MF (1989), Pharmacokinetics of acrivastine after oral and colonic administration, *J Clin Pharm*, 29(5): 444–7.

Chang SY, Nelson FR, Findlay JW, and Taylor LC (1989), Quantitative gas chromatographic-mass spectrometric analysis of acrivastine and a metabolite in human plasma, *J Chromatogr*, 29(497): 288–95.

Cohen AF, Hamilton MJ, Liao SH, Findlay JW, and Peck AW (1985), Pharmacodynamic and pharmacokinetics of BW 825C: A new antihistamine, *Eur J Clin Pharm*, 28(2): 197–204.

Simons FER and Simons KJ (1999), Clinical pharmacology of new histamine H receptor antagonists, *Clin Pharmacokinetics*, 36(5): 329–52.

Albuterol

Brand names: Proventil, Ventolin
Alternate names: salbutamol
Classification: β agonist
λ: 2–6 hrs
V_d: 1.3–2.7 L/kg
Usual dosage: Inhaled: two inhalations q 4–6 hrs
Oral: 2–4 mg tid/qid; 0.1–0.2 mg/kg/dose

Source	Therapeutic/ Nontoxic	Toxic	Lethal
Blood	0.001–0.06 mg/L	0.02–0.45 mg/L	See comments

Comments

- Fatalities usually attributed to asthma rather than drug overdose

Selected Sources

Bexar County Medical Examiner's Office data 1996–2007.
Couper FJ and Drummer OH (1999), Postmortem stability and interpretation of β_2 agonist concentrations, *J For Sci*, 44(3): 523–6.
Lewis LD, Essex E, Volans GN, and Cochrane GM (1993), A study of self poisoning with oral salbutamol—Laboratory and clinical features, *Hum Exper Tox*, 12(5): 397–401.
Lewis LD, McLaren M, Essex E, and Cochrane GM (1990) Plasma concentrations of salbutamol in acute severe asthmatics, *Australian New Zealand J Med*, 20(3): 204–7.
Physicians' Desk Reference 61 Edition (2007), Thomson PDR, Montvale, NJ, p. 3055.

Alfentanil

Brand names: Alfenta
Alternate names: alphamethylfentanyl
Classification: narcotic
λ: 1–2 hrs
V_d: 0.3–1 L/kg
Usual dosage: 8–75 μg/kg im/iv

Source	Therapeutic/ Nontoxic	Toxic	Lethal
Blood	0.03–0.48 mg/L	0.09–0.1 mg/L	0.03 mg/L
Bile			0.06 mg/L
Liver			0.08 mg/kg

Comments

- Therapeutic concentrations can be fatal if drug not administered in a monitored medical setting
- Causes respiratory depression and decreased heart rate
- Commonly used for surgical anesthesia

Selected Sources

Gillespie TJ, Gandolfi AJ, Davis TP, and Morano RA (1982), Identification and quantification of alpha-methylfentanyl in post mortem specimens, *J Anal Tox*, 6(3): 139–42.

Mahla ME, White SE, and Moneta MD (1988), Delayed respiratory depression after alfentanil, *Anesthesiology*, 69(4): 593–5.

Michiels M, Hendriks R, and Heykants J (1983), Radioimmunoassay of the new opiate analgesics alfentanil and sufentanil: Preliminary pharmacokinetic profile in man, *J Pharm Pharmacol*, 35(2), 86–93.

Sebel RS, Lalor JM, Flynn PJ, and Simpson BA (1984), Respiratory depression after alfentanil infusion, *Brit Med J (Clin Res Ed.)*, 289: 1581–2.

Stanski DR (1987), The clinical pharmacology of alfentanil, *Eur J Anaesthesiology—Supplement*, 1: 3–11.

Stanski DR and Hug CC (1982), Alfentanil—A kinetically predictable narcotic analgesic, *Anesthesiology*, 57(6): 435–8.

Alprazolam

Brand names: Xanax
Classification: benzodiazepine
λ: 6–27 hrs
V_d: 0.9–1.3 L/kg
Usual dosage: 0.25–0.5 mg tid

Source	Therapeutic/ Nontoxic	Toxic	Lethal
Blood	0.002–0.07 mg/L	0.04–0.6 mg/L	0.13–2.1 mg/L
Vitreous			0.6 mg/L
Urine			1.0 mg/L
Bile			2.8 mg/L
Liver			0.2–9.2 mg/kg
Kidney			3.8 mg/kg
Stomach contents			13 mg

Comments

- Tolerance can develop and should be considered when interpreting drug concentrations
- Sudden withdrawal can cause seizures and death
- Metabolized by CYP 3A

Selected Sources

Bexar County Medical Examiner's Office data 1996–2007.

Glue P, Fang A, Gandelman K, and Klee B (2006), Pharmacokinetics of an extended release formulation of alprazolam (Xanax XR) in healthy normal adolescent and adult volunteers, *Am J Ther*, 13(5): 418–22.

Jenkins AJ, Levine B, Locke JL, and Smialek JE (May–June 1997), A fatality due to alprazolam intoxication, *J Anal Toxicol*, 21(3): 218–20.

Physicians' Desk Reference 61 Edition (2007), Thomson PDR, Montvale, NJ, pp. 3092–6.

Wolf BC, Lavezzi WA, Sullivan LM, Middleberg RA, and Flannagan LM (2005), Alprazolam-related deaths in Palm Beach County, *Am J For Med Path*, 26(1): 24–7.

Wright CE, Sisson TL, Fleishaker JC, and Antal EJ (1997), Pharmacokinetics and psychomotor performance of alprazolam: Concentration-effect relationship, *J Clin Pharmacol*, 37(4): 321–9.

Aluminum

Brand names: not applicable
Classification: metal
λ: 8 hrs–8 yrs
V_d: unknown
Usual dosage: not applicable

Source	Therapeutic/ Nontoxic	Toxic	Lethal
Blood	0.004–0.09 mg/L	0.05–0.25 mg/L	0.4–24 mg/L
Urine	0.04–0.08 mg/L	0.2–0.5 mg/L	
Bile			404 mg/L
Liver	0.6–2.4 mg/kg		4.7–90 mg/kg
Kidney	0.07–0.4 mg/kg		15–32 mg/kg
Brain	0.2–0.9 mg/kg		1.7–5 mg/kg
Skeletal muscle	0.07–0.9 mg/kg		
Bone			1.1–30 mg/kg

Selected Sources

Arieff AI, Cooper JD, Armstrong D, and Lazarowitz VC (1979), Dementia, renal failure, and brain aluminum, *Ann Int Med*, 90(5): 741–7.

Berend K, van der Voet G, and Boer WH (2001), Acute aluminum encephalopathy in a dialysis center caused by a cement mortar water distribution pipe, *Kid Intl*, 59(2): 746–53.

Berman E (1980), *Toxic Metals and Their Analysis*, Heyden, Philadelphia.

de Wolff FA, Berend K, and van der Voet GB (2002), Subacute fatal aluminum poisoning in dialyzed patients: Post-mortem toxicological findings, *For Sci Intl*, 128(1–2): 41–3.

Flanagan RJ (1998), Guidelines for the interpretation of analytical toxicology results and unit of measurement conversion factors, *Ann Clin Biochem*, 35: 261–7.

Kosier JH (1999), Aluminum toxicity in the 1990s, *Anna J*, 26(4): 423–4.

McLaughlin AI, Kazantzis G, King E, Teare D, Porter RJ, and Owen R (1962), Pulmonary fibrosis and encephalopathy associated with the inhalation of aluminium dust, *Brit J Ind Med*, 19: 253–63.

Rahil-Khazen R, Bolann BJ, Myking A, and Ulvik RJ (2002), Multi-element analysis of trace element levels in human autopsy tissues by using inductively coupled atomic emission spectrometry technique (ICP-AES), *J Trace Elements Med Bio*, 16(1): 15–25.

Reusche E, Pilz P, Oberascher G, Lindner B, Egensperger R, and Gloeckner K (2001), Subacute fatal aluminum encephalopathy after reconstructive otoneurosurgery: A case report, *Hum Path*, 32(10): 1136–40.

Shirabe T, Irie K, and Uchida M (2002), Autopsy case of aluminum encephalopathy, *Neuropathology*, 22(3): 206–10.

Versieck J (1985), Trace elements in human body fluids and tissues, *Crit Rev Clin Lab Sci*, 22(2): 97–184.

Zatta P, Zambenedetti P, Reusche E, Stellmacher F, Cester A, and Albanese P (2004), A fatal case of aluminium encephalopathy in a patient with severe chronic renal failure not on dialysis, *Nephrology Dialysis Transplantation*, 19(11): 2929–31.

Amanitin

Brand names: not applicable
Classification: poison
λ: unknown
V_d: ~1 L/kg
Usual dosage: not applicable

Source	Therapeutic/ Nontoxic	Toxic	Lethal
Blood	No data available		0.008–0.19 mg/L

Comments

- Found in *Amanita, Galerina,* and *Conocyte* ("death cap") mushrooms
- Generally found in blood for 1–5 days, 4 days in urine, 5 days in liver/kidney
- Symptoms/signs of toxicity: nausea/vomiting/diarrhea, renal failure, hepatic necrosis
- Symptoms start 5–15 hrs after ingestion

Selected Sources

Jaeger A, Jehl F, Flesch F, Sauder P, and Kopferschmitt J (1993), Kinetics of amatoxins in human poisoning: Therapeutic implications, *J Tox Clin Tox*, 31(1): 63–80.
Vesconi S, Langer M, Iapichino G, Costantino D, Busi C, and Fiume L (1985), Therapy of cytotoxic mushroom intoxication, *Crit Care Med*, 13(5): 402–6.

Amantadine

Brand names: Symmetrel
Classification: antiviral/anti-Parkinson's
λ: 9–31 hrs
V_d: 2.9–11 L/kg
Usual dosage: 100–200 mg bid/qd

Source	Therapeutic/ Nontoxic	Toxic	Lethal
Blood	0.06–1.1 mg/L	1.5–5.0 mg/L	4.8–48 mg/L
Urine			1330 mg/L
Bile			419 mg/L
Liver			135 mg/kg

Comments

- May prolong QT interval

Selected Sources

Bexar County Medical Examiner's Office data 1996-2007.
Cook PE, Dermer SW, and McGurk T (1986), Fatal overdose with amantadine, *Can J Psychiatry*, 31(8): 757–8.
Deleu D, Northway MG, and Hanssens Y (2002), Clinical pharmacokinetic and pharmacodynamic properties of drugs used in the treatment of Parkinson's disease, *Clin Pharmacokinet*, 41(4): 261–309.
Fahn S, Craddock G, and Kumin G (1971), Acute toxic psychosis from suicidal overdosage of amantadine, *Arch Neurol*, 25(1): 45–8.
Ing TS, Daugirdes JT, and Soung LS (1979), Toxic effects of amantadine in patients with renal failure, *Can Med Assoc J*, 120: 695–8.
Reynolds PC and Van Meter S (1984), A death involving amantadine, *J Anal Tox*, 8: 100.

Amisulpride

Brand names: Socian, Solian
Classification: antipsychotic
λ: 11–27 hrs
V_d: 5.4–6.2 L/kg
Usual dosage: 50–400 mg/d

Source	Therapeutic/ Nontoxic	Toxic	Lethal
Blood	0.05–0.4 mg/L	9.6 mg/L	13 mg/L

Comments

- Not available in the United States

Selected Sources

Kratzsch C, Peters FT, Kraemer T, Weber AA, and Maurer HH (2003), Screening, library-assisted identification and validated quantification of fifteen neuroleptics and three of their metabolites in plasma by liquid chromatography/mass spectrometry with atmospheric pressure chemical ionization, *J Mass Spectrum,* 38(3): 283–95.

Rosenzweig P, Canal M, Patat A, Bergougnan L, Zieleniuk I, and Bianchetti G (2002), A review of the pharmacokinetics, tolerability and pharmacodynamics of amisulpride in healthy volunteers, *Hum Psychopharmacol,* 17(1): 1–13.

Tracqui A, Mutter-Schmidt C, Kintz P, Berton C, and Mangin P (1995), Amisulpride poisoning: A report on two cases, *Hum Exp Tox,* 14(3): 294–8.

Amitriptyline

Brand names: Elavil, Vanatrip, Endep
Classification: antidepressant (TCA)
λ: 8–50 hrs
V_d: 12–18 L/kg
Usual dosage: 75–150 mg qd

Source	Therapeutic/ Nontoxic	Toxic	Lethal
Blood	0.02–0.24 mg/L	0.5–2.2 mg/L	1.8–39 mg/L
Vitreous			0.8–6.1 mg/L
Urine	5–15 mg/L		2.5–28 mg/L
Bile			8–48 mg/L
Liver	3.2–10 mg/kg	>50 mg/kg	26–518 mg/kg
Kidney			5–98 mg/kg
Brain			4.8–22 mg/kg
Skeletal muscle	0.08–0.28 mg/kg		1.2–11 mg/kg
Stomach contents			14–2000 mg

Comments

- Active metabolite: nortriptyline
- Metabolized by CYP 2D6, 3A, 1A2, and 2C19
- Acute overdoses usually have a 2:1 amitriptyline: nortriptyline ratio
- May prolong QT interval, associated with cardiac arrhythmias

Selected Sources

Apple FS (1989), Postmortem tricyclic antidepressant concentrations: Assessing cause of death using parent drug to metabolite ratio, *J Anal Tox*, 13(4): 197–8.

Bailey DN and Shaw RF (1980), Interpretation of blood and tissue concentrations in fatal self-ingested overdose involving amitriptyline: An update, *J Anal Tox*, 4(5): 232–6.

Bexar County Medical Examiner's Office data 1996–2007.

Biggs JT, Spiker DG, Petit JM, and Ziegler VE (1977), Tricyclic antidepressant overdose: Incidence of symptoms, *JAMA*, 238(2): 135–8.

Cooper TB, Allen D, and Simpson GM (1976), A sensitive method for determination of amitriptyline and nortriptyline in human plasma, *Psychopharmacol Commun*, 2(2): 105–16.

Garland WA (1977), Quantitative determination of amitriptyline and its principal metabolite, nortriptyline, by GLC–Chemical ionization mass spectrometry, *J Pharm Sci*, 66(1): 77–81.

Langford AM and Pounder DJ (1997), Possible markers for postmortem drug redistribution, *J For Sci*, 42(1): 88–92.

Paterson SC (1985), Drug levels found in cases of fatal self-poisoning, *Forensic Science Intl*, 27(2): 129–33.
Royds RB and Knight AH (1970), Tricyclic antidepressant poisoning, *Practitioner*, 204(220): 282–6.
Tracqui A, Kintz P, Ritter-Lohner S, Mangin P, Lugnier A, and Chaumont A (1990), Toxicological findings after fatal amitriptyline self-poisoning, *Hum Exper Tox*, 9(4): 257–61.
Vasiliades J and Bush KC (1976), Gas liquid chromatographic determination of therapeutic and toxic levels of amitriptyline in human serum with a nitrogen-sensitive detector, *Anal Chem*, 48(12): 1708–4.
Wallace JE, Blum K, and Singh JM (1974), Determination of drugs in biological specimens—A review, *J Tox Clin Tox*, 7(5): 477–95.

Amlodipine

Brand names: Norvasc
Classification: calcium channel blocker
λ: 32–44 hrs
V_d: 17–25 L/kg
Usual dosage: 2.5–10 mg qd

Source	Therapeutic/ Nontoxic	Toxic	Lethal
Blood	0.001–0.02 mg/L	0.07–0.14 mg/L	0.19–2.7 mg/L
Urine			1.1 mg/L
Bile			69–77 mg/L
Liver			8.7–91 mg/kg
Kidney			40 mg/kg
Brain			5.4 mg/kg
Skeletal muscle			2.9 mg/kg
Stomach contents			17–583 mg/kg

Selected Sources

Adams BD and Browne WT (1998), Amlodipine overdose causes prolonged calcium channel blocker toxicity, *Am J Emer Med*, 16(5): 527–8.

Cosbey SH and Carson DJ (1997), A fatal case of amlodipine poisoning, *J Anal Tox*, 21(3): 221–2.

Faulkner JK, McGibney D, Chasseaud LF, Perry JL, and Taylor IW (1986), The pharmacokinetics of amlodipine in healthy volunteers after single intravenous and oral doses and after 14 repeated oral doses given once daily, *Brit J Clin Pharm*, 22(1): 21–5.

Johansen SS and Genner J (2003), A fatal case of amlodipine poisoning, *J Clin For Med*, 10: 169–172.

Lehmann G, Reiniger G, Beyerle A, and Rudolph W (1993), Pharmacokinetics and additional anti-ischaemic effectiveness of amlodipine, a once-daily calcium antagonist, during acute and long-term therapy of stable angina pectoris in patients pre-treated with a beta-blocker, *Eur Heart J*, 14(11): 1531–5.

Poggenborg RP, Videbaek L, and Jacobsen IA (2006), A case of amlodipine overdose, *Basic Clin Pharm and Tox*, 99(3): 209–12.

Sklerov JH, Levine B, Ingwersen KM, Aronica-Pollack PA, and Fowler D (2006), Two cases of fatal amlodipine overdose, *J Anal Tox*, 30(5): 346–51.

Stanek EJ, Nelson CE, and DeNofrio D (1997), Amlodipine overdose, *Ann Pharmacotherapy*, 31(7–8): 853–6.

Amobarbital

Brand names: Amytal, Tuinal
Classification: barbiturate
λ: 10–40 hrs
V_d: 0.9–2.3 L/kg
Usual dosage: 60–150 mg bid/qid

Source	Therapeutic/ Nontoxic	Toxic	Lethal
Blood	0.6–7.7 mg/L	5.0–50 mg/L	11–100 mg/L
Vitreous			8–26 mg/L
Urine	1.6–3.7 mg/L		
Liver			19–50 mg/kg
Kidney			10–30 mg/kg
Brain			11–24 mg/kg

Comments

- Not available in the United States
- Tolerance can develop and should be considered when interpreting drug concentrations

Selected Sources

Balasubramaniam K, Lucas SB, Mawer GE, and Simons PJ (1970), The kinetics of amylobarbitone metabolism in healthy men and women, *Brit J Pharm*, 39(3): 564–72.

Gupta RC and Kofoed J (1966), Toxicological statistics for barbiturates, other sedatives, and tranquilizers in Ontario, *Can Med Assoc J*, 94: 863–5.

Parker KD, Elliott HW, Wright JA, Nomof H, and Hine CH (1970), Blood and urine concentrations of subjects receiving barbiturates, meprobamate, glutethimide, or diphenylhydantoin, *Clin Tox*, 3(1): 131–45.

Wallace JE, Blum K, and Singh JM (1974), Determination of drugs in biological specimens—A review, *J Tox—Clin Tox*, 7(5): 477–95.

Ziminski KR, Wemyss CT, Bidanset JH, Manning TJ, and Lukash L (1984), Comparative study of postmortem barbiturates, methadone, and morphine in vitreous humor, blood, and tissue, *J For Sci*, 29(3): 903–9.

Amoxapine

Brand names: Asendin
Classification: antidepressant (TCA)
λ: 8 hrs
V_d: unknown
Usual dosage: 150–400 mg qd

Source	Therapeutic/ Nontoxic	Toxic	Lethal
Blood	0.03–0.2 mg/L	0.3–2.1 mg/L	0.89–18 mg/L
Vitreous			0.2 mg/L
Urine			13–28 mg/L
Bile			14–1264 mg/L
Liver			17–150 mg/kg
Brain			2.5–52 mg/kg
Stomach contents			75–134 mg

Comments

- Active metabolites: 8-hydroxyamoxapine (λ 30 hrs) and 7-hydroxyamoxapine
- Is a metabolite of loxapine
- May prolong QT interval

Selected Sources

Beierle FA and Hubbard RW (1983), Liquid chromatographic separation of antidepressant drugs. II. Amoxapine and maprotiline, *Ther Drug Monit,* 5(3): 293–301.
Kinney JL and Evans RK Jr (1982), Evaluation of amoxapine, *Clin Pharm* 1(5): 417–24.
Sedgwick P, Spiehler VR, and Lowe DR (1982), Toxicological findings in amoxapine overdose, *J Anal Tox,* 6(2): 82–4.
Taylor RL, Crooks CR, and Caplan YH (1982), The determination of amoxapine in human fatal overdoses, *J Anal Tox,* 6(6): 309–11.
Winek CL, Wahba WW, and Rozin L (1984), Amoxapine fatalities: Three case studies, *For Sci Intl,* 26(1): 33–8.

Amphetamine

Brand names: Adderall, Dexedrine, Dextrostat
Street names: Bennies, Uppers, Speed, Pep Pills, CoPilots
Classification: stimulant
λ: 9–12 hrs
V_d: 3.2–6 L/kg
Usual dosage: 2.5–20 mg bid

Source	Therapeutic/ Nontoxic	Toxic	Lethal
Blood	0.02–0.07 mg/L	0.2–3 mg/L	0.5–41 mg/L
Urine			25–700 mg/L
Liver			4.3–45 mg/kg
Kidney			3.8–48 mg/kg
Brain			2.8–41 mg/kg
Skeletal muscle			4 mg/kg
Stomach contents			10–134 mg

Comments

- Deaths are due to cardiovascular and central nervous system effects
  - Minimal concentration for CNS effects = 0.005 mg/L
  - Minimal concentration for CV effect = 0.02 mg/L
- Metabolized by CYP 2D6
- Metabolite of benzphetamine, clobenzorex, famprofazone, fencamfamine, fenethylline, fenproporex, mefenorex, mesocarb, and prenylamine

Selected Sources

Adjutantis G, Coutselinis A, and Dimopoulos G (1975), Fatal intoxication with amphetamines, *Med Sci and Law*, 15(1): 62–3.

Angrist B, Corwin J, Bartlik B, and Cooper T (1987), Early pharmacokinetics and clinical effects of oral D-amphetamine in normal subjects, *Biological Psychiatry*, 22(11): 1357–68.

Bexar County Medical Examiner's Office data 1996–2007.

Cravey RH and Jain NC (1973), Testing for amphetamines: Medico-legal hazards, *Trauma*, 15(1): 49–94.

Heinemann A, Miyaishi S, Iwersen S, Schmoldt A, and Püschel K (1998), Body-packing as cause of unexpected sudden death, *For Sci Intl*, 92(1): 1–10.

Meyer E, Van Bocxlaer JF, Dirinck IM, Lambert WE, Thienpont L, and De Leenheer AP (1997), Tissue distribution of amphetamine isomers in a fatal overdose, *J Anal Tox*, 21(3): 236–9.

Morselli PL, Placidi GF, Maggini C, Gomeni R, Guazelli M, DeLisio G, Standen S, and Tognoni G (1976), An integrated approach for the evaluation of psychotrophic drug in man: I. Studies on amphetamine relationship between drug levels and psychophysiological measurements, *Psychopharmacologia,* 46(2): 211–7.

Orrenius S and Maehly AC (1970), Lethal amphetamine intoxication: A report of three cases, *Zeitschrift für Rechtsmedizin/J Legal Med*, 67(3): 184–9.

Physicians' Desk Reference 60 Edition (2006), Thomson PDR, Montvale, NJ, pp. 1386–7, 3168–3172.

van Hoof F, Heyndrickx A, and Timperman J (1974), Report of a human fatality due to amphetamine, *Arch Tox*, 32(4): 307–12.

Aripiprazole

Brand names: Abilify
Classification: antipsychotic
λ: 47–75 hrs
V_d: 4.9 L/kg
Usual dosage: 10–30 mg qd

Source	Therapeutic/ Nontoxic	Toxic	Lethal
Blood	0.03–0.45 mg/L	0.72–1.4 mg/L	No data available

Comments

- Active metabolite: dehydro-aripiprazole
- Metabolized by CYP 2D6 and 3A

Selected Sources

Carstairs SD and Williams SR (2005), Overdose of aripiprazole, a new type of antipsychotic, *J Emerg Med,* 28(3): 311–3.

Mallikaarjun S, Salazar DE, and Bramer SL (2004), Pharmacokinetics, tolerability, and safety of aripiprazole following multiple oral dosing in normal healthy volunteers, *J Clin Pharmacol,* 44(2): 179–87.

Physicians' Desk Reference 60 Edition (2006), Thomson PDR, Montvale, NJ, pp. 2472–8.

Seifert SA, Schwartz MD, and Thomas JD (2005), Aripiprazole (Abilify) overdose in a child, *Clin Tox,* 43(3): 193–6.

Armodafinil

Brand names: Nuvigil
Classification: stimulant
λ: 5–36 hrs
V_d: 0.6 L/kg
Usual dosage: 150–250 mg qam

Source	Therapeutic/ Nontoxic	Toxic	Lethal
Blood	2.0–9.9 mg/L	No data available	

Comments

- Is the R-enantiomer of modafinil

Selected Sources

Darwish M, Kirby M, Robertson P, and Hellriegel ET (2008), Interaction profile of armodafinil with medications metabolized by cytochrome P450 enzymes 1a2, 3a4, and 2c19 in healthy subjects, *Clin Pharm*, 47(1): 61–74.

Dinges DF, Arora S, Darwish M, and Niebler GE (2006), Pharmacodynamic effects on alertness of single doses of armodafinil in healthy subjects during a nocturnal period of acute sleep loss, *Curr Med Res Opin*, 22(1): 159–67.

Arsenic

Brand names: component of some pesticides
Classification: metalloid
λ: 10–30 hrs
V_d: unknown
Usual dosage: not applicable

Source	Therapeutic/ Nontoxic	Toxic	Lethal
Blood	0.03–0.07 mg/L	0.05–1 mg/L	0.3–10 mg/L
Urine	0.01–0.13 mg/L		>1 mg/L
Bile			2.4 mg/L
Liver	0.02–0.07 mg/kg		2–400 mg/kg
Kidney	0.02–0.1 mg/kg		0.2–100 mg/kg
Brain	0.02–0.07 mg/kg		0.2–20 mg/kg
Skeletal muscle	0.04–0.1 mg/kg		12 mg/kg
Nail	0.88 mg/kg		50–67 mg/kg
Stomach contents			1–40000 mg/L

Comments

- Elemental arsenic (AS^o) is not toxic
- Arsenate (As^{+5}), arsenite (As^{+3}), and Arsine gas (AsH_3) are toxic; As^{+5} < As^{+3} < AsH_3
- Binds to hair and nails
- Metabolized to dimethylarsinic acid

Selected Sources

Adelson L (1974), Chapter XIII, Murder by poison, in *The Pathology of Homicide,* Charles C Thomas, Springfield, IL, pp. 725–875.
Benramdane L, Accominotti M, Fanton L, Malicier D, and Vallon JJ (1999), Arsenic speciation in human organs following fatal arsenic trioxide poisoning—A case report, *Clin Chem,* 45(2): 301–6.
Bexar County Medical Examiner's Office data 1996–2007.
Knight B (1991), *Forensic Pathology,* Oxford University Press. New York, pp. 530–2.
McBay AJ (1973), Toxicological findings in fatal poisonings, *Clin Chem,* 19(4): 361–5.
Sumino K, Hayakawa K, Shibata T, and Kitamura S (1975), Heavy metals in normal Japanese tissues: Amounts of 15 heavy metals in 30 subjects, *Arch Environ Health,* 30(10): 487–94.

Atenolol

Brand names: Tenormin
Classification: β-blocker
λ: 5–8 hrs
V_d: 0.7–0.8 L/kg
Usual dosage: 50–200 mg qd

Source	Therapeutic/ Nontoxic	Toxic	Lethal
Blood	0.04–0.7 mg/L	2.5–9.4 mg/L	No data available

Selected Sources

Amery A, De Plaen JF, Lijnen P, McAinsh J, and Reybrouck T (1977), Relationship between blood level of atenolol and pharmacologic effect, *Clin Pharm Thera,* 21(6): 691–9.

Czendlik CH, Sioufi A, Preiswerk G, and Howald H (1997), Pharmacokinetic and pharmacodynamic interaction of single doses of valsartan and atenolol, *Eur J Clin Pharm,* 52(6): 451–9.

DeLima LG, Kharasch ED, and Butler S (1995), Successful pharmacologic treatment of massive atenolol overdose: Sequential hemodynamics and plasma atenolol concentrations, *Anesthesiology,* 83(1): 204–7.

Gerkin R and Curry S (1987), Significant bradycardia following acute self-poisoning with atenolol, *Vet Hum Tox,* 29: 479.

Montgomery AB, Stager MA, and Schoene RB (1985), Marked suppression of ventilation while awake following massive ingestion of atenolol, *Chest,* 88(6): 920–1.

Saitz R, Williams BW, and Farber HW (1991), Atenolol-induced cardiovascular collapse treated with hemodialysis, *Crit Care Med,* 19(1): 116–8.

Atomoxetine

Brand names: Strattera
Classification: norepinephrine reuptake inhibitor
λ: 5 hrs
V_d: 0.85–2.3 L/kg
Usual dosage: 0.3–1.2 mg/kg bid/qd

Source	Therapeutic/ Nontoxic	Toxic	Lethal
Blood	0.04–0.9 mg/L	No data available	5.4–8.3 mg/L[a]
Vitreous			0.96 mg/L[a]
Bile			33 mg/L[a]
Liver			29 mg/kg[a]
Stomach contents			17 mg/L[a]

[a] Co-intoxicant venlafaxine (100 mg/L).

Comments

- Metabolized by CYP 2D6
- May prolong QT interval

Selected Sources

Garside D, Ropero-Miller JD, and Riemer EC (2006), Postmortem tissue distribution of atomoxetine following fatal and nonfatal doses—Three case reports, *J For Sci,* 51(1): 179–82
Sauer JM, Ring BJ, and Witcher JW (2005), Clinical pharmacokinetics of atomoxetine, *Clin Pharmacokinet*, 44(6): 571–90.

Atracurium

Brand names: Tracrium
Classification: neuromuscular blocker
λ: 15–20 min
V_d: 0.1–0.2 L/kg
Usual dosage: 0.08–0.5 mg/kg/dose; iv only

Source	Therapeutic/ Nontoxic	Toxic	Lethal
Blood	0.36–1.5 mg/L	No data available	

Comments

- Therapeutic concentrations can be fatal if drug not administered in a monitored medical setting

Selected Sources

Beemer G (1990), Pharmacokinetics of atracurium during continuous infusion, *Br J Anaesth*, 65(5): 668–74.

Fisher DM, Canfell PC, Spellman MJ, Miller RDH, Bjorksten AR, and Crankshaw DP (1990), Pharmacokinetics and pharmacodynamics of atracurium in infants and children, *Anesthesiology*, 73(1): 33–7.

Atropine

Brand names: AtroPen, Sal-Tropine
Classification: antimuscarinic
λ: 2–3 hrs
V_d: 0.9–3.1 L/kg
Usual dosage: 0.4–0.6 mg q 4–6 hrs

Source	Therapeutic/ Nontoxic	Toxic	Lethal/ Comatose
Blood	0.006–0.3 mg/L	0.02–0.24 mg/L	0.2–3.1 mg/L
Urine		0.19–1.8 mg/L	1.5–11 mg/L
Liver			0.7 mg/kg

Comments

- Used to treat organophosphate poisoning
- Physostigmine is an antidote to atropine poisoning

Selected Sources

Berghem L, Bergman U, Schildt B, and Sorbo B (1980), Plasma atropine concentrations determined by radioimmunoassay after single-dose I.V. and I.M. administration, *Br J Anaesth*, 52(6): 597–601.

Boumba VA, Mitselou A, and Vougiouklakis T (2004), Fatal poisoning from ingestion of *Datura stramonium* seeds, *Vet Hum Tox*, 46(2): 81–2.

Hayden PW, Larson SM, and Lakshminarayanan S (1979), Atropine clearance from human plasma, *J Nucl Med*, 20(4): 366–7.

Kehe CR, Lasseter KC, Miller NC, Wick KA, Shamblen EC, Ekholm BP, Sandahl JH, Chang SF, Goldlust MB, and Kvam DC (1992), Comparative absorption of atropine from a metered-dose inhaler and an intramuscular injection, *Ther Drug Monit*, 14(2): 132–4.

Schneider F, Lutun P, Kintz P, Astruc D, Flesch F, and Tempe JD (1996), Plasma and urine concentrations of atropine after the ingestion of cooked deadly nightshade berries, *J Tox Clin Tox*, 34(1): 113–7.

Baclofen

Brand names: Lioresal, Kemstro
Classification: muscle relaxant
λ: 2–8 hrs
V_d: 0.7–0.9 L/kg
Usual dosage: 5–15 mg tid

Source	Therapeutic/ Nontoxic	Toxic	Lethal
Blood	0.05–0.6 mg/L	0.4–6 mg/L	17–106 mg/L
Urine			760–774 mg/L

Selected Sources

Chapple D, Johnson D, and Connors R (2001), Baclofen overdose in two siblings, *Ped Emer Care*, 17(2): 110–2.

De Giovanni N and d'Aloja E (2001), Death due to baclofen and dipyrone ingestion, *For Sci Intl*, 123(1): 26–32.

Fraser AD, MacNeil D, and Isner AF (1991), Toxicological analysis of a fatal baclofen (Lioresal®) ingestion, *J For Sci* 36: 1596–602.

Perry HE, Wright RO, Shannon MW, and Woolf AD (1998), Baclofen overdose: Drug experimentation in a group of adolescents, *Pediatrics*, 1(6): 1045–8.

Wall GC, Wasiak W, and Hicklin GA (2006), An initially unsuspected case of baclofen overdose (clinical report), *Am J Crit Care*, 15(6): 611–3.

Wiersma HE, van Boxtel CJ, Butter JJ, van Aalderen WM, Omari T, and Benninga MA (2003), Pharmacokinetics of a single oral dose of baclofen in pediatric patients with gastroesophageal reflux disease, *Thera Drug Monitoring*, 25(1): 93–8.

Wu VC, Lin SL, Lin SM, and Fang CC (2005), Treatment of baclofen overdose by haemodialysis: A pharmacokinetic study, *Nephrol Dial Transplant*, 20(2): 441–3.

Benzene

Brand names: component in paint remover, solvents, gasoline
Classification: volatile (aromatic hydrocarbon)
λ: 8–12 hrs
V_d: unknown
Usual dosage: not applicable

Source	Therapeutic/ Nontoxic	Toxic	Lethal
Blood	0.000005–0.35 mg/L	No data available	0.9–120 mg/L
Urine			0.6–2.3 mg/L
Bile			11–45 mg/L
Liver			2.6–379 mg/kg
Kidney			5.5–75 mg/kg
Brain			14–179 mg/kg
Lung			22 mg/kg
Adipose tissue			22–120 mg/kg
Stomach contents			10 mg/L

Comments

- Cardiotoxic: intoxication associated with arrhythmias

Selected Sources

Avis SP and Hutton CJ (1993), Acute benzene poisoning: A report of three fatalities, *J For Sci*, 38(3): 599–602.
Barbera N, Bulla G, and Romano G (1998), A fatal case of benzene poisoning, *J For Sci*, 43(6): 1250–1.
Brugnone F, Perbellini L, Romeo L, Bianchin M, Tonello A, and Pianalto G (1998), Benzene in environmental air and human blood, *Intl Arch Occupational and Environmental Health*, 71(8): 554–9.
Sato A, Nakajima T, Fujiwara Y, and Murayama N (1975), Kinetic studies on sex difference in susceptibility to chronic benzene intoxication—With special reference to body fat content, *Br J Ind Med*, 32(4): 321–8.
Stephens BG (2004), Chapter XXII, Investigation of deaths from drug abuse, in *Spitz and Fisher's Medicolegal Investigation of Death Fourth Edition*, Spitz WU (Ed.), Charles C Thomas, Springfield, IL, pp. 1166–1217.
Tauber J (1970), Instant benzol death, *J Occ Med*, 12(3): 91–2.
Winek CL and Collom WD (1971) Benzene and toluene fatalities, *J Occ Med*, 13(5): 259–61.
Winek CL, Collom WD, and Wecht CH (1967), Fatal benzene exposure by glue-sniffing, *Lancet*, 1: 683.

Benzocaine

Brand names: Cetacaine, Orajel, Cepacol, Anbesol
Classification: local anesthetic
λ: unknown
V_d: unknown
Usual dosage: 10%–20% gel applied tid/qid

Source	Therapeutic/ Nontoxic	Toxic	Lethal
Blood	0.05–0.48 mg/L	1.0 mg/L	3.5 mg/L
Urine	1.5 mg/L	3.8 mg/L	

Comments

- Toxicity results in methemoglobinemia

Selected Sources

Bexar County Medical Examiner's Office data 1996–2007.
Logan BK and Gordon AM (2005), Death of an infant involving benzocaine, *J For Sci*, 50(6): 1486–8.
McKinney CD, Postiglione KF, and Herold DA (1992), Benzocaine-adultered street cocaine in association with methemoglobinemia, *Clin Chem*, 38(4): 596–7.
Potter JL and Hillman JV (1979), Benzocaine-induced methemoglobinemia, *JACEP*, 8(1): 26–7.

Benzphetamine

Brand names: Didrex
Classification: stimulant/anorectic
λ: unknown
V_d: unknown
Dosage: 25–50 mg tid/bid/qd

Source	Therapeutic/ Nontoxic	Toxic	Lethal[a]
Blood	0.02–0.5 mg/L	No data available	14 mg/L
Vitreous			21 mg/L
Urine	0.14–0.96 mg/L methamphetamine 0.21–3.8 mg/L amphetamine		8 mg/L
Bile			83 mg/L
Liver			106 mg/kg
Kidney			38 mg/kg
Brain			31 mg/kg
Stomach contents			53 mg

[a] Values are for parent drug (benzphetamine) except where otherwise indicated.

Comments

- Metabolized to *d*-amphetamine and *d*-methamphetamine

Selected Sources

Brooks JP, Phillips M, Stafford DT, and Bell JS (1982), A case of benzphetamine poisoning, *Am J For Med Path*, 3(3): 245–7.

Cody JT and Valtier S (1998), Detection of amphetamine and methamphetamine following administration of benzphetamine, *J Anal Tox*, 22(4): 299–309.

Kraemer T and Maurer HH (2002), Toxicokinetics of amphetamines: Metabolism and toxicokinetic data of designer drugs, amphetamine, methamphetamine, and their N-alkyl derivatives, *Ther Drug Monit*, 24(2): 277–89.

Benztropine

Brand names: Cogentin
Classification: anti-Parkinson's agent
λ: unknown
V_d: unknown
Dosage: 1–2 mg qd

Source	Therapeutic/ Nontoxic	Toxic	Lethal
Blood	0.004–0.13 mg/L	0.05–0.1 mg/L	0.18–1.1 mg/L
Vitreous			0.3 mg/L
Urine			5.6–7.1 mg/L
Liver			8.7 mg/kg

Comments

- Metabolized by CYP 2D6

Selected Sources

Fahy P, Arnold P, Curry SC, and Bond R (1989), Serial serum drug concentrations and prolonged anticholinergic toxicity after benztropine (cogentin) overdose, *Am J Emer Med*, 7(2): 199–202.

Jindal SP, Lutz T, Hallstrom C, and Vestergaard P (1981), A stable isotope dilution assay for the antiparkinsonian drug benztropine in biological fluids, *Clinica Chimica Acta*, 112(3): 267–73.

Lynch MJ and Kotsos A (2001), Fatal benztropine toxicity, *Med Sci Law*, 41(2): 155–8.

Rosano TG, Meola JM, Wolf BC, Guisti LW, and Jindal SP (1994), Benztropine identification and quantitation in a suicidal overdose, *J Anal Tox*, 18(6): 348–53.

Bromazepam

Brand names: Compendium, Lectopam
Classification: benzodiazepine
λ: 18–65 hrs
V_d: 0.8–1.5 L/kg
Usual dosage: 1.5–3 mg qHS

Source	Therapeutic/ Nontoxic	Toxic	Lethal
Blood	0.08–0.26 mg/L	0.3–0.4 mg/L	0.82–7.7 mg/L

Comments

- Tolerance can develop and should be considered when interpreting drug concentrations

Selected Sources

Escande M, Monjanel-Mouterde S, Diadema B, Coassolo P, Orluc A, Aubert C, Durand A, and Cano JP (1989), Determination of the optimal dose of bromazepam in the elderly, *Therapie*, 44(3): 219–22.

Fujii J, Inotsume N, and Nakano M (1990), Effect of food on the bioavailability of bromazepam following oral administration in healthy volunteers, *Journal of Pharmacobio-Dynamics*, 13(5): 269–71.

Laurito TL, Mendes GD, Santagada V, Caliendo G, de Moraes ME, and De Nucci G (2004), Bromazepam determination in human plasma by high-performance liquid chromatography coupled to tandem mass spectrometry: A highly sensitive and specific tool for bioequivalence studies, *J Mass Spect*, 39(2): 168–76.

Marrache F, Megarbane B, Pirnay S, Rhaoui A, and Thuong M (2004), Difficulties in assessing brain death in a case of benzodiazepine poisoning with persistent cerebral blood flow, *Hum Exp Tox*, 23(10): 503–5.

Michaud K, Romain N, Giroud C, Brandt C, and Mangin P (2001), Hypothermia and undressing associated with non-fatal bromazepam intoxication, *For Sci Intl*, 124(2–3): 112–4.

Brompheniramine

Brand names: component of BroveX, Dallergy, Lodrane, Dimetapp, Bromfed
Classification: antihistamine
λ: 12–35 hrs
V_d: 8.6–15 L/kg
Dosage: 4 mg q 4–6 hrs

Source	Therapeutic/ Nontoxic	Toxic	Lethal
Blood	0.004–0.02 mg/L	No data available	0.4–0.99 mg/L[a]
Liver			4.2 mg/kg[a]
Skeletal muscle			2.3 mg/kg[a]

[a] Co-intoxicant phenylpropanolamine (6.3 mg/L blood).

Selected Sources

Bruce RB, Pitts JE, and Pinchbeck FM (1968), Determination of brompheniramine in blood and urine by gas–liquid chromatography, *Anal Chem*, 40(8): 1246–50.

Jumbelic MI, Hanzlick R, and Cohle S (1997), Alkylamine antihistamine toxicity and review of pediatric toxicology registry of the National Association of Medical Examiners, Report 4: Alkylamines, *Am J For Med Path*, 18(1): 65–9.

Simons FE, Frith EM, and Simons KJ (1982), The pharmacokinetics and antihistaminic effects of brompheniramine, *J Allergy Clin Immunol*, 70(6): 458–64.

Buprenorphine

Brand names: Buprenex, Subutex, Suboxone (with naloxone)
Classification: opiate agonist–antagonist
λ: 3–44 hrs
V_d: 1.3–1.5 L/kg
Usual dosage: 2–16 mg qd

Source	Therapeutic/ Nontoxic	Toxic	Lethal
Blood	0.001–0.01 mg/L	0.02–0.2 mg/L	0.14–13 mg/L
Urine			0.06–3.4 mg/L
Bile			0.8–2.0 mg/L
Brain			6.4 mg/kg

Comments

- Interacts with HIV protease inhibitors and antifungals (azoles) resulting in increased buprenorphine concentrations
- Metabolized by CYP 3A4

Selected Sources

Compton P, Ling W, Moody D, and Chiang N (2006), Pharmacokinetics, bioavailability and opioid effects of liquid versus tablet buprenorphine, *Drug Alcohol Dependence*, 82(1): 25–31.

Elkader A and Sproule B (2005), Buprenorphine: Clinical pharmacokinetics in the treatment of opioid dependence, *Clinical Pharmacokinetics*, 44(7): 661–80.

Gaulier JM, Marquet P, Lacassie E, Dupuy JL, and Lachatre G (2000), Fatal intoxication following self-administration of a massive dose of buprenorphine, *J For Sci*, 45(1): 226–8.

Kintz P (2002), A new series of 13 buprenorphine-related deaths, *Clinical Biochemistry*, 35(7): 513–6.

Physicians' Desk Reference 61 Edition (2007), Thomson PDR, Montvale, NJ, pp. 2717–21.

Tracqui A, Kintz P, and Ludes B (1998), Buprenorphine-related deaths among drug addicts in France: A re-report on 20 fatalities, *J Anal Toxicol*, 22: 43.

Walsh SL, Preston KL, Stitzer ML, Cone EJ, and Bigelow GE (1994), Clinical pharmacology of buprenorphine: Ceiling effects at high doses, *Clin Pharm Ther*, 55(5): 569–80.

Bupropion

Brand names: Wellbutrin, Zyban
Classification: antidepressant
λ: 12–30 hrs
V_d: 17–20 L/kg
Usual dosage: 100 mg bid/tid

Source	Therapeutic/ Nontoxic	Toxic	Lethal
Blood	0.01–0.2 mg/L	1.2 mg/L	1.5–21 mg/L
Liver			14 mg/kg
Skeletal muscle	0.08–0.16 mg/kg		
Stomach contents			1582 mg

Comments

- Has multiple active metabolites
- Metabolized by CYP 2B6

Selected Sources

Daviss WB, Perel JM, Birmaher B, Rudolph GR, Melhem I, Axelson DA, and Brent DA (2006), Steady-state clinical pharmacokinetics of bupropion extended-release in youths, *J Am Academy Child Adol Psych*, 45(12): 1503–9.

Friel PN, Logan BK, and Fligner CL (1993), Three fatal drug overdoses involving bupropion, *J Anal Tox*, 17(7): 436–8.

Harris CR, Gualtieri J, and Stark G (1997), Fatal bupropion overdose, *J Tox Clin Tox*, 35(3): 321–4.

Linder MW and Keck PE (1998), Standards of laboratory practice: Antidepressant drug monitoring. National Academy of Clinical Biochemistry, *Clin Chem*, 44(5): 1073–84.

Preskorn SH (1983), Antidepressant response and plasma concentrations of bupropion, *J Clin Psych*, 44(5 Pt 2): 137–9.

Rohrig TP and Ray NG (1992), Tissue distribution of bupropion in a fatal overdose, *J Anal Tox*, 16(5): 343–5.

White RS and Langford JR (2002), Sustained release bupropion: Overdose and treatment, *Am J Emer Med*, 20(4): 388–9.

Buspirone

Brand names: Buspar
Classification: anxiolytic
λ: 2–6 hrs
V_d: 2.7–7.9 L/kg
Usual dosage: 15–30 mg qd

Source	Therapeutic/ Nontoxic	Toxic	Lethal
Blood	0.0002–0.01 mg/L	No data available	2–7.3 mg/L

Comments

- Active metabolite: 6-hydroxybuspirone

Selected Sources

Dockens RC, Salazar DE, Fulmor IE, Wehling M, Arnold ME, and Croop R (2006), Pharmacokinetics of a newly identified active metabolite of buspirone after administration of buspirone over its therapeutic dose range, *J Clin Pharm*, 46(11): 1308–13.

Mahmood I and Sahajwalla C (1999), Clinical pharmacokinetics and pharmacodynamics of buspirone: An anxiolytic drug, *Clin Pharmacokinet*, 36(4): 277–87.

Roman M, Kronstrand R, Lindstedt D, and Josefsson M (2008), Quantitation of seven low-dosage antipsychotic drugs in human postmortem blood using LC-MS-MS, *J Anal Tox*, 32(2): 147–55.

Salazar DE, Frackiewicz EJ, Dockens R, Kollia G, Fulmor IE, Tigel PD, Uderman HD, Shiovitz TM, Sramek JJ, and Cutler NR (2001), Pharmacokinetics and tolerability of buspirone during oral administration to children and adolescents with anxiety disorder and normal healthy adults, *J Clin Pharmacol*, 41: 1351–8.

Butalbital

Brand names: Bupap, Esgic, Floricet (w/ aceta, caffeine), Fiorinal (w/ caffeine)
Classification: barbiturate
λ: 30–40 hrs
V_d: unknown
Usual dosage: 50–100 mg per dose

Source	Therapeutic/ Nontoxic	Toxic	Lethal
Blood	0.2–11 mg/L	7.0–40 mg/L	13–50 mg/L
Liver	0.48–24 mg/kg		50 mg/kg
Kidney	0.21–11 mg/kg		
Brain	0.22–0.56 mg/kg		
Skeletal muscle	0.13–7.1 mg/kg		
Cardiac muscle	0.23–8.7 mg/kg		

Comments

- Tolerance can develop and should be considered when interpreting drug concentrations

Selected Sources

Baselt RC and Cravey RH (1977), A compendium of therapeutic and toxic concentrations of toxicologically significant drugs in human biofluids, *J Anal Tox,* 1: 81–103.
Bexar County Medical Examiner's Office data 1996–2007.
Lewis RJ, Johnson RD, Southern TL, and Canfield DV (2003), Distribution of butalbital in postmortem tissues and fluids from non-overdose cases, *J Anal Tox*, 27(3): 145–8.

Butane

Brand names: component of aerosol propellants, cigarette lighters, camping stoves
Classification: volatile (aliphatic hydrocarbon)
λ: unknown
V_d: unknown
Usual dosage: not applicable

Source	Therapeutic/ Nontoxic	Toxic	Lethal
Blood	No data available		0.11–129 mg/L
Urine			0.01 mg/L
Liver			0.48–27 mg/kg
Kidney			0.43–14 mg/kg
Brain			0.44–13 mg/kg
Lung			0.03–7.5 mg/kg
Adipose tissue			1.8 mg/kg
Stomach contents			0.05–0.47 mg/L

Comments

- Cardiotoxic: intoxication associated with arrhythmias

Selected Sources

Ago M, Ago K, and Ogata M (2002), A fatal case of n-butane poisoning after inhaling anti-perspiration aerosol deodorant, *Legal Med*, 4(2): 113–8.

Jackowski C, Römhild W, Aebi B, Bernhard W, Krause D, and Dirnhofer R (2005), Autoerotic accident by inhalation of propane-butane gas mixture, *Am J For Med Path*, 26(4): 355–9.

Stephens BG (2004), Chapter XXII, Investigation of deaths from drug abuse in *Spitz and Fisher's Medicolegal Investigation of Death Fourth Edition*, Spitz WU (Ed.), Charles C Thomas, Springfield, IL, pp. 1166–217.

Sugie H, Sasaki C, Hashimoto C, Takeshita H, Nagai T, and Nakamura S (2004), Three cases of sudden death due to butane or propane gas inhalation: Analysis of tissues for gas components, *For Sci Intl*, 143(2–3): 211–4.

Butorphanol

Brand names: Stadol
Classification: opiate agonist–antagonist
λ: 2–8 hrs
V_d: 6.6–11 L/kg
Usual dosage: 1 mg iv; 2 mg im; 1–2 mg intranasal q 3–4 hrs

Source	Therapeutic/ Nontoxic	Toxic	Lethal
Blood	0.0009–0.004 mg/L	No data available	4–9 mg/L

Selected Sources

Davis GA, Rudy AC, Archer SM, and Wermeling DP (2004), Pharmacokinetics of butorphanol tartrate administered from single-dose intranasal sprayer, *Am J Health Syst Pharm,* 61(3): 261–6.

Ramsey R, Higbee M, Maesner J, and Wood J (1988), Influence of age on the pharmacokinetics of butorphanol, *Acute Care,* 12(Suppl. 1): 8–16.

Schulz M and Schmoldt A (2003), Therapeutic and toxic blood concentrations of more than 800 drugs and other xenobiotics, *Pharmazie,* 58(7): 447–74.

Caffeine

Brand names: Cafcit
Classification: methylxanthine (stimulant)
λ: 2–10 hrs
V_d: 0.5–0.9 L/kg
Usual dosage: 5 mg/kg qd

Source	Therapeutic/ Nontoxic	Toxic	Lethal
Blood	2–15 mg/L	15–50 mg/L	79–1040 mg/L
Vitreous			100–159 mg/L
Urine		15 mg/L	21–280 mg/L
Bile			64–312 mg/L
Liver			58–670 mg/kg
Kidney			13–352 mg/kg
Brain			75–188 mg/kg
Stomach contents			5.2–319 mg

Comments

- Metabolized by CYP 1A2

Selected Sources

Alstott RL, Miller AJ, and Forney RB (1973), Report of a human fatality due to caffeine, *J For Sci*, 18(2): 135–7.

Dimaio VJ and Garriott JC (1974), Lethal caffeine poisoning in a child, *For Sci*, 3(3): 275–8.

Garriott JC, Simmons LM, Poklis A, and Mackell MA (1985), Five cases of fatal overdose from caffeine-containing "look-alike" drugs, *J Anal Tox*, 9(3): 141–3.

Kerrigan S and Lindsey T (2005), Fatal caffeine overdose: Two case reports, *For Sci Intl*, 153(1): 67–9.

Physicians' Desk Reference 61 Edition (2007), Thomson PDR, Montvale, NJ, pp. 1886–9.

Winek CL, Wahba W, Williams K, Blenko J, and Janssen J (1985), Caffeine fatality: A case report, *For Sci Intl*, 29(3–4): 207–11.

Carbamazepine

Brand names: Tegretol, Carbatrol, Equetro, Epitol
Classification: anticonvulsant
λ: 12–65 hrs
V_d:0.8–1.4 L/kg
Usual dosage: 200–800 mg bid

Source	Therapeutic/ Nontoxic	Toxic	Lethal
Blood	1.9–13 mg/L	10–15 mg/L	20–73 mg/L
Liver			123 mg/kg
Kidney			72 mg/kg
Brain			78–86 mg/kg
Cardiac muscle			64 mg/kg

Comments

- Metabolized by CYP 3A

Selected Sources

Bexar County Medical Examiner's Office data 1996–2007.

Denning DW, Matheson L, Bryson SM, Streete J, Berry DJ, and Henry JA (1985), Death due to carbamazepine self-poisoning: Remedies reviewed, *Hum Tox*, 4(3): 255–60.

Druid H and Holmgren P (1997), A compilation of fatal and control concentrations of drugs in postmortem femoral blood, *J For Sci*, 42(1): 79–87.

Fisher RS and Cysyk BJ (1988), A fatal overdose of carbamazepine: Case report and review of literature, *J Tox Clin Tox*, 26(7): 477–86.

Graves NM, Brundage RC, Wen Y, Cascino G, So E, Ahman P, Rarick J, Krause S, and Leppik IE (1998), Population pharmacokinetics of carbamazepine in adults with epilepsy, *Pharmacotherapy*, 18(2): 273–81.

Physicians' Desk Reference 60 Edition (2006), Thomson PDR, Montvale, NJ, pp. 2278–81.

Rawlins MD, Collste P, Bertilsson L, and Palmer L (1975), Distribution and elimination kinetics of carbamazepine in man, *Eur J Clin Pharmacol*, 8(2): 91–6.

Spiller HA and Carlisle RDJ (2001), Timely antemortem and postmortem concentrations in a fatal carbamazepine overdose, *For Sci*, 46(6): 510–2.

Carbinoxamine

Brand names: Palgic, Pediox
Classification: antihistamine
λ: 10–20 hrs
V_d: unknown
Usual dosage: 4–24 mg qd

Source	Therapeutic/ Nontoxic	Toxic	Lethal
Blood	0.002–0.03 mg/L	No data available	0.25[a]–15 mg/L
Liver	2.5 mg/kg		

[a] Infant.

Comments

- Elevated concentrations may be associated with sudden unexplained deaths in infants

Selected Sources

Bexar County Medical Examiner's Office data 1996–2007.

Hoffman DJ, Leveque MJ, and Thomson T (1983), Capillary GLC assay for carbinoxamine and hydrocodone in human serum using nitrogen-sensitive detection, *J Pharm Sci*, 72(11): 1342–4.

Schulz M and Schmoldt A (2003), Therapeutic and toxic blood concentrations of more than 800 drugs and other xenobiotics, *Pharmazie*, 58(7): 447–74.

Stockis A, Deroubaix X, Jeanbaptiste B, Lins R, Allemon AM, and Laufen H (1995), Relative bioavailability of carbinoxamine and phenylephrine from a retard capsule after single and repeated dose administration in healthy subjects, *Arzneimittelforschung*, 45(9): 1009–12.

Stockis A, Lebacq E, Deroubaix X, Allemon AM, and Laufen H (1992), Relative bioavailability of carbinoxamine and phenylpropanolamine from a retard suspension after single dose administration in healthy subjects, *Arzneimittelforschung*, 42(12): 1478–81.

Carbon Monoxide

Brand names: not applicable
Classification: gas (combustion product of organic material)
λ: 5–6 hrs (21% O_2); 30–90 min (100% O_2)
V_d: unknown
Usual dosage: not applicable

Source	Therapeutic/ Nontoxic	Toxic	Lethal
Blood	0%–3% nonsmoker 3%–8% smoker 0.5%–4.7% infant 3.5%–10% hemolytic anemia	15%–30%	33%–72%
Spleen	<10%	30%–50%	29%–72%

Comments

- Binds to ferrous ion to form carboxyhemoglobin (COHb)
- Has 200–300 times greater affinity to hemoglobin (Hb) molecule than O_2
- Can be detected by Conway cell

Selected Sources

Bexar County Medical Examiner's Office data 1996–2007.
Hampson NB (2007), Carboxyhemoglobin elevation due to hemolytic anemia, *J Emer Med*, 33(1): 17–9.
Levine B (Ed.) (2002), *Principles of Forensic Toxicology*, American Association for Clinical Chemistry, Washington, DC, USA. pp. 330–7.

Carbon Tetrachloride

Brand names: component of dry cleaning chemicals, solvents, degreasers
Alternate names: tetrachloromethane
Classification: volatile (halogenated hydrocarbon)
λ: unknown
V_d: unknown
Usual dosage: not applicable

Source	Therapeutic/ Nontoxic	Toxic	Lethal
Blood	0.003–0.007 mg/L	0.1–31 mg/L	57–260 mg/L
Vitreous			170 mg/L
Urine			328 mg/L
Bile			170 mg/L
Liver			59–142 mg/kg
Kidney			150 mg/kg
Brain			175–243 mg/kg
Lung			39–127 mg/kg
Skeletal muscle			71 mg/kg
Cardiac muscle			78 mg/kg

Comments

- Cardiotoxic: intoxication associated with arrhythmias
- Heptatotoxic

Selected Sources

Broussard L (2002), Chapter 19, Inhalants, in *Principles of Forensic Toxicology*, Levine B (Ed.), American Association for Clinical Chemistry, Washington, DC, USA, pp. 345–353.

Brugnone F, Apostoli P, Perbellini L, Silvestri R, and Cocheo V (1983), Monitoring of occupational exposure to low concentration of carbon tetrachloride, *Dev Tox Environ Sci*, 11: 575–8.

Knight B (1991), *Forensic Pathology*, Chapter 34, Deaths from organic solvents, Oxford University Press, New York, pp. 533–6.

Mathieson PW, Williams G, and MacSweeney JE (1985), Survival after massive ingestion of carbon tetrachloride treated by intravenous infusion of acetylcysteine, *Hum Tox*, 4(6): 627–31.

Ruprah M, Mant TG, and Flanagan RJ (1985), Acute carbon tetrachloride poisoning in 19 patients: Implications for diagnosis and treatment, *Lancet*, 1: 1027–9.

Stephens BG (2004), Chapter XXII, Investigation of deaths from drug abuse in *Spitz and Fisher's Medicolegal Investigation of Death Fourth Edition*, Spitz WU (Ed.), Charles C Thomas, Springfield, IL, pp. 1166–217.

Tombolini A and Cingolani M (1996), Fatal accidental ingestion of carbon tetrachloride: A postmortem distribution study, *J For Sci*, 41(1): 166–8.

Carisoprodol

Brand names: Soma, Vanadom
Classification: muscle relaxant
λ: 1–8 hrs
V_d: unknown
Usual dosage: 350 mg tid

Source	Therapeutic/ Nontoxic	Toxic	Lethal
Blood	10–40 mg/L	30–50 mg/L	39–110 mg/L
Urine			13–165 mg/L
Bile			64 mg/L
Liver			127 mg/kg
Kidney			110 mg/kg
Skeletal muscle			103 mg/kg
Stomach contents			350 mg/L

Comments

- Active metabolite: meprobamate
- Metabolized by CYP 2C19
- Tolerance can develop and should be considered when interpreting drug concentrations

Selected Sources

Backer RC, Zumwalt R, McFeeley P, Veasey S, and Wohlenberg N (1990), Carisoprodol concentrations from different anatomical sites: Three overdose cases, *J Anal Tox*, 14(5): 332–4.
Bexar County Medical Examiner's Office data 1996–2007.
Davis GG and Alexander CB (1998), A review of carisoprodol deaths in Jefferson County, Alabama, *South Med J*, 91(8): 726–30.
Maes R, Hodnett N, Landesman H, Kananen G, Finkle B, and Sunshine I (1969), The gas chromatographic determination of selected sedatives (ethchlorvynol, paraldehyde, meprobamate, and carisoprodol) in biological material, *J For Sci*, 14(2): 235–54.
Olsen H, Koppang E, Alvan G, and Mørland J (1994), Carisoprodol elimination in humans, *Ther Drug Monit*, 16(4): 337–40.

Cetirizine

Brand names: Zyrtec
Classification: antihistamine
λ: 5.5–9 hrs
V_d: 0.4–0.6 L/kg
Usual dosage: 2.5–10 mg qd

Source	Therapeutic/ Nontoxic	Toxic	Lethal
Blood	0.11–0.36 mg/L	2.4 mg/L	No data available
Vitreous		129 mg/L	

Selected Sources

Lefebvre RA, Rosseel MT, and Bernheim J (1988), Single dose pharmacokinetics of cetirizine in young and elderly volunteers, *Int J Clin Pharmacol Res,* 8(6): 463–70.

Pandya KK, Bangaru RA, Gandhi TP, Modi IA, Modi RI, and Chakravarthy BK (1996), High-performance thin layer chromatography for the determination of cetirizine in human plasma and its use in pharmacokinetic studies, *J Pharm Pharmacol,* 48(5): 510–3.

Ridout SM and Tariq SM (1997), Cetirizine overdose in a young child, *J Allergy Clin Immunol,* 99(6 Pt 1): 860–1.

Wood SG, John BA, Chasseaud LF, Yeh J, and Chung M (1987), The metabolism and pharmacokinetics of 14c cetirizine in humans, *Ann Allergy,* 59(6 Pt 2): 31–4.

Chloral Hydrate

Brand names: Somnote, Aquachloral, Noctec
Classification: sedative/hypnotic
λ: 3–4 min
V_d: 0.3–1 L/kg
Usual dosage: 500–2000 mg tid/qid

Source	Therapeutic/ Nontoxic[a]	Toxic[a]	Lethal[a]
Blood	1.5–15 mg/L	40–50 mg/L	60–1700 mg/L
Vitreous			73 mg/L
Urine			128 mg/L
Stomach contents			25 mg

[a] All concentrations are for trichloroethanol.

Comments

- Active metabolite: trichloroethanol (λ 8–30 hrs)

Selected Sources

Benson R (2000), *Concise International Chemical Assessment Document No, 25: Choral Hydrate International Programme on Chemical Safety*. World Health Organization, Geneva.

Benson R (2000), *Toxicological Review of Chloral Hydrate (CAS No.302-17-0)* US EPA, Washington, DC.

Bexar County Medical Examiner's Office data 1996–2007.

Gaulier JM, Merle G, Lacassie E, Courtiade B, Haglund P, Marquet P, and Lachâtre GJ (2001), Fatal intoxications with chloral hydrate, *For Sci*, 46(6): 1507–9.

Heller PF, Goldberger BA, and Caplan YH (1992), Chloral hydrate overdose: Trichloroethanol detection by gas chromatography/mass spectrometry, *For Sci Intl*, 52(2): 231–4.

Levine B, Park J, Smith TD, and Caplan YH (1985), Chloral hydrate: Unusually high concentrations in a fatal overdose, *J Anal Tox*, 9(5): 232–3.

Chlordiazepoxide

Brand names: Librium, Librax (with Clidinium)
Street names: Lib
Classification: benzodiazepine
λ: 24–48 hrs
V_d: 0.3–0.6 L/kg
Usual dosage: 5–10 mg tid/qid

Source	Therapeutic/ Nontoxic	Toxic	Lethal
Blood	1–3 mg/L	3–60 mg/L	7.7[a]–20 mg/L
Urine		1 mg/L	2.2[a]–8 mg/L
Liver			10 mg/kg
Stomach contents			239 mg/L

[a] Ethanol was cointoxicant (BAC 0.19 g/dL).

Comments

- Tolerance can develop and should be considered when interpreting drug concentrations
- Active metabolite: nordiazepam (λ 38–135 hrs)

Selected Sources

Cate JC and Jatlow PI (1973), Chlordiazepoxide overdose: Interpretation of serum drug concentrations, *Clin Tox*, 6(4): 533 61.
Druid H and Holmgren P (1997), A compilation of fatal and control concentrations of drugs in postmortem femoral blood, *J For Sci*, 42(1): 79–87.
Rada RT, Kellner R, and Buchanan JG (1975), Chlordiazepoxide and alcohol: A fatal overdose, *J For Sci*, 20(3): 544–7.
Stanski DR, Greenblatt DJ, Selwyn A, Shader RI, Franke K, and Koch-Weser J (1976), Plasma and cerebrospinal fluid concentrations of chlordiazepoxide and its metabolites in surgical patients, *Clin Pharmacol Ther*, 20(5): 571–8.
Wallace JE, Blum K, and Singh JM (1974), Determination of drugs in biological specimens—A review, *J Tox Clin Tox*, 7(5): 477–95.

Chloroform

Brand names: not applicable
Alternate names: trichloromethane
Classification: solvent/volatile (halogenated hydrocarbon)
λ: 1.5 hrs
V_d: 2.2–2.5 L/kg
Usual dosage: not applicable

Source	Therapeutic/ Nontoxic	Toxic[a]	Lethal
Blood	0.001–5 mg/L	60–250 mg/L	60–834 mg/L
Urine			9.7 mg/L
Bile			16–149 mg/L
Liver			64–298 mg/kg
Kidney			38–124 mg/kg
Brain			54–133 mg/kg
Lung			14–92 mg/kg
Adipose tissue			79 mg/kg
Stomach contents			7.1–540 mg/kg

[a] Same range as therapeutic concentrations for anesthesia

Selected Sources

Chiou WL (1975), Quantitation of hepatic and pulmonary first-pass effects and its implications in pharmacokinetic study. I. Pharmacokinetics of chloroform in man, *J Pharmaco Biopharm*, 3(3): 193–201.

Fry BJ, Taylor T, and Hathway DE (1972), Pulmonary elimination of chloroform and its metabolite in man, *Archives Internationales de Pharmacodynamie et de Therapie*, 196(1): 98–111.

Gaillard Y, Masson-Seyer MF, Giroud M, Roussot JF, and Prevosto JM (2006), A case of drug-facilitated sexual assault leading to death by chloroform poisoning, *Intl J Legal Med*, 120(4): 241–5.

Hajimiragha H, Ewers U, Jansen-Rosseck R, and Brockhaus A (1986), Human exposure to volatile halogenated hydrocarbons from the general environment, *Intl Arch Occ Environ Health*, 58(2): 141–50.

Kim NY, Park SW, and Suh JK (1996), Two fatal cases of dichloromethane or chloroform poisoning, *J For Sci*, 41(3): 527–9.

Kohr RM (1990), Suicide by chloroform ingestion following self-mutilation, *Am J For Med Path*, 11(4): 324–8.

McGee MB, Jejurikar SG, and VanBerkom LC (1987), A double homicide as a result of chloroform poisoning, *J For Sci*, 32(5): 1453–9.

Poobalasingham N and Payne JP (1978), The uptake and elimination of chloroform in man, *Br J Anaesthesia*, 50(4): 325–9.

Stephens BG (2004), Chapter XXII, Investigation of deaths from drug abuse in *Spitz and Fisher's Medicolegal Investigation of Death Fourth Edition*, Spitz WU (Ed.), Charles C Thomas, Springfield, IL, pp. 1166–217.

Chloroquine

Brand names: Aralen
Classification: antimalarial/antiarthritic
λ: 72–300 hrs
V_d: 116–285 L/kg
Usual dosage: 150–600 mg qd

Source	Therapeutic/ Nontoxic	Toxic	Lethal
Blood	0.02–0.5 mg/L	0.5–1.0 mg/L	3–460 mg/L
Vitreous			5.3 mg/L
Urine			20–1700 mg/L
Bile			18–8410 mg/L
Liver	2.9–58 mg/kg		16–1307 mg/kg
Kidney	0.6–5.8 mg/kg		11–1690 mg/kg
Brain	0.7–7.3 mg/kg		1–100 mg/kg
Skeletal muscle			10–132 mg/kg
Cardiac muscle			23–24 mg/kg
Stomach contents			193–1900 mg/L

Comments

- Prolongs QT interval

Selected Sources

Gustafsson LL, Walker O, Alván G, Beermann B, Estevez F, and Gleisner L (1983), Disposition of chloroquine in man after single intravenous and oral doses, *Br J Clin Pharm*, 15(4): 471–9.
Keller T, Schneider A, Lamprecht R, Aderjan R, Tutsch-Bauer E, and Kisser W (1998), Fatal chloroquine intoxication, *For Sci Intl*, 96(1): 21–8.
Kuhlman JJ, Mayes RW, Levine B, Jones R, Wagner GN, and Smith ML (1991), Cloroquine distribution in postmortem cases, *J For Sci*, 36(5): 1572–9.
Muhm M, Stimpfl T, Malzer R, Mortinger H, Binder R, Vycudilik W, Berzlanovich A, Bauer G, and Laggner AN (1996), Suicidal chloroquine poisoning: Clinical course, autopsy findings, and chemical analysis, *J For Sci*, 41(6): 1077–9.
Noirfalise A (1978), Chloroquine intoxication: Two case reports, *For Sci*, 11(3): 177–9.

Chlorpheniramine

Brand names: component of OTC cold medications including Tylenol Cold, Vicks 44, Tussionex, Chlor-trimeton
Classification: antihistamine
λ: 12–43 hrs
V_d: 2.5–3.8 L/kg
Usual dosage: 4 mg q 4–6 hrs

Source	Therapeutic/ Nontoxic	Toxic	Lethal
Blood	0.01–0.04 mg/L	0.5 mg/L	1.1 mg/L
Bile			1.5 mg/L
Liver	0.5–2.5 mg/kg		6.6 mg/kg
Kidney			1.4 mg/kg
Brain			2.5 mg/kg
Lung			5.2 mg/kg

Selected Sources

Huang SM, Athanikar NK, Sridhar K, Huang YC, and Chiou WL (1982), Pharmacokinetics of chlorpheniramine after intravenous and oral administration in normal adults, *Eur J Clin Pharm*, 22(4): 359–65.
Reed D (1981), A fatal case involving chlorpheniramine, *Clin Tox*, 18(8): 941–3.
Soper JW, Chaturvedi AK, and Canfield DV (2000), Prevalence of chlorpheniramine in aviation accident pilot fatalities, 1991–1996, *Aviat Space Environ Med*, 71(12): 1206–9.

Chlorpromazine

Brand names: Thorazine, Largactil, Ormazine
Classification: antipsychotic
λ: 23–37 hrs
V_d: 10–35 L/kg
Usual dosage: 300–800 mg qd

Source	Therapeutic/ Nontoxic	Toxic	Lethal
Blood	0.01–0.3 mg/L	0.5–3 mg/L	3–35 mg/L
Urine			62–750 mg/L
Bile			23 mg/L
Liver	7–17 mg/kg		45–2110 mg/kg
Kidney			4–740 mg/kg
Brain			125–200 mg/kg
Skeletal muscle			12 mg/kg
Stomach contents			373 mg/kg

Comments

- Prolongs QT interval
- Metabolized by CYP 2D6

Selected Sources

Algeri EJ, Katsas GG, and McBay AJ (1959), Toxicology of some new drugs: Glutethimide, meprobamate and chlorpromazine, *J For Sci*, 4: 111–35.

Bailey DN and Guba JJ (1979), Gas-chromatographic analysis for chlorpromazine and some of its metabolites in human serum, with use of a nitrogen detector, *Clin Chem*, 25(7): 1211–5.

Bexar County Medical Examiner's Office data 1996–2007.

Bonnichsen R, Geertinger P, and Maehly AC (1970), Toxicological data on phenothiazine drugs in autopsy cases, *Zeitschrift für Rechtsmedizin/J Legal Med*, 67(3): 158–69.

Coutselinis A, Dimopoulos G, and Dritsas C (1974), Fatal intoxication with chlorpromazine with special regard to the influence of putrefaction on its toxicological analysis, *For Sci*, 4(2): 191–4.

Dahl SG and Strandjord RE (1977), Pharmacokinetics of chlorpromazine after single and chronic dosage, *Clin Pharm Ther*, 21(4): 437–48.

Chlorprothixene

Brand names: Taractan, Truxal
Classification: antipsychotic
λ: 11–39 hrs
V_d: 11–23 L/kg
Usual dosage: 25–50 mg tid/qid

Source	Therapeutic/ Nontoxic	Toxic	Lethal
Blood	0.04–0.5 mg/L	0.5–0.8 mg/L	0.4–1.8 mg/L
Urine			0.4 mg/L
Bile			3.9 mg/L
Liver			5–42 mg/kg
Stomach contents			25–340 mg

Selected Sources

Bagli M, Rao ML, Höflich G, Kasper S, Langer M, Barlage U, Beneke M, Süverkrüp R, and Möller HJ (1996), Pharmacokinetics of chlorprothixene after single intravenous and oral administration of three galenic preparations, *Arzneimittelforschung*, 46(3): 47–50.

Christensen H (1974), Chlorprothixene and its metabolites in blood, liver and urine from fatal poisoning, *Acta Pharmacol Toxicol (Copenh)*, 34(1): 16–26.

Druid H and Holmgren P (1997), A compilation of fatal and control concentrations of drugs in postmortem femoral blood, *J For Sci*, 42(1): 79–87.

Poklis A, Maginn D, and Mackell MA (1983), Chlorprothixene and chlorprothixene-sulfoxide in body fluids from a case of drug overdose, *J Anal Tox*, 7(1): 29–32.

Chlorzoxazone

Brand names: Paraflex, Parafon, Forte DSC, Remular-S, Relaxazone
Classification: muscle relaxant
λ: 1.1–1.8 hrs
V_d: 0.4–0.6 L/kg
Usual dosage: 500–750 mg tid/qid

Source	Therapeutic/ Nontoxic	Toxic	Lethal
Blood	5–20 mg/L	39 mg/L	No data available

Comments

- Metabolized by CYP 2E1

Selected Sources

Conney AH and Burns JJ (1960), Physiological disposition and metabolic fate of chlorzoxazone (paraflex) in man, *J Pharm Exper Ther*, 128: 340–3.

Prompila N, Wittayalertpanya S, and Komolmit P (2007), A study on the pharmacokinetics of chlorzoxazone in healthy Thai volunteers, *J Med Assoc Thai*, 90(1): 160–6.

Roberge RJ, Atchley B, Ryan K, and Krenzelok EP (1998), Two chlorzoxazone (parafon forte) overdoses and coma in one patient: Reversal with flumazenil, *Am J Emerg Med*, 16(4): 393–5.

Citalopram

Brand names: Celexa
Classification: antidepressant (SSRI)
λ: 12–37 hrs
V_d: 10–18 kg/L
Usual dosage: 20–60 mg qd

Source	Therapeutic/ Nontoxic	Toxic	Lethal
Blood	0.01–0.4 mg/L	1–4 mg/L	4–49 mg/L
Vitreous	0.1–0.2 mg/L		0.3 mg/L
Urine			0.5–276 mg/L
Bile	1.3–2.1 mg/L		3.3–6 mg/L
Liver	0.4–21 mg/kg		12–55 mg/kg
Kidney			13 mg/kg
Brain			2–22 mg/kg
Skeletal muscle	0.06–0.8 mg/kg		

Comments

- Prolongs QT interval
- Metabolized by CYP 2C19, 2D6, and 3A

Selected Sources

Anastos N, McIntyre IM, Lynch MJ, and Drummer OH (2002), Postmortem concentrations of citalopram, *J For Sci*, 47(4): 882–4.
Bexar County Medical Examiner's Office data 1996–2007.
Druid H and Holmgren P (1997), A compilation of fatal and control concentrations of drugs in postmortem femoral blood, *J For Sci*, 42(1): 79–87.
Gutierrez M and Abramowitz W (2000), Steady-state pharmacokinetics of citalopram in young and elderly subjects, *Pharmacotherapy*, 20(12): 1441–7.
Jonasson B and Saldeen T (2002), Citalopram in fatal poisoning cases, *For Sci Intl*, 126(1): 1–6.
Luchini D, Morabito G, and Centini F (2005), Case report of a fatal intoxication by citalopram, *Am J For Med Path*, 26(4): 352–4.
Öström M, Eriksson A, Thorson J, and Spigset O (1996), Fatal overdose with citalopram, *Lancet*, 348(9023): 339–40.
Segura LJ and Bravo B (2004), Postmortem citalopram concentrations: Alone or along with other compounds, *J For Sci*, 49(4): 814–9.
Worm K, Dragsholt C, Simonsen K, and Kringsholm B (1998), Citalopram concentrations in samples from autopsies and living persons, *Intl J Legal Med*, 111(4): 188–90.

Clemastine

Brand names: Tavist, Dayhist, Meclastin
Classification: antihistamine
λ: 10–34 hrs
V_d: 7–15 L/kg
Usual dosage: 1.34 mg bid

Source	Therapeutic/ Nontoxic	Toxic	Lethal
Blood	0.0007–0.002 mg/L	No data available	

Selected Sources

Davydova NN, Yasuda SU, Woosley RL, and Wainer IW (2000), Determination of clemastine in human plasma by gas chromatography with nitrogen-phosphorus detection, *J Chromatogr B Biomed Sci Appl*, 744(1): 177–81.

Schran HF, Petryk L, Chang CT, O'Connor R, and Gelbert MB (1996), The pharmacokinetics and bioavailability of clemastine and phenylpropanolamine in single-component and combination formulations, *J Clin Pharmacol*, 36(10): 911–22.

Clobazam

Brand names: Frisium, Urbanyl
Classification: benzodiazepine
λ: 10–40 hrs
V_d: 1 L/kg
Usual dosage: 5–15 mg qd

Source	Therapeutic/ Nontoxic	Toxic	Lethal
Blood	0.14–0.41 mg/L	No data available	3.9 mg/L

Comments

- Active metabolite: desmethylclobazam
- Not available in the United States
- Tolerance can develop and should be considered when interpreting drug concentrations

Selected Sources

Monjanel-Mouterde S, Antoni M, Bun H, Botta-Frindlund D, Gauthier A, Durand A, and Cano JP (1994), Pharmacokinetics of a single oral dose of clobazam in patients with liver disease, *Pharmacol Toxicol*, 74(6): 345–50.

Proença P, Teixeira H, Pinheiro J, Marques EP, and Vieira DN (2004), Forensic intoxication with clobazam: HPLC/DAD/MSD analysis, *For Sci Intl*, 143(2–3): 205–9.

Rouini M, Ardakani YH, Hakemi L, Mokhberi M, and Badri G (2005), Simultaneous determination of clobazam and its major metabolite in human plasma by a rapid HPLC method, *J Chromatogr B Analyt Technol Biomed Life Sci*, 823(2): 167–71.

Clobenzorex

Brand names: Asenlix, Dinintel, Finedal, Rexigen
Street name: Greenies
Classification: stimulant/anorectic
λ: unknown
V_d: unknown
Dosage: 30 mg qd

Source	Therapeutic/ Nontoxic	Toxic	Lethal[a]
Blood	No data available		1.9 mg/L Clo[a] 1.3–3.1 mg/L amph[a]
Urine	0.001–0.05 mg/L Clo 0.01–4.7 mg/L amph		1.3 mg/L Clo 2.0 mg/L amph
Bile			14 mg/L Clo 15 mg/L amph
Liver			174 mg/kg Clo 15 mg/kg amph
Stomach contents			4.9 mg Clo 0.22 mg amph

[a] Co-intoxicant methamphetamine (0.5 mg/L)

Comments

- Metabolized to *d*- and *l*-amphetamine
- Not available in United States; available in Mexico

Selected Sources

Anderson D, New Drugs, California Association of Toxicologists, accessed at http://www.cal-tox.org/Downloads/Monographs/Clobenzorex.pdf on September 3, 2008.
Cody JT and Valtier S (2001), Amphetamine, clobenzorex, and 4-hydroxyclobenzorex levels following multidose administration of clobenzorex, *J Anal Tox*, 25(3): 158–65.
Kraemer T and Maurer HH (2002), Toxicokinetics of amphetamines: Metabolism and toxicokinetic data of designer drugs, amphetamine, methamphetamine, and their N-alkyl derivatives, *Ther Drug Monit*, 24(2): 277–89.

Clomipramine

Brand names: Anafranil
Classification: antidepressant (TCA)
λ: 19–37 hrs
V_d: 9–25 L/kg
Usual dosage: 25 mg qd

Source	Therapeutic/ Nontoxic	Toxic	Lethal
Blood	0.2–0.4 mg/L	0.6–1.6 mg/L	1.7–3.3 mg/L
Urine			0.35–0.48 mg/L
Liver	7–20 mg/kg		12–320 mg/kg
Brain			4.9–8 mg/kg
Stomach contents			4–21 mg

Comments

- Can cause serotonin syndrome
- Active metabolite: *N*-desmethylclomipramine
- Metabolized by CYP 1A2, 2D6, 3A, and 2C19
- May prolong QT interval

Selected Sources

Bexar County Medical Examiner's Office data 1996–2007.

Druid H and Holmgren P (1997), A compilation of fatal and control concentrations of drugs in postmortem femoral blood, *J For Sci*, 42(1): 79–87.

Gex-Fabry M, Haffen E, Paintaud G, Bizouard P, Sechter D, Bechtel PR, and Balant LP (2000), Population pharmacokinetics of clomipramine, desmethylclomipramine and hydroxylated metabolites in patients with depression receiving chronic treatment: model evaluation, *Ther Drug Monit*, 22(6): 701–11.

McIntyre IM, King CV, Cordner SM, and Drummer OH (1994), Postmortem clomipramine: Therapeutic or toxic concentrations? *J For Sci*, 39(2): 486–93.

Meatherall RC, Guay DR, Chalmers JL, and Keenan JR (1983), A fatal overdose with clomipramine, *J Anal Tox*, 7(4): 168–71.

Stolk LM and van der Geest S (1998), Plasma concentrations after a clomipramine intoxication, *J Anal Tox*, 22(7): 612–3.

Clonazepam

Brand names: Klonopin
Classification: benzodiazepine
λ: 19–60 hrs
V_d: 1.5–4.4 L/kg
Usual dosage: 0.25–5 mg bid

Source	Therapeutic/ Nontoxic	Toxic	Lethal
Blood	0.004–0.08 mg/L	0.1–0.6 mg/L	0.68–1.4 mg/L

Comments

- Tolerance can develop and should be considered when interpreting drug concentrations

Selected Sources

Berlin A and Dahlström H (1975), Pharmacokinetics of the anticonvulsant drug clonazepam evaluated from single oral and intravenous doses and by repeated oral administration, *Eur J Clin Pharmacol*, 9(2–3): 155–9.

Bexar County Medical Examiner's Office data 1996–2007.

Burrows DL, Hagardorn AN, Harlan GC, Wallen ED, and Ferslew KE (2003), A fatal drug interaction between oxycodone and clonazepam, *J For Sci*, 48(3): 683–6.

Greenblatt DJ, Blaskovich PD, Nuwayser ES, Harmatz JS, Chen G, and Zinny MA (2005), Clonazepam pharmacokinetics: Comparison of subcutaneous microsphere injection with multiple-dose oral administration, *J Clin Pharmacol*, 45(11): 1288–93.

Welch TR, Rumack BH, and Hammond K (1977), Clonazepam overdose resulting in cyclic coma, *Clin Tox*, 10(4): 433–6.

Clonidine

Brand names: Catapres, Duraclon
Classification: central α-agonist
λ: 6–20 hrs
V_d: 0.9–2.2 L/kg
Usual dosage: 0.1–0.3 mg bid/tid

Source	Therapeutic/ Nontoxic	Toxic	Lethal
Blood	0.0002–0.004 mg/L	0.01–0.23 mg/L	No data available
Urine		3.4–6.5 mg/L	

Selected Sources

Domino LE, Domino SE, and Stockstill MS (1986), Relationship between plasma concentrations of clonidine and mean arterial pressure during an accidental clonidine overdose, *Br J Clin Pharm*, 21(1): 71–4.
Frisk-Holmberg M, Paalzow L, and Edlund PO (1981), Clonidine kinetics in man—Evidence for dose dependency and changed pharmacokinetics during chronic therapy, *Br J Clin Pharm*, 12(5): 653–8.
Lusthof KJ, Lameijer W, and Zweipfenning PG (2000), Use of clonidine for chemical submission, *J Tox Clin Tox*, 38(3): 329–32.
Moore MA and Phillipi P (1976), Letter: Clonidine overdose, *Lancet*, 2: 694.
Neuvonen PJ, Vilska J, and Keränen A (1979), Severe poisoning in a child caused by a small dose of clonidine, *Clin Tox*, 14(4): 369–74.
Rotellar JAO, Monasterio ES, de la Cruz JS, and Gene CG (1981), Clonidine in thousand-fold overdose, *Lancet*, 1: 1312.
Velasquez MT, Rho J, Maronde RF, and Barr J (1983), Plasma clonidine levels in hypertension, *Clin Pharm Thera*, 34(3): 341–6.
Wasserman GS, Mydler TT, and Watson WA (1992), Pediatric clonidine levels and toxicity, *Vet Hum Tox*, 34: 335.

Clorazepate

Brand names: Tranxene
Classification: benzodiazepine
λ: 2.3–2.4 hrs
V_d: 1–1.7 L/kg
Usual dosage: 7.5 mg tid

Source	Therapeutic/ Nontoxic	Toxic	Lethal
Blood	0.1–2.6 mg/L	2–5 mg/L	No data available

Comments

- Active metabolite: nordiazepam (λ 38–135 hrs)
- Tolerance can develop and should be considered when interpreting drug concentrations

Selected Sources

Bertler A, Lindgren S, Magnusson JO, and Malmgren H (1983), Pharmacokinetics of chlorazepate after intravenous and intramuscular administration, *Psychopharmacology (Berl)*, 80(3): 236–9.

Greenblatt DJ, Divoll MK, Soong MH, Boxenbaum HG, Harmatz JS, and Shader RI (1988), Desmethyldiazepam pharmacokinetics: Studies following intravenous and oral desmethyldiazepam, oral clorazepate and intravenous diazepam, *J Clin Pharmacol*, 28(9): 853–9.

Clorazepate (tranxene). Another benzodiazepine (1972), *Medical Letter on Drugs Therapeutics*, 14(23): 85–6.

Clozapine

Brand names: Clozaril, FazaClo
Classification: antipsychotic
λ: 4–66 hrs
V_d: 4.6–5 L/kg
Usual dosage: 300–450 mg qd

Source	Therapeutic/ Nontoxic	Toxic	Lethal
Blood	0.04–0.8 mg/L	0.9–7.0 mg/L	1.3–13 mg/L
Vitreous			1.3 mg/L
Urine		4.3 mg/L	11 mg/L
Bile			1844 mg/L
Liver	0.8–1.5 mg/kg	5.9–17 mg/kg	6.5–85 mg/kg
Stomach contents			6.5–2420 mg

Comments

- Prolongs QT interval
- Metabolized by CYP 1A2, 3A4, and 2D6

Selected Sources

Bexar County Medical Examiner's Office data 1996–2007.

Druid H and Holmgren P (1997), A compilation of fatal and control concentrations of drugs in postmortem femoral blood, *J For Sci*, 42(1): 79–87.

Flanagan RJ, Spencer EP, Morgan PE, Barnes TR, and Dunk L (2005), Suspected clozapine poisoning in the UK/Eire, 1992–2003, *For Sci Intl*, 155(2–3): 91–9.

Ishii A, Mizoguchi K, Kageoka M, Seno H, Kumazawa T, and Suzuki O (1997), Nonfatal suicidal intoxication by clozapine, *J Tox Clin Tox*, 35(2): 195–7.

Keller T, Miki A, Binda S, and Dirnhofer R (1997), Fatal overdose of clozapine, *For Sci Intl*, 86(1–2): 119–25.

Kratzsch C, Peters FT, Kraemer T, Weber AA, and Maurer HH (2003), Screening, library-assisted identification and validated quantification of fifteen neuroleptics and three of their metabolites in plasma by liquid chromatography/mass spectrometry with atmospheric pressure chemical ionization, *J Mass Spectrum*, 38(3): 283–95.

Meeker JE, Herrmann PW, Som CW, and Reynolds PC (1992), Clozapine tissue concentrations following an apparent suicidal overdose of clozaril, *J Anal Tox*, 16(1): 54–6.

Physicians' Desk Reference 61 Edition (2007), Thomson PDR, Montvale, NJ, pp. 2184–9.

Worm K, Kringsholm B, and Steentoft A (1993), Clozapine cases with fatal, toxic or therapeutic concentrations, *Int J Legal Med*, 106(3): 115–8.

Cocaine

Brand names: Cocaine hydrochloride
Street names: Coke, Crack, Snow Crack; w/ heroin: Dynamite, Belushi, Eightball, Moonrock, Speedball; w/ PCP: Jim Jones, Parachute, Spaceball
Classification: local anesthetic (ENT)/stimulant
λ: 0.7–1.5 hrs
V_d: 1.7–2.7 L/kg
Usual dosage: 1%–10% solutions used topically; 1–2 mg/kg/dose

Source	Therapeutic/ Nontoxic	Toxic	Lethal
Blood	0.1–0.3 mg/L	0.1–5 mg/L	0.1–330 mg/L
Vitreous			0.8–13 mg/L
Urine			0.05–402 mg/L
Bile			2–468 mg/L
Liver			0.2–393 mg/kg
Kidney			3.8–28 mg/kg
Brain			0.04–74 mg/kg
Skeletal muscle			0.1–48 mg/kg

Comments

- Can be metabolized *in vitro* (and *in vivo*) to ecgonine methyl ester and benzoylecgonine
- Active metabolites: cocaethylene, norcocaine
- Metabolized by CYP 3A

Selected Sources

Amon CA, Tate LG, Wright RK, and Matusiak W (1986), Sudden death due to ingestion of cocaine, *J Anal Tox*, 10(5): 217–8.

Bednarczyk LR, Gressmann EA, and Wymer RL (1980), Two cocaine-induced fatalities, *J Anal Tox*, 4(5): 263–5.

Bexar County Medical Examiner's Office data 1996–2007.

Giroud C, Michaud K, Sporkert F, Eap C, Augsburger M, Cardinal P, and Mangin P (2004), A fatal overdose of cocaine associated with coingestion of marijuana, buprenorphine and fluoxetine. Body fluid and tissue distribution of cocaine and its metabolites determinded by hydrophilic interaction chromatography-mass spectrometry (HILIC-MS), *J Anal Toxicol*, Sep 28(6), 464–74.

Hart CL, Jatlow P, Sevarino KA, and McCance-Katz EF (2000), Comparison of intravenous cocaethylene and cocaine in humans, *Psychopharmacology (Berl)*, 149(2): 153–62.

Heinemann A, Miyaishi S, Iwersen S, Schmoldt A, and Püschel K (1998), Body-packing as cause of unexpected sudden death, *For Sci Intl*, 92(1): 1–10.

Jenkins AJ, Levine B, Titus J, and Smialek JE (1999), The interpretation of cocaine and benzoylecgonine concentrations in postmortem cases, *For Sci Intl*, 101(1): 17–25.

Mackey-Bojack S, Kloss J, Apple F (2000), Cocaine, cocaine metabolite, and ethanol concentrations in postmortem blood and vitreous humor, *J Anal Toxicol*, 24(1), 59–65.

Peretti FJ, Isenschmid DS, Levine B, Caplan YH, and Smialek JE (1990), Cocaine fatality: An unexplained blood concentration in a fatal overdose, *For Sci Intl*, 48(2): 135–8.

Poklis A, Maginn D, and Barr JL (1987), Tissue disposition of cocaine in man: A report of five fatal poisonings, *For Sci Intl*, 33(2): 83–8.

Spiehler VR and Reed D (1985), Brain concentrations of cocaine and benzoylecgonine in fatal cases, *J For Sci*, 30(4):1003–11.

Terndrup TE, Walls HC, Mariani PJ, Gavula DP, Madden CM, Cantor RM (1992), Plasma cocaine and tetracaine levels following application of topical anesthesia in children, *Ann Emerg Med* Feb 21(2), 162–6.

Winek CL, Wahba WW, Rozin L, and Janssen JK (1987), An unusually high blood cocaine concentration in a fatal case, *J Anal Tox*, 11(1): 43–6.

Codeine

Brand names: often combined with aceta or ASA (Tylenol w/ codeine, Empirin w/ codeine)
Classification: narcotic
λ: 1.1–4 hrs
V_d: 2.2–4.7 L/kg
Usual dosage: 15–60 mg q 4 hrs

Source	Therapeutic/ Nontoxic	Toxic	Lethal
Blood	0.03–0.4 mg/L	0.5–1 mg/L	1–48 mg/L
Urine	5–20 mg/L	25 mg/L	6.2–370 mg/L
Bile			1.4–60 mg/L
Liver			13–128 mg/kg
Kidney			2.3–36 mg/kg
Brain			4.8–33 mg/kg
Stomach contents			150–280 mg/L

Comments

- Metabolized to morphine by CYP 2D6
- Tolerance can develop and should be considered when interpreting drug concentrations

Selected Sources

Findlay JW, Butz RF, and Welch RM (1977), Codeine kinetics as determined by radioimmunoassay, *Clin Pharmacol Ther,* 22(4): 439–46.
Gerostamoulos J, Burke MP, and Drummer OH (1996), Involvement of codeine in drug-related deaths, *Am J For Med Path,* 17(4): 327–35.
Guay DR, Awni WM, Findlay JW, Halstenson CE, Abraham PA, Opsahl JA, Jones EC, and Matzke GR (1988), Pharmacokinetics and pharmacodynamics of codeine in end-stage renal disease, *Clin Pharmacol Ther,* 43(1): 63–71.
Kim I, Barnes AJ, Oyler JM, Schepers R, Joseph RE Jr, Cone EJ, Lafko D, Moolchan ET, and Huestis MA (2002), Plasma and oral fluid pharmacokinetics and pharmacodynamics after oral codeine administration, *Clin Chem,* 48(9): 1486–96.
Kintz P, Tracqui A, and Mangin P (1991), Codeine concentrations in human samples in a case of fatal ingestion, *Int J Legal Med,* 104(3): 177–8.
Pearson MA, Poklis A, and Morrison RR (1979), A fatality due to the ingestion of (methyl morphine) codeine, *Clin Tox,* 15(3): 267–71.
Peat MA and Sengupta A (1977), Toxicological investigations of cases of death involving codeine and dihydrocodeine, *For Sci,* 9(1): 21–32.

Cyanide

Brand names: component of some insecticides
Classification: poison
λ: 1 hr
V_d: 0.4 L/kg
Usual dosage: not applicable

Source	Therapeutic/ Nontoxic	Toxic	Lethal
Blood	<0.25 mg/L	0.25–5 mg/L	1–100 mg/L
Vitreous			0.5–1.4 mg/L
Urine			0.1–5 mg/L
Bile			2.6–7.9 mg/L
Liver			0.1–43 mg/kg
Kidney			0.5–55 mg/kg
Brain			0.6–30 mg/kg
Stomach contents			2–4000 mg/L

Comments

- Associated with bright red lividity and musculature at autopsy
- Has a distinct bitter almond smell

Selected Sources

Adelson L (1974), Chapter XIII, Murder by poison, in *The Pathology of Homicide*, Charles C Thomas, Springfield, IL, pp. 725–875.

Bexar County Medical Examiner's Office data 1996–2007.

Hall AH, Doutre WH, Ludden T, Kulig KW, and Rumack BH (1987), Nitrite/thiosulfate treated acute cyanide poisoning: Estimated kinetics after antidote, *J Tox Clin Tox*, 25(1–2): 121–33.

Knight B (1991), *Forensic Pathology*, Oxford University Press, New York, pp. 526–7.

Levine B (Ed.) (2002), *Principles of Forensic Toxicology*, American Association for Clinical Chemistry, Washington, DC, USA, pp. 337–44.

Wallace JE, Blum K, and Singh JM (1974), Determination of drugs in biological specimens—A review, *J Tox Clin Tox*, 7(5): 477–95.

Cyclizine

Brand names: Marezine
Classification: antihistamine
λ: 7–24 hrs
V_d: 13–21 L/kg
Usual dosage: 50 mg q 4–6 hrs

Source	Therapeutic/ Nontoxic	Toxic	Lethal
Blood	0.01–0.3 mg/L	0.75–1 mg/L	15–80 mg/L
Liver			37 mg/kg
Brain			3 mg/kg

Selected Sources

Backer RC, McFeeley P, and Wohlenberg N (1989), Fatality resulting from cyclizine overdose, *J Anal Tox*, 13(5): 308–9.

Battista HJ, Henn R, and Schnabel F (1978), Clinical course, morphological and toxicological findings in a fatal case of cyclizine poisoning in a child, *Beitrage zur Gerichtlichen Medizin*, 36: 429–31.

Griffin DS and Baselt RC (1984), Blood and urine concentrations of cyclizine by nitrogen-phosphorus gas-liquid chromatography, *J Anal Tox*, 8(2): 97–9.

Land G, Dean K, and Bye A (1981), Determination of cyclizine and norcyclizine in plasma and urine using gas-liquid chromatography with nitrogen selective detection, *J Chromatogr*, 222(1): 135–40.

Schulz M and Schmoldt A (2003), Therapeutic and toxic blood concentrations of more than 800 drugs and other xenobiotics, *Pharmazie*, 58(7): 447–74.

Cyclobenzaprine

Brand names: Flexeril, Amrix, Fexmid
Classification: muscle relaxant
λ: 8.3–47 hrs
V_d: unknown
Usual dosage: 5 mg tid

Source	Therapeutic/ Nontoxic	Toxic	Lethal
Blood	0.002–0.05 mg/L	No data available	0.3–1.8 mg/L
Bile			17 mg/L
Liver			3.1 mg/kg
Skeletal muscle			0.59 mg/kg

Comments

- Metabolized by CYP 1A2

Selected Sources

Bexar County Medical Examiner's Office data 1996–2007.
Spiller HA and Cutino L (2003), Fatal cyclobenzaprine overdose with postmortem values, *J For Sci*, 48(4): 883–4.
Winchell GA, King JD, Chavez-Eng CM, Constanzer ML, and Korn SH (2002), Cyclobenzaprine pharmacokinetics, including the effects of age, gender and hepatic insufficiency, *J Clin Pharmacol*, 42(1): 61–9.

Cyproheptadine

Brand names: Periactin
Classification: antihistamine
λ: 8.6 hrs
V_d: unknown
Usual dosage: 4 mg tid

Source	Therapeutic/ Nontoxic	Toxic	Lethal
Blood	0.003–0.03 mg/L	No data available	0.49[a]–0.62[b] mg/L
Urine			0.23[a]–0.75[b] mg/L
Bile			8.1[b]–31[a] mg/L
Liver			7.6[b] mg/kg
Kidney			1.8[b] mg/kg
Stomach contents			2.3[b] mg

[a] Citalopram co-intoxicant (2.3 mg/L)
[b] Blood alcohol content 0.09 mg/L

Selected Sources

Bexar County Medical Examiner's Office data 1996–2007.

Gunja N, Collins M, and Graudins A (2004), A comparison of the pharmacokinetics of oral and sublingual cyproheptadine, *J Tox Clin Tox*, 42(1): 79–83.

Levine B, Green-Johnson D, Hogan S, and Smialek JE (1998), A cyproheptadine fatality, *J Anal Tox*, 22(1): 72–4.

Dantrolene

Brand names: Dantrium
Classification: muscle relaxant
λ: 4–10 hrs
V_d: unknown
Usual dosage: 25–100 mg tid

Source	Therapeutic/ Nontoxic	Toxic	Lethal
Blood	0.7–8 mg/L	No data available	

Comments

- Active metabolite: 5-hydroxydantrolene
- Associated with malignant hyperthermia

Selected Sources

Lerman J, McLeod ME, and Strong HA (1989), Pharmacokinetics of intravenous dantrolene in children, *Anesthesiology*, 70(4): 625–9.

Physicians' Desk Reference 61 Edition (2007), Thomson PDR, Montvale, NJ, pp. 2694–5.

Podranski T, Bouillon T, Schumacher PM, Taguchi A, Sessler DI, and Kurz A (2005), Compartmental pharmacokinetics of dantrolene in adults: Do malignant hyperthermia association dosing guidelines work? *Anesth Analg*, 101(6): 1695–9.

Desipramine

Brand names: Norpramin
Classification: antidepressant (TCA)
λ: 12–28 hrs
V_d: 24–60 L/kg
Usual dosage: 75–150 mg qd

Source	Therapeutic/ Nontoxic	Toxic	Lethal
Blood	0.04–0.25 mg/L	0.4–1.7 mg/L	3–36 mg/L
Urine			0.21–34 mg/L
Liver			107–140 mg/kg
Stomach contents			118–180 mg

Comments

- Metabolite of imipramine
- Prolongs QT interval
- Metabolized by CYP 2D6

Selected Sources

Amitai Y and Frischer H (2004), Excess fatality from desipramine and dosage recommendations, *Ther Drug Monit*, 26(5): 468–73.
Bexar County Medical Examiner's Office data 1996–2007.
Bickel MH, Brochon R, Friolet B, Herrmann B, and Stofer AR (1967), Clinical and biochemical results of a fatal case of desipramine intoxication, *Psychopharmacologia*, 10(5): 431–6.
Burke MJ, Harvey AT, and Preskorn SK (1996), Pharmacokinetics of the newer antidepressants, *Am J Med*, 100(1): 119–21.
Chaturvedi AK, Hidding JT, Rao NG, Smith JC, and Bredehoeft SJ (1987), Two tricyclic antidepressant poisonings: Levels of amitriptyline, nortriptyline and desipramine in post-mortem biological samples, *For Sci Intl*, 33(2): 93–101.
Furlanut M, Benetello P, and Spina E (1993), Pharmacokinetic optimisation of tricyclic antidepressant therapy, *Clinical Pharmacokinetics*, 24(4): 301–18.
Linder MW and Keck PE (1998), Standards of laboratory practice: Antidepressant drug monitoring, National Academy of Clinical Biochemistry, *Clin Chem*, 44(5): 1073–84.
Sawyer WT, Caudill JL, and Ellison MJ (1984), A case of severe acute desipramine overdose, *Am J Psychiatry*, 141(1): 122–3.
von Moltke LL, Greenblatt DJ, and Shader RI (1993), Clinical pharmacokinetics of antidepressants in the elderly. Therapeutic implications, *Clin Pharmacokinet*, 24(2): 141–60.

Desloratadine

Brand names: Clarinex
Classification: antihistamine
λ: 27–36 hrs
V_d: 49 L/kg
Usual dosage: 2.5–10 mg qd

Source	Therapeutic/ Nontoxic	Toxic	Lethal
Blood	0.003–0.006 mg/L	No data available	

Comments

- May prolong QT interval
- Active metabolite: 3-hydroxydesloratadine
- Metabolized by CYP 3A

Selected Sources

Affrime M, Banfield C, Gupta S, Cohen A, Boutros T, Thonoor M, and Cayen M (2002), Comparison of pharmacokinetics and metabolism of desloratadine, fexofenadine, levocetirizine and mizolastine in humans, *Clin Pharmacokinet,* 41(Suppl. 1): 21–8.

Molimard M, Diquet B, and Benedetti MS (2004), Comparison of pharmacokinetics and metabolism of desloratadine, fexofenadine, levocetirizine and mizolastine in humans, *Fundam Clin Pharmacol*, 18(4): 399–411.

Dexfenfluramine

Brand names: Redux
Classification: anorectic
λ: 13–20 hrs
V_d: 10–14 L/kg
Usual dosage: 15 mg bid

Source	Therapeutic/ Nontoxic	Toxic	Lethal
Blood	0.013–0.05 mg/L	0.15–0.78 mg/L	3.3 mg/L[a]

[a] Postmortem sample in suicide case; exact cause of death not given

Comments

- No longer available in the United States
- Associated with pulmonary hypertension
- Active metabolite: *d*-norfenfluramine
- Metabolized by CYP 2D6

Selected Sources

Cheymol G, Weissenburger J, Poirier JM, and Gellee C (1995), The pharmacokinetics of dexfenfluramine in obese and non-obese subjects, *Br J Clin Pharm*, 39(6): 684–7.
Redux™ [package insert] (1996) Philadelphia, PA, Wyeth-Ayerst Laboratories.
LoVecchio F and Curry SC (1998), Dexfenfluramine overdose, *Ann Emer Med*, 32(1): 102–3.

Dexmethylphenidate

Brand names: Focalin
Classification: stimulant
λ: 2–4.5 hrs
V_d: 1.5–3.7 L/kg
Usual dosage: 2.5 mg bid

Source	Therapeutic/ Nontoxic	Toxic	Lethal
Blood	0.01–0.03 mg/L	No data available	

Selected Sources

Physicians' Desk Reference 60 Edition (2006), Thomson PDR, Montvale, NJ, pp. 2214–20.
Teo SK, Scheffler MR, Wu A, Stirling DI, Thomas SD, and Stypinski D (2004), A single-dose, two-way crossover, bioequivalence study of dexmethylphenidate HCl with and without food in healthy subjects, *J Clin Pharm*, 44(2): 173–8.

Dextromethorphan

Brand names: common component of OTC cough medicines including: Balamine, Tylenol Cold, Vicks
Classification: antitussive
λ: 3–4 hrs
V_d: 255–316 L/kg
Usual dosage: 10–20 mg q 4 hrs

Source	Therapeutic/ Nontoxic	Toxic	Lethal
Blood	0.005–0.06 mg/L	No data available	3.5–9.7 mg/L
Liver			31–230 mg/kg

Comments

- Metabolized by CYP 2D6

Selected Sources

Rammer L, Holmgren P, and Sandler H (1988), Fatal intoxication by dextromethorphan: A report on two cases, *For Sci Intl*, 37(4): 233–6.

Schadel M, Wu D, Otton SV, Kalow W, and Sellers EM (1995), Pharmacokinetics of dextromethorphan and metabolites in humans: Influence of the CYP2D6 phenotype and quinidine inhibition, *J Clin Psychopharmacology*, 15(4): 263–9.

Vetticaden SJ, Cabana BE, Prasad VK, Purich ED, Jonkman JH, and de Zeeuw R (1989), Phenotypic differences in dextromethorphan metabolism, *Pharmaceutical Research*, 6(1): 13–9.

Dextromoramide

Brand names: Palfium, Jetrium, Dimorlin
Classification: narcotic
λ: 2.2–4.9 hrs
V_d: 0.6–2.4 L/kg
Usual dosage: 5–20 mg q 4 hrs

Source	Therapeutic/ Nontoxic	Toxic	Lethal
Blood	0.01–0.18 mg/L	0.2–0.5 mg/L	0.87–1.9 mg/L
Urine			0.1 mg/L
Bile			0.05–0.49 mg/L
Liver			0.39 mg/kg
Kidney			0.13–0.25 mg/kg
Brain			0.03–0.07 mg/kg
Stomach contents			0.05-0.06 mg/L

Comments

- Tolerance can develop and should be considered when interpreting drug concentrations

Selected Sources

Brewer E (1990), A dextromoramide-related fatality, *J For Sci*, 35(2): 483–9.
Kintz P, Tracqui A, Mangin P, Lugnier AA, and Chaumont AJ (1989), Fatal intoxication by dextromoramide: A report on two cases, *J Anal Tox*, 13(4): 238–9.
Kintz P, Tracqui A, Mangin P, Lugnier A, and Chaumont A (1989), Toxicological findings after fatal dextromoramide injection, *J Tox Clin Tox*, 27(6): 385–8.
Pagani I, Barzaghi N, Crema F, Perucca E, Ego D, and Rovei V (1989), Pharmacokinetics of dextromoramide in surgical patients, *Fundamental Clinical Pharmacology*, 3(1): 27–35.
Rop PP, Grimaldi F, Bresson M, Fornaris M, and Viala A (1993), Simultaneous determination of dextromoramide, propoxyphene and norpropoxyphene in necropsic whole blood by liquid chromatography, *J Chromatography*, 615(2): 357–64.

Diazepam

Brand names: Valium, Valrelease
Street names: V
Classification: benzodiazepine
λ: 30–66 hrs
V_d: 1–2 L/kg
Usual dosage: 2–10 mg bid/qid

Source	Therapeutic/ Nontoxic	Toxic	Lethal
Blood	0.02–4 mg/L	3–20 mg/L	5–30 mg/L
Urine			3 mg/L
Bile			0.8 mg/L
Liver			16 mg/kg
Skeletal muscle			16 mg/kg

Comments

- Sudden withdrawal can lead to anxiety, seizures, and death
- Tolerance can develop and should be considered when interpreting drug concentrations
- Metabolized by CYP 2C19 and 3A
- Active metabolite: nordiazepam (λ 38–135 hrs)

Selected Sources

Cardauns H and Iffland R (1973), Fatal intoxication of a young drug addict with diazepam, *Archiv für Toxikologie*, 31(2): 147–51.
Finkle BS, McCloskey KL, and Goodman LS (1979), Diazepam and drug-associated deaths: A survey in the United States and Canada, *JAMA*, 242(5): 429–34.
Greenblatt DJ, Harmatz JS, Friedman H, Locniskar A, and Shader RI (1989), A large-sample study of diazepam pharmacokinetics, *Ther Drug Mon*, 11(6): 652–7.
Tada K, Moroji T, Sekiguchi R, Motomura H, and Noguchi T (1985), Liquid-chromatographic assay of diazepam and its major metabolites in serum, and application to pharmacokinetic study of high doses of diazepam in schizophrenics, *Clin Chem*, 31(10): 1712–5.

Dibenzepine

Brand names: Noveril
Classification: antidepressant (TCA)
λ: 3.5–5 hrs
V_d: 3–4 L/kg
Usual dosage: 240 mg bid/qd

Source	Therapeutic/ Nontoxic	Toxic	Lethal
Blood	0.02–0.15 mg/L	3 mg/L	3.3–153 mg/L
Urine			12–350 mg/L
Bile			63–113 mg/L
Liver			20–550 mg/kg
Brain			9.1–43 mg/kg
Kidney			31–63 mg/kg
Skeletal muscle			1–38 mg/kg
Stomach contents			220–1500 mg/kg

Selected Sources

Bonnichsen R and Schubert B (1971), Determination of dibenzepine in autopsy material, *Zeitschrift für Rechtsmedizin*, 68(5): 253–60.

Brochon R, Lehner H, Gauch R, and Rudin O (1969), The detection and determination of dibenzepine and its metabolites in autopsy material, *Archiv für Toxikologie*, 24(4): 249–59.

Christensen H and Felby S (1975), Dibenzepine and its metabolites in blood, muscle, liver, vitreous body and urine from fatal poisoning, *Acta Pharmacologica et Toxicologica*, 37(5): 393–401.

Robinson AE, Coffer AI, and McDowall RD (1974), Toxicology of some autopsy cases involving tricyclic antidepressant drugs, *Zeitschrift für Rechtsmedizin*, 74(4): 261–6.

Schlicht HJ and Gelbke HP (1978), Gas chromatographic determination of dibenzepine and its basic metabolites in biological material, *J Chromatography A*, 166(2): 599–603.

Dicyclomine

Brand names: Bentyl, Byclomine, Dibent
Classification: antimuscarinic/antispasmotic
λ: 1.8 hrs
V_d: 3.6 L/kg
Usual dosage: 20 mg qid

Source	Therapeutic/ Nontoxic	Toxic	Lethal
Blood	0.02–0.1 mg/L	0.2 mg/L	0.2–0.5 mg/L
Vitreous			0.1 mg/L
Bile			0.6 mg/L

Selected Sources

Garriott JC, Rodriquez R, and Norton LE (1984), Two cases of death involving dicyclomine in infants measurement of therapeutic and toxic concentrations in blood, *J Tox Clin Tox*, 22(5): 455–62.
Physicians' Desk Reference 60 Edition (2006), Thomson PDR, Montvale, NJ, pp. 724–6.

Diethylpropion

Brand names: Tenuate
Classification: stimulant/anorectic
λ: unknown
V_d: unknown
Usual dosage: 25 mg tid

Source	Therapeutic/ Nontoxic	Toxic	Lethal
Blood	0.02–1.8 mg/L	2 mg/L	5.4 mg/L

Selected Sources

Schulz M and Schmoldt A (2003), Therapeutic and toxic blood concentrations of more than 800 drugs and other xenobiotics, *Pharmazie*, 58(7): 447–74.

Wright GJ, Lang JF, Lemieux RE, and Goodfriend MJ (1975), The objective and timing of drug disposition studies, appendix III. Diethylpropion and its metabolites in the blood plasma of the human after subcutaneous and oral administration, *Drug Metabolism Reviews*, 4(2): 267–76.

Digitoxin

Brand names: Digitaline
Classification: cardiac glycoside
λ: 6–12 dys
V_d: 0.49–0.82 L/kg
Usual dosage: 0.05–0.2 mg qd

Source	Therapeutic/ Nontoxic	Toxic	Lethal
Blood	0.01–0.03 mg/L	0.03–0.63 mg/L	0.2–0.3 mg/L

Comments

- Overdose treated with Digibind® (Digoxin Immune Fab)

Selected Sources

Krappweis J, Petereit G, Justus J, Altmann E, and Kirch W (1996), Digitoxin intoxication with lethal outcome, *Eur J Med Res*, 1(12): 551–3.

MacFarland RT, Marcus FI, Fenster PE, Graves PE, and Perrier D (1984), Pharmacokinetics and bioavailability of digitoxin by a specific assay, *Eur J Clin Pharm*, 27(1): 85–9.

Ochs HR, Grube E, Greenblatt DJ, Arendt R, and Bodem G (1981), Pharmacokinetics and pharmacodynamics of intravenous digoxin and digitoxin, *Klinische Wochenschrift*, 59(16): 889–97.

Schmitt K, Tulzer G, Häckel F, Sommer R, and Tulzer W (1994), Massive digitoxin intoxication treated with digoxin-specific antibodies in a child, *Ped Card*, 15(1): 48–9.

Woolf AD, Wenger T, Smith TW, and Lovejoy FH (1992), The use of digoxin-specific Fab fragments for severe digitalis intoxication in children, *NEJM*, 326(26): 1739–44.

Digoxin

Brand names: Lanoxin, Lanoxicaps, Digitalis
Classification: cardiac glycoside
λ: 1.5–2 d
V_d: 4.1–8 L/kg
Usual dosage: 0.125–0.5 mg qd

Source	Therapeutic/ Nontoxic	Toxic	Lethal
Blood	0.0008–0.002 mg/L	0.002–0.03 mg/L	0.01–1.3 mg/L
Vitreous	0.002–0.007 mg/L		0.003–0.05 mg/L
Urine			0.01–1.3 mg/L
Bile			0.86–2.4 mg/L
Liver	0.03–0.2 mg/kg		0.03–0.73 mg/kg
Kidney	0.05–0.4 mg/kg		0.13–1.7 mg/kg
Brain	0.003–0.07 mg/kg		0.009–0.05 mg/kg
Skeletal muscle	0.008–0.06 mg/kg		0.01–0.37 mg/kg
Cardiac muscle	0.03–0.5 mg/kg		0.14–1.2 mg/kg

Comments

- Causes increased potassium
- Overdose treated with Digibind® (Digoxin Immune Fab)

Selected Sources

Aderjan R, Buhr H, and Schmidt G (1979), Investigation of cardiac glycoside levels in human post mortem blood and tissues determined by a special radioimmunoassay procedure, *Arch Tox*, 42(2): 107–14.

Andersson KE, Bertler A, and Wettrell G (1975), Post-mortem distribution and tissue concentrations of digoxin in infants and adults, *Acta Paediatrica Scandinavica*, 64(3): 497–504.

Citrin DL (1973), Fatal intoxication with digoxin, *Lancet* 1: 376.

Dickson SJ and Blazey ND (1977), Post-mortem digoxin levels—Two unusual case reports, *For Sci*, 9(2): 145–50.

DiMaio VJ, Garriott JC, and Putnam R (1975), Digoxin concentrations in postmortem specimens after overdose and therapeutic use, *J For Sci*, 20(2): 340–7.

Hastreiter AR, Kim PW, and van der Horst R (1983), Accidental digoxin overdose in an infant: Postmortem tissue concentrations, *J For Sci*, 28(2): 482–8.

Hinderling PH and Hartmann D (1991), Pharmacokinetics of digoxin and main metabolites/derivatives in healthy humans, *Ther Drug Monitoring*, 13(5): 381–401.

Iisalo E, Nuutila M (1973), Myocardial digoxin concentrations in fatal intoxications, *Lancet*, 1:257.

Nicholls DP (1977), Fatal digoxin overdose, *Postgraduate Medical Journal*, 53(619): 280–1.

Physicians' Desk Reference 60 Edition (2006), Thomson PDR, Montvale, NJ, pp. 1458–72.

Rietbrock N, Wojahn H, Weinmann J, Hasford J, and Kuhlmann J (1978), Suicide with beta-methyldigoxin, *Deutsche Medizinische Wochenschrift*, 103(46): 1841–4.

Ritz S, Harding P, Martz W, Schütz HW, and Kaatsch HJ (1992), Measurement of digitalis-glycoside levels in ocular tissues: A way to improve postmortem diagnosis of lethal digitalis-glycoside poisoning? I. Digoxin, *Intl J Legal Med*, 105(3): 149–54.

Selesky M, Spiehler V, Cravey RH, and Elliot HW (1977), Digoxin concentrations in fatal cases, *J For Sci*, 22(2): 409–17.

Smolarz A, Roesch E, Lenz E, Neubert H, and Abshagen P (1985), Digoxin specific antibody (Fab) fragments in 34 cases of severe digitalis intoxication, *J Tox Clin Tox*, 23(4–6): 327–40.

Steentoft A (1973), Fatal digitalis poisoning, *Acta Pharmacologica et Toxicologica*, 32(5): 353–7.

Dihydrocodeine

Brand names: Codicontin, Synalgos (w/ ASA, caffeine), Novahistine (w/ phenylephrine), HydroTussin (w/ pseudoephedrine, chlorpheniramine)
Classification: narcotic
λ: 3.3–4.5 hrs
V_d: 1.1–1.3 L/kg
Usual dosage: 16–32 mg q 4 hrs

Source	Therapeutic/ Nontoxic	Toxic	Lethal
Blood	0.03–0.3 mg/L	0.5–1 mg/L	0.8–18 mg/L
Liver			1.3 mg/kg
Kidney			11 mg/kg
Brain			0.8 mg/kg

Comments

- Metabolite of hydrocodone
- Active metabolite: dihydromorphone
- Tolerance can develop and should be considered when interpreting drug concentrations

Selected Sources

Klinder K, Skopp G, Mattern R, and Aderjan R (1999), The detection of dihydrocodeine and its main metabolites in cases of fatal overdose, *Intl J Legal Med*, 112(3): 155–8.

Rowell FJ, Seymour RA, and Rawlins MD (1983), Pharmacokinetics of intravenous and oral dihydrocodeine and its acid metabolites, *Eur J Clin Pharm*, 25(3): 419–24.

Schulz M and Schmoldt A (2003), Therapeutic and toxic blood concentrations of more than 800 drugs and other xenobiotics, *Pharmazie*, 58(7): 447–74.

Skopp G, Klinder K, Pötsch L, Zimmer G, Lutz R, and Aderjan R (1998), Postmortem distribution of dihydrocodeine and metabolites in a fatal case of dihydrocodeine intoxication, *For Sci Intl*, 95(2): 99–107.

Diltiazem

Brand names: Cardizem, Tiazac
Classification: calcium channel blocker
λ: 2–13 hrs
V_d: 3.6–11 L/kg
Usual dosage: 60–120 mg bid

Source	Therapeutic/ Nontoxic	Toxic	Lethal
Blood	0.05–0.4 mg/L	0.56–6.1 mg/L	0.92–31 mg/L
Vitreous			5.5 mg/L
Urine			5.4–60 mg/L
Bile			0.3–295 mg/L
Liver			0.18–182 mg/kg
Kidney			0.05–49 mg/kg
Brain			0.03–33 mg/kg
Stomach contents			0.12–3.3 g

Comments

- Metabolized by CYP 3A

Selected Sources

Bexar County Medical Examiner's Office data 1996–2007.

Boyd RA, Chin SK, Don-Pedro O, Verotta D, Sheiner LB, and Williams RL (1989), The pharmacokinetics and pharmacodynamics of diltiazem and its metabolites in healthy adults after a single oral dose, *Clin Pharm Thera*, 46(4): 408–19.

Cantrell FL and Williams SR (2005), Fatal unintentional overdose of diltiazem with antemortem and postmortem values, *Clin Tox*, 43(6): 587–8.

Druid H and Holmgren P (1997), A compilation of fatal and control concentrations of drugs in postmortem femoral blood, *J For Sci*, 42(1): 79–87.

Kaliciak HA, Huckin SN, and Cave WS (1992), A death attributed solely to diltiazem, *J Anal Tox*, 16(2): 102–3.

Kalin JR, Wood KM, and Lee QJ (1994), A possible suicide by diltiazem overdose, *J Anal Tox*, 18(3): 180–2.

Luomanmäki K, Tiula E, Kivistö KT, and Neuvonen PJ (1997), Pharmacokinetics of diltiazem in massive overdose, *Ther Drug Monit*, 19(2): 240–2.

Ochs HR and Knüchel M (1984), Pharmacokinetics and absolute bioavailability of diltiazem in humans, *Klinische Wochenschrift*, 62(7): 303–6.

Physicians' Desk Reference 60 Edition (2006), Thomson PDR, Montvale, NJ, pp. 1699–701.

Romano G, Barbera N, Rossitto C, and Spadaro G (2002), Lethal diltiazem poisoning, *J Anal Tox*, 26(6): 374–7.

Roper TA, Sykes R, and Gray C (1993), Fatal diltiazem overdose: Report of four cases and review of the literature, *Postgrad Med J*, 69(812): 474–6.

Dimethyltryptamine

Brand names: not applicable
Street name: DMT
Classification: hallucinogen
λ: 0.25–2 hrs
V_d: 35–50 L/kg
Usual dosage: not applicable

Source	Therapeutic/ Nontoxic	Toxic	Lethal
Blood	0.012–0.017 mg/L DMT 0.023–0.39 mg/L THH 0.002–0.004 mg/L harmaline	No data available	0.01–0.02 mg/L DMT 0.24–0.38 mg/L THH 0.04–0.07 mg/L harmaline
Urine			0.89 mg/L DMT 6.02 mg/L THH 2.26 mg/L harmaline
Bile			0.57 mg/L DMT 4.78 mg/L THH 0.41 mg/L harmaline
Liver			13.24 mg/kg THH 3.6 mg/kg harmaline
Kidney			6.89 mg/kg THH 2.24 mg/kg harmaline
Brain			0.43 mg/kg THH 0.04 mg/kg harmaline

Comments

- Found in *ayahuasca* and *hoasca* plants
- Smoked or insufflated
- Major metabolites: tetrahydroharmine (THH) and harmaline

Selected Sources

Riba J, Valle M, Urbano G, Yritia M, Morte A, and Barbanoj MJ (2003), Human pharmacology of ayahuasca: Subjective and cardiovascular effects, monoamine metabolite excretion, and pharmacokinetics, *J Pharm Exp Ther*, 306(1): 73–83.

Sklerov J, Levine B, Moore KA, King T, and Fowler D (2005), A fatal intoxication following the ingestion of 5-methoxy-N,N-dimethyltryptamine in an ayahuasca preparation, *J Anal Tox*, 29(8): 838–41.

Diphenhydramine

Brand names: Benadryl, Nytol, Simply Sleep, Sominex, Compoz
Classification: antihistamine
λ: 2–13 hrs
V_d: 2–5 L/kg
Usual dosage: 25–50 mg q 4–6 hrs

Source	Therapeutic/ Nontoxic	Toxic	Lethal
Blood	0.004–0.26 mg/L	1–5 mg/L	5–39 mg/L
Vitreous			10–15 mg/L
Urine			6.4–376 mg/L
Liver			34–260 mg/kg
Kidney			50–114 mg/kg
Brain			16–32 mg/kg
Skeletal muscle			7.3–22 mg/kg
Stomach contents			0.82–705 mg

Comments

- Prolongs QT interval
- Metabolized by CYP 2D6

Selected Sources

Aderjan R, Bösche J, and Schmidt G (1982), Poisoning by diphenhydramine—Forensic-toxicologic interpretation of analytic results, *Zeitschrift für Rechtsmedizin*, 88(4): 263–70.

Albert KS, Hallmark MR, Sakmar E, Weidler DJ, and Wagner JG (1975), Pharmacokinetics of diphenhydramine in man, *J Pharm Biopharm*, 3(3): 159–70.

Backer RC, Pisano RV, and Sopher IM (1977), Diphenhydramine suicide—Case report, *J Anal Tox*, 1:227–8.

Bexar County Medical Examiner's Office data 1996–2008.

Blyden GT, Greenblatt DJ, Scavone JM, and Shader RI (1986), Pharmacokinetics of diphenhydramine and a demethylated metabolite following intravenous and oral administration, *J Clin Pharm*, 26(7): 529–33.

Hausmann E, Wewer H, Wellhöner HH, and Weller JP (1983), Lethal intoxication with diphenhydramine. Report of a case with analytical follow-up, *Arch Tox*, 53(1): 33–9.

Karch SB (1998), Diphenhydramine toxicity: Comparisons of postmortem findings in diphenhydramine-, bcocaine-, and heroin-related deaths, *Am J For Med Path*, 19(2): 143–7.

Pragst F, Herre S, and Bakdash A (2006), Poisonings with diphenhydramine—A survey of 68 clinical and 55 death cases, *For Sci Intl*, 161(2–3): 189–97.

Scavone JM, Greenblatt DJ, Harmatz JS, Engelhardt N, and Shader RI (1998), Pharmacokinetics and pharmacodynamics of diphenhydramine 25 mg in young and elderly volunteers, *J Clin Pharm*, 38(7): 603–9.

Dipyrone

Brand names: Analgin, Conmel, Novalgin, Metamizole
Classification: NSAID
λ: 2.6–3.7 hrs
V_d: 1.1 L/kg
Usual dosage: 500–1000 mg tid

Source	Therapeutic/ Nontoxic	Toxic	Lethal
Blood	4–11 mg/L[a]	3.3[b]–20 mg/L	No data available
Urine	4–10 mg/L[a]	3.2 mg/L[b]	

[a] Concentrations are of active metabolite (MAA)
[b] Infant

Comments

- Not available in United States
- Causes agranulocytosis
- Active metabolite: 4-methyl-amino-antipyrine (MAA)

Selected Sources

Levy M, Zylber-Katz E, and Rosenkranz B (1995), Clinical pharmacokinetics of dipyrone and its metabolites, *Clin Pharmacokinetics*, 28(3): 216–34.

Rizzoni G and Furlanut M (1984), Cyanotic crises in a breast-fed infant from mother taking dipyrone, *Hum Tox*, 3(6): 505–7.

Sistovaris N, Pola W, and Wolhoff H (1983), Thin-layer chromatographic determination of major metamizole metabolites in serum and urine, *J Chromatography A*, 274: 289–98.

Vlahov V, Badian M, Verho M, and Bacracheva N (1990), Pharmacokinetics of metamizol metabolites in healthy subjects after a single oral dose of metamizol sodium, *Eur J Clin Pharm*, 38(1): 61–5.

Disopyramide

Brand names: Norpace
Classification: antiarrhythmic
λ: 4–10 hrs
V_d: 2.2–4.1 L/kg
Usual dosage: 400–800 mg bid/tid

Source	Therapeutic/ Nontoxic	Toxic	Lethal
Blood	0.4–4.8 mg/L	7–9 mg/L	16–146 mg/L
Urine			430–1500 mg/L
Bile			6.2–435 mg/L
Liver			17–115 mg/kg
Kidney			147 mg/kg
Brain			24 mg/kg
Stomach contents			0.9–15 mg

Comments

- Prolongs QT interval

Selected Sources

Anderson WH, Stafford DT, and Bell JS (1980), Disopyramide (Norpace) distribution at autopsy of an overdose case, *J For Sci*, 25(1): 33–9.

Hayler AM, Holt DW, and Volans GN (1978), Fatal overdosage with disopyramide, *Lancet*, 1: 968–9.

Le Corre P, Gibassier D, Sado P, and Le Verge R (1988), Stereoselective metabolism and pharmacokinetics of disopyramide enantiomers in humans, *Drug Metab Dispos*, 16(6): 858–64.

Michalek RW, Rejent TA, and Spencer RA (1982), Disopyramide fatality: Case report and GC/FID analysis, *J Anal Tox*, 6(5): 255–7.

Sathyavagiswaran L (1987), Fatal disopyramide intoxication from suicidal/accidental overdose, *J For Sci*, 32(6): 1813–8.

Singer P and Mozayani A (1995), An overdose fatality in a child involving disopyramide and sulindac, *J Anal Tox*, 19(6): 529–30.

Wayne K, Manolas E, and Sloman G (1980), Fatal overdose with disopyramide, *Med J Aust*, 1(5):231–2.

Yukawa E, Orio K, Yukawa M, Terao K, and Kinoshita H (2005), Population pharmacokinetic investigation of disopyramide by mixed effect modelling using routine clinical pharmacokinetic data in Japanese patients, *J Clin Pharm Thera*, 30(4): 401–5.

Disulfiram

Brand names: Antabuse
Classification: alcohol aversion therapy
λ: unknown
V_d: unknown
Usual dosage: 125–500 mg qd

Source	Therapeutic/ Nontoxic	Toxic	Lethal
Blood	0.05–0.4 mg/L	1.8–5 mg/L	8 mg/L

Comments

- Heptatotoxic
- When combined with ETOH causes nausea, vomiting, hypotension, tachycardia
- Metabolized to diethyldithiocarbamate and diethyldithiocarbamate methyl ester

Selected Sources

Faiman MD, Jensen JC, and Lacoursiere RB (1984), Elimination kinetics of disulfiram in alcoholics after single and repeated doses, *Clin Pharm Thera*, 36(4): 520–6.
Kirubakaran V, Liskow B, Mayfield D, and Faiman MD (1983), Case report of acute disulfiram overdose, *Am J Psychiatry*, 140(11): 1513–4.
Schulz M and Schmoldt A (2003), Therapeutic and toxic blood concentrations of more than 800 drugs and other xenobiotics, *Pharmazie*, 58(7): 447–74.

Donepezil

Brand names: Aricept
Classification: acetylcholinesterase inhibitor (Alzheimer's treatment)
λ: 50–70 hrs
V_d: 12 L/kg
Usual dosage: 5–10 mg qd

Source	Therapeutic/ Nontoxic	Toxic	Lethal
Blood	0.003–0.03 mg/L	0.55 mg/L	No data available

Comments

- Toxicities treated with atropine
- Metabolized by CYP 2D6 and 3A

Selected Sources

Rogers SL, Cooper NM, Sukovaty R, Pederson JE, Lee JN, and Friedhoff LT (1998), Pharmacokinetic and pharmacodynamic profile of donepezil HCl following multiple oral doses, *Br J Clin Pharm*, 46(Suppl. 1): 7–12.

Rogers SL and Friedhoff LT (1998), Pharmacokinetic and pharmacodynamic profile of donepezil HCl following single oral doses, *Br J Clin Pharm*, 46(Suppl. 1): 1–6.

Xie Z, Liao Q, Xu X, Yao M, Wan J, and Liu D (2006), Rapid and sensitive determination of donepezil in human plasma by liquid chromatography/tandem mass spectrometry: Application to a pharmacokinetic study, *Rapid Commun Mass Spectrom*, 20(21): 3193–8.

Yano H, Fukuhara Y, Wada K, Kowa H, and Nakashima K (2003), A case of acute cholinergic adverse effects induced by donepezil overdose: A follow-up of clinical course and plasma concentration of donepezil, *Rinsho Shinkeigaku*, 43(8): 482–6.

Dothiepin

Brand names: Dosulepin, Prothiaden
Classification: antidepressant (TCA)
λ: 11–24 hrs
V_d: 19–195 L/kg
Usual dosage: 75–300 mg bid/tid

Source	Therapeutic/ Nontoxic	Toxic	Lethal
Blood	0.003–0.12 mg/L	0.8–4.7 mg/L	2.3–62 mg/L
Vitreous			0.3–0.9 mg/L
Urine			3.8–33 mg/L
Bile			12–268 mg/L
Liver			2–52 mg/kg
Kidney			3.1–10 mg/kg
Brain			2.8 mg/kg
Skeletal muscle			0.4–18 mg/kg
Cardiac muscle			2.9–17 mg/kg
Stomach contents			0.002–20 mg

Comments

- Active metabolite: desmethyldothiepin

Selected Sources

Cirimele V, Kintz P, Tracqui A, and Mangin P (1995), A fatal dothiepin overdose, *For Sci Intl*, 76(3), 205–9.

Ilett KF, Hackett LP, Dusci LJ, and Paterson JW (1991), Disposition of dothiepin after overdose: Effects of repeated-dose activated charcoal, *Ther Drug Monit*, 13(6): 485–9.

Keller T and Schneider A. Tutsch-Bauer E (2000), Fatal intoxication due to dothiepin, *For Sci Intl*, 109(2): 159–66.

Langford AM, Taylor KK, and Pounder DJ (1998), Drug concentration in selected skeletal muscles, *J For Sci*, 43(1): 22–7.

Maguire KP, Burrows GD, Norman TR, and Scoggins BA (1981), Metabolism and pharmacokinetics of dothiepin, *Br J Clin Pharm*, 12(3): 405–9.

Paterson SC (1985), Drug levels found in cases of fatal self-poisoning, *For Sci Intl*, 27(2): 129–33.

Pounder DJ, Hartley AK, and Watmough PJ (1994), Postmortem redistribution and degradation of dothiepin. Human case studies and an animal model, *Am J For Med Path*, 15(3): 231–5.

Robinson AE, Coffer AI, and McDowall RD (1974), Toxicology of some autopsy cases involving tricyclic antidepressant drugs, *Zeitschrift für Rechtsmedizin*, 74(4): 261–6.

Williams KR and Pounder DJ (1997), Site-to-site variability of drug concentrations in skeletal muscle, *Am J For Med Path*, 18(3): 246–50.

Doxapram

Brand names: Dopram
Classification: stimulant
λ: 6.6–9.9 hrs
V_d: 3.2–3.6 L/kg
Usual dosage: 0.5–2 mg/kg/dose iv

Source	Therapeutic/ Nontoxic	Toxic	Lethal
Blood	1.6–5.2 mg/L	7–14 mg/L	No data available

Selected Sources

Barbé F, Hansen C, Badonnel Y, Legagneur H, Vert P, and Boutroy MJ (1999), Severe side effects and drug plasma concentrations in preterm infants treated with doxapram, *Ther Drug Monit*, 21(5): 547–52.
Clements JA, Robson RH, and Prescott LF (1979), The disposition of intravenous doxapram in man, *Eur J Clin Pharm*, 16(6): 411–6.

Doxepin

Brand names: Sinequan, Adapin
Classification: antidepressant (TCA)
λ: 6–23 hrs
V_d: 17–31 L/kg
Usual dosage: 30–150 mg qd

Source	Therapeutic/ Nontoxic	Toxic	Lethal
Blood	0.009–0.15 mg/L	0.2–2.1 mg/L	0.9–150 mg/L
Vitreous			2.9 mg/L
Urine			1.4–16 mg/L
Bile			38–195 mg/L
Liver			22–500 mg/kg
Kidney			3.3–70 mg/kg
Brain			9–42 mg/kg
Skeletal muscle			6.8–38 mg/kg
Cardiac muscle			2.7–16 mg/kg
Stomach contents			3.7–750 mg

Comments

- Metabolized by CYP 2D6 and 2C19
- May prolong QT interval
- Active metabolite: desmethyldoxepin

Selected Sources

Apple FS (1989), Postmortem tricyclic antidepressant concentrations: Assessing cause of death using parent drug to metabolite ratio, *J Anal Tox*, 13(4): 197–8.

Bexar County Medical Examiner's Office data 1996–2007.

Biggs JT, Spiker DG, Petit JM, and Ziegler VE (1977), Tricyclic antidepressant overdose: Incidence of symptoms, *JAMA*, 238(2): 135–8.

Caplan YH, Ottinger WE, and Crooks CR (1983), Therapeutic and toxic drug concentrations in post mortem blood: A six year study in the State of Maryland, *J Anal Tox*, 7(5): 225–30.

Cordonnier J, Heyndrickx A, Jordaens L, Brijs R, and De Keyser R (1983), A fatal intoxication due to doxepin, *J Anal Tox*, 7(4): 161–4.

de Groot G, Maes RAA, Hodnett CN, Kelly RC, Bost RO, and Sunshine I (1978), Four cases of fatal doxepin poisoning, *J Anal Tox*, 2:18–20.

Kirchheiner J, Meineke I, Müller G, Roots I, and Brockmöller J (2002), Contributions of CYP2D6, CYP2C9 and CYP2C19 to the biotransformation of E- and Z-doxepin in healthy volunteers, *Pharmacogenetics*, 12(7): 571–80.

Norheim G (1973), Determination of doxepin in autopsy material, *Archiv fur Toxikologie*, 31(1): 7–12.
Pounder DJ, Jones GR (1990), Post-mortem drug redistribution — A toxicological nightmare, *For Sci Intl*, 43(3): 253–63.
Quai I, Fagarasan M, Fagarasan E, and Usineviciu I (1985), Tricyclic antidepressants: Clinical considerations, tissue concentrations and morphopathologic changes in the acute intoxication in man, *Acta Medicinae Legalis et Socialis*, 35(1): 107–9.
Ziegler VE, Biggs JT, Wylie LT, Rosen SH, Hawf DJ, and Coryell WH (1978), Doxepin kinetics, *Clin Pharm Thera*, 23(5): 573–9.

Doxylamine

Brand names: Bendectin, Unisom
Classification: antihistamine
λ: 10–12 hrs
V_d: 1.8–2.6 L/kg
Usual dosage: 25–50 mg qHS

Source	Therapeutic/ Nontoxic	Toxic	Lethal
Blood	0.05–0.12 mg/L	1–2 mg/L	0.7–165 mg/L
Urine			16–509 mg/L
Bile			3.2 mg/L
Liver			14–300 mg/kg
Kidney			22 mg/kg
Skeletal muscle			6.3 mg/kg
Stomach contents			5–900 mg

Selected Sources

Bayley M, Walsh FM, and Valaske MJ (1975). Fatal overdose from Bendectin, *Clin Pediat,* 14(5): 507–9, 514.

Bexar County Medical Examiner's Office data 1996–2007.

Bockholdt B, Klug E, and Schneider V (2001), Suicide through doxylamine poisoning, *For Sci Intl,* 119(1): 138.

Friedman H and Greenblatt DJ (1985), The pharmacokinetics of doxylamine: Use of automated gas chromatography with nitrogen-phosphorus detection, *J Clin Pharm,* 25(6): 448–51.

Friedman H, Greenblatt DJ, Scavone JM, Burstein ES, Ochs HR, and Harmatz JS (1989), Clearance of the antihistamine doxylamine. Reduced in elderly men but not in elderly women, *Clin Pharmacokinet,* 16(5): 312–6.

Siek TJ and Dunn WA (1993), Documentation of a doxylamine overdose death: Quantitation by standard addition and use of three instrumental techniques, *J For Sci,* 38(3): 713–20.

Wu Chen NB, Schaffer MI, Lin RL, Kurland ML, Donoghue ER, and Stein RJ (1983), The general toxicology unknown. II. A case report: doxylamine and pyrilamine intoxication, *J For Sci,* 28(2): 398–403.

Duloxetine

Brand names: Cymbalta
Classification: antidepressant (SNRI)
λ: 8–17 hrs
V_d: 16–23 L/kg
Usual dosage: 20–60 mg qd

Source	Therapeutic/ Nontoxic	Toxic	Lethal
Blood	0.023–0.08 mg/L	No data available	
Bile	0.57 mg/L		
Liver	0.28–22 mg/kg		

Comments

- Metabolized by CYP 2D6 and 1A2
- May cause liver failure

Selected Sources

Anderson D, Reed S, Lintemoot J, Kegler S, DeQuintana S, and Sandberg M (2006), A first look at duloxetine (Cymbalta) in a postmortem laboratory, *J Anal Tox*, 30(8): 576–80.

Hanje AJ, Pell LJ, Votolato NA, Frankel WL, and Kirkpatrick RB (2006), Case report: Fulminant hepatic failure involving duloxetine hydrochloride, *Clin Gastroenterol Hepatol*, 4(7): 912–7.

Ning M, Zhang B, Li H, Chen B, Xu P, and Wang F (2007), Determination of duloxetine in human plasma via LC/MS and subsequent application to a pharmacokinetic study in healthy Chinese volunteers, *Clinica Chimica Acta*, 380(1–2): 100-5.

Emetine

Brand names: Syrup of Ipecac
Classification: emetic
λ: unknown
V_d: unknown
Usual dosage: 1.2–2.4 mg/dose

Source	Therapeutic/ Nontoxic	Toxic	Lethal
Blood	0.006–0.01 mg/L	No data available	0.85–2.5 mg/L
Bile			1.9 mg/L
Liver			14 mg/kg
Kidney			7.4 mg/kg

Comments

- Can cause myocarditis

Selected Sources

Adler AG, Walinsky P, Krall RA, and Cho SY (1980), Death resulting from ipecac syrup poisoning, *JAMA,* 243(19): 1927–8.

Friedman EJ (1984), Death from ipecac intoxication in a patient with anorexia nervosa, *Am J Psychiatry,* 141(5): 702–3.

Scharman EJ, Hutzler JM, Rosencrance JG, and Tracy TS (2000), Single dose pharmacokinetics of syrup of ipecac, *Ther Drug Monit*, 22(5): 566–73.

Schneider DJ, Perez A, Knilamus TE, Daniels SR, Bove KE, and Bonnell H (1996), Clinical and pathologic aspects of cardiomyopathy from ipecac administration in Munchausen's syndrome by proxy, *Pediatrics,* 97(6 Pt 1): 902–6.

Enflurane

Brand names: Ethrane
Classification: halogenated anesthetic
λ: 0–1 hr
V_d: 10–23 L/kg
Usual dosage: 0.25%–4.5% inhaled

Source	Therapeutic/ Nontoxic	Toxic	Lethal
Blood	25–203 mg/L	No data available	80–710 mg/L
Brain			270–450 mg/kg

Comments

- Can cause hepatic necrosis
- Metabolized by CYP 2E1

Selected Sources

Goucke CR, Hackett LP, Barrett PH, and Ilett KF (2007), Blood concentrations of enflurane before, during, and after hypothermic cardiopulmonary bypass, *J Cardiothorac Vasc Anesth*, 21(2): 218–23.

Jacob B, Heller C, Daldrup T, Bürrig KF, Barz J, and Bonte W (1989), Fatal accidental enflurane intoxication, *J For Sci*, 34(6): 1408–12.

Strum DP, Eger EI, Unadkat JD, Johnson BH, and Carpenter RL (1991), Age affects the pharmacokinetics of inhaled anesthetics in humans, *Anesth Analg*, 73(3): 310–8.

Walker FB and Morano RA (1990), Fatal recreational inhalation of enflurane, *J For Sci*, 35(1): 197–8.

Ephedrine

Brand names: Primatene, Rynatuss (w/ chlorpheniramine, phenylephrine, carbetapentane)
Street names: Ma Huang, herbal Ecstasy
Classification: stimulant/decongestant
λ: 3–11 hrs
V_d: 2.2–3.4 L/kg
Usual dosage: 10–20 mg bid

Source	Therapeutic/ Nontoxic	Toxic	Lethal
Blood	0.05–0.12 mg/L	0.11–23 mg/L	3.5–20 mg/L
Urine			547 mg/L
Liver			24 mg/kg
Kidney			14 mg/kg
Brain	<0.2 mg/kg		8.9 mg/kg

Comments

- May be associated with sudden unexplained infant deaths

Selected Sources

Backer R, Tautman D, Lowry S, Harvey CM, and Poklis A (1997), Fatal ephedrine intoxication, *J For Sci*, 42(1): 157–9.

Garriott JC, Simmons LM, Poklis A, and Mackell MA (1985), Five cases of fatal overdose from caffeine-containing "look-alike" drugs, *J Anal Tox*, 9(3): 141–3.

Gurley BJ, Gardner SF, White LM, and Wang PL (1998), Ephedrine pharmacokinetics after the ingestion of nutritional supplements containing *Ephedra Sinica* (Ma Huang), *Ther Drug Monit*, 20(4): 439–45.

Haller CA and Benowitz NL (2000), Adverse cardiovascular and central nervous system events associated with dietary supplements containing ephedra alkaloids, *NEJM*, 343(25): 1833–8.

Marinetti L, Lehman L, Casto B, Harshbarger K, Kubiczek P, and Davis J (2005), Over-the-counter cold medications-postmortem findings in infants and the relationship to cause of death, *J Anal Tox*, 29(7): 738–43.

Epinephrine

Brand names: EpiPen, Twinject
Classification: stimulant
λ: 2 min
V_d: unknown
Usual dosage: 0.3 mg im (anaphylaxis); 1–5 mg iv (cardiac arrest)

Source	Endogenous	Toxic	Lethal
Blood	0.005–0.6 ng/mL	1.6 ng/mL	No data available

Note: Units are ng/mL

Comments

- Causes increased blood pressure and tachycardia
- Associated with cardiac arrhythmias

Selected Sources

Galbo H, Holst JJ, Christensen NJ (1975), Glucagon and plasma catecholamine responses to graded and prolonged exercise in man, *J Applied Physiology*, 38(1): 70–6.

Karch SB (1989), Coronary artery spasm induced by intravenous epinephrine overdose, *Am J Emer Med*, 7(5): 485–8.

Lindner KH, Haak T, Keller A, Bothner U, and Lurie KG (1996), Release of endogenous vasopressors during and after cardiopulmonary resuscitation, *Heart*, 75(2): 145–50.

Willemsen JJ, Ross HA, Jacobs MC, Lenders JW, Thien T, and Swinkels LM (1995), Highly sensitive and specific HPLC with fluorometric detection for determination of plasma epinephrine and norepinephrine applied to kinetic studies in humans, *Clin Chem*, 41(10): 1455–60.

Escitalopram

Brand names: Lexapro, Cipralex
Classification: antidepressant (SSRI)
λ: 27–32 hrs
V_d: 11–16 L/kg
Usual dosage: 10–20 mg qd

Source	Therapeutic/ Nontoxic	Toxic	Lethal
Blood	0.01–0.06 mg/L	See comments	

Comments

- Is pure S-enantiomer of citalopram
- Laboratories usually do not differentiate between escitalopram and citalopram
- May compare to citalopram concentrations for toxic/lethal levels but must consider that escitalopram is more active and lower concentrations may result in toxicity
- Prolongs QT interval

Selected Sources

Physicians' Desk Reference 61 Edition (2007), Thomson PDR, Montvale, NJ, pp. 1190–4.

Rao N (2007), The clinical pharmacokinetics of escitalopram, *Clin Pharmacokinet*, 46(4): 281–90.

Estazolam

Brand names: Prosom
Classification: benzodiazepine
λ: 10–30 hrs
V_d: 0.46–0.66 L/kg
Usual dosage: 1–2 mg qHS

Source	Therapeutic/ Nontoxic	Toxic	Lethal
Blood	0.055–0.19 mg/L	1.25 mg/L	No data available

Comments

- Tolerance can develop and should be considered when interpreting drug concentrations
- Metabolized by CYP 3A

Selected Sources

Aoshima T, Fukasawa T, Otsuji Y, Okuyama N, Gerstenberg G, and Miura M (2003), Effects of the CYP2C19 genotype and cigarette smoking on the single oral dose pharmacokinetics and pharmacodynamics of estazolam, *Prog Neuropsychopharmacol Biol Psychiatry*, 27(3): 535–8.

Gustavson LE and Carrigan PJ (1990), The clinical pharmacokinetics of single doses of estazolam, *Am J Med*, 88(3A): 2S–5S.

Physicians' Desk Reference 61 Edition (2007), Thomson PDR, Montvale, NJ, pp. 517–20.

Scotto di Tella A, Ricci P, Di Nunzio C, and Cassandro P (1986), A new method for the determination in blood and urine of a novel triazolobenzodiazepine (estazolam) by HPLC, *J Anal Tox*, 10(2): 65–7.

Ethanol

Brand names: drinking alcohol
Classification: CNS depressant
λ: 2–14 hrs
V_d: 0.4–0.6 L/kg
Usual dosage: not applicable

Blood Ethanol Content	Findings		
0.02 g/dL	Decreased inhibitions		
0.05 g/dL	Relaxed, less alert, coordination slightly impaired		
0.08 g/dL	Impaired coordination and judgment		
0.1 g/dL	Decreased reaction time		
0.15 g/dL	Decreased balance and gait functioning		
0.3–0.4	Unconsciousness		
>0.4 g/dL	Coma/death		
Lethal Concentrations			
Blood	0.32–1.8 g/dL	Liver	0.2–1.2 g/100 g
Urine	0.5–0.9 g/dL	Brain	0.3–0.9 g/100 g
Bile	0.1–2.8 g/dL	Kidney	0.3–1.0 g/100 g

Comments

- Specimen to whole blood ratios have been established
  - Serum 1.1–1.35, saliva 1.1, vitreous 1.2, bile 1.0, CSF 1.1
  - Liver 0.6, kidney 0.7, brain 0.8
- Can get ethanol production with decomposition especially in the setting of diabetes
  - Decomposition only: blood 0.07–0.22 g/dL
  - Diabetes and decomposition: blood 0.51 g/dL; brain 0.04 g/100 g; liver 0.08 g/100 g; urine 0.05 g/dL; acetone > 15 g/dL
- Metabolized by CYP 2E1

Selected Sources

Bexar County Medical Examiner's Office data 1996–2007.

Christopoulos G, Kirch ER, and Gearien JE (1973), Determination of ethanol in fresh and putrefied post mortem tissues, *J Chromatography A*, 87(2): 454–72.

Collison IB (2005), Elevated postmortem ethanol concentrations in an insulin-dependent diabetic, *J Anal Tox*, 29: 762–4.

Gilliland MG and Bost RO (1993), Alcohol in decomposed bodies: Postmortem synthesis and distribution, *J For Sci*, 38: 1266–74.

Levine B (1999), *Principles of Forensic Toxicology*, American Association for Clinical Chemistry, Washington, DC, USA, pp. 170–84.

Zumwalt RE, Bost RO, and Sunshine I (1982), Evaluation of ethanol concentration in decomposed bodies, *J For Sci*, 27: 549–54.

Ethchlorvynol

Brand names: Placidyl
Classification: sedative/hypnotic
λ: 10–20 hrs
V_d: 3–4 L/kg
Usual dosage: 500–1000 mg qHS

Source	Therapeutic/ Nontoxic	Toxic	Lethal
Blood	1–18 mg/L	20–135 mg/L	39–260 mg/L
Vitreous			10 mg/L
Urine	0.3–10 mg/L		10–200 mg/L
Bile			125–240 mg/L
Liver			18–1600 mg/kg
Kidney			18–860 mg/kg
Brain			13–285 mg/kg
Stomach contents			10–940 mg

Selected Sources

Caplan YH, Ottinger WE, and Crooks CR (1983), Therapeutic and toxic drug concentrations in post mortem blood: A six year study in the State of Maryland, *J Anal Tox*, 7(5): 225–30.

Cummins LM, Martin YC, and Scherfling EE (1971), Serum and urine levels of ethchlorvynol in man, *J Pharm Sci*, 6(2): 261–3.

Maes R, Hodnett N, Landesman H, Kananen G, Finkle B, and Sunshine I (1969), The gas chromatographic determination of selected sedatives (ethchlorvynol, paraldehyde, meprobamate, and carisoprodol) in biological material, *J For Sci*, 14(2): 235–54.

Wallace JE, Blum K, and Singh JM (1974), Determination of drugs in biological specimens—A review, *J Tox Clin Tox*, 7(5): 477–95.

Winek CL and Wahba WW (1989), Body distribution of ethchlorvynol, *J For Sci*, 34(3): 687–90.

Ethosuximide

Brand names: Zarontin
Classification: anticonvulsant
λ: 30–60 hrs
V_d: unknown
Usual dosage: 250–500 mg bid

Source	Therapeutic/ Nontoxic	Toxic	Lethal
Blood	31–130 mg/L	100–200 mg/L	250 mg/L
Urine			120 mg/L
Liver	200 mg/kg		280 mg/kg
Brain	160 mg/kg		

Comments

- Associated with agranulocytosis

Selected Sources

Fraser AD, Isner AF, and Heifetz SA (1988), Tissue distribution of ethosuximide and clobazam in a seizure related fatality, *J For Sci*, 33(4): 1058–63.

French J (1994), The long-term therapeutic management of epilepsy, *Ann Int Med*, 120(5): 411–22.

Schulz M and Schmoldt A (2003), Therapeutic and toxic blood concentrations of more than 800 drugs and other xenobiotics, *Pharmazie*, 58(7): 447–74.

Solow EB and Green JB (1971), The determination of ethosuximide in serum by gas chromatography: Preliminary results of clinical application, *Clinica Chimica Acta*, 33(1): 87–90.

Ethylene Glycol

Brand names: component of antifreeze
Classification: alcohol
λ: 2.5–4.5 hrs
V_d: 0.5–0.8 L/kg
Usual dosage: not applicable

Source	Nontoxic	Toxic	Lethal
Blood	94–182 mg/L	500–1400 mg/L	289–7120 mg/L
Vitreous			454–535 mg/L
Urine	21–77 mg/L		888–2700 mg/L
Bile			786–4174 mg/L
Liver			300–15120 mg/kg
Kidney			225–1134 mg/kg
Brain			135–1960 mg/kg
Skeletal muscle			643 mg/kg
Cardiac muscle			58 mg/kg
Stomach contents			859 mg/L

Comments

- Associated with calcium oxalate crystals in kidneys and blood vessels
- Metabolized to glycoaldehyde by alcohol dehydrogenase

Selected Sources

Bexar County Medical Examiner's Office data 1996–2007.
Bowen DA, Minty PS, and Sengupta A (1978), Two fatal cases of ethylene glycol poisoning, *Med Sci Law*, 18(2): 101–7.
Flanagan RJ (1998), Guidelines for the interpretation of analytical toxicology results and unit of measurement conversion factors, *Ann Clin Biochem*, 35: 261–7.
Hantson P, Vanbinst R, and Mahieu P (2002), Determination of ethylene glycol tissue content after fatal oral poisoning and pathologic findings, *Am J For Med Path*, 23(2): 159–61.
Harris LS (1980), Case 38-1979: Ethylene glycol poisoning, *NEJM*, 302(8): 466.
Klendshoj NC and Rejent TA (1966), Tissue levels of some poisoning agents less frequently encountered, *J For Sci*, 11(1): 75–80.
Verrilli M R, Deyling CL, Pippenger CE, Van Lente F, Vidt DG, and Sivak ED (1987), Fatal ethylene glycol intoxication. Report of a case and review of the literature, *Cleveland Clinic J Med*, 54(4): 289–95.
Wills JH, Coulston F, Harris ES, McChesney EW, Russell JC, and Serrone DM (1974), Inhalation of aerosolized ethylene glycol by man, *Clin Tox*, 7(5): 463–76.

Ethylmorphine

Brand names: Dionine
Classification: narcotic
λ: 2–3 hrs
V_d: 3–4 L/kg
Usual dosage: 20–50 mg/dose

Source	Therapeutic/ Nontoxic	Toxic	Lethal
Blood	0.3–0.6 mg/L	No data available	1.3–3.0 mg/L

Selected Sources

Aasmundstad TA, Xu BQ, Johansson I, Ripel A, Bjørneboe A, and Christophersen AS (1995), Biotransformation and pharmacokinetics of ethylmorphine after a single oral dose, *Br J Clin Pharm,* 39(6): 611–20.

Jonasson B, Jonasson U, Holmgren P, and Saldeen T (1999), Fatal poisonings where ethylmorphine from antitussive medications contributed to death, *Intl J Legal Med,* 112(5): 299–302.

Etomidate

Brand names: Amidate
Classification: anesthetic
λ: 1-1.5 hrs
V_d: 2.5–3.6 L/kg
Usual dosage: 20–40 mg/dose (0.3–0.6 mg/kg/dose)

Source	Therapeutic/ Nontoxic	Toxic	Lethal
Blood	0.06–0.5 mg/L	No data available	0.4 mg/L
Vitreous			0.3 mg/L
Bile			0.46 mg/L

Comments

- Therapeutic concentrations can be fatal if not administered in a monitored, medical setting

Selected Sources

Bexar County Medical Examiner's Office data 1996–2007.

Schüttler J, Schwilden H, and Stoeckel H (1985), Infusion strategies to investigate the pharmacokinetics and pharmacodynamics of hypnotic drugs: Etomidate as an example. *Eur J Anaesthesiology*, 2(2): 133–42.

Van Hamme MJ, Ghoneim MM, and Ambre JJ (1978), Pharmacokinetics of etomidate, a new intravenous anesthetic, *Anesthesiology*, 49(4): 274–7.

Felbamate

Brand names: Felbatol
Classification: anticonvulsant
λ: 18–34 hrs
V_d: 0.7–0.8 L/kg
Usual dosage: 300–400 mg tid/qid

Source	Therapeutic/ Nontoxic	Toxic	Lethal
Blood	35–157 mg/L	111–200 mg/L	No data available
Brain	13–74 mg/kg		

Comments

- Associated with hepatic necrosis and aplastic anemia
- Prolongs QT interval
- Metabolized by CYP 2E1 and 3A

Selected Sources

Adusumalli VE, Wichmann JK, Kucharczyk N, Kamin M, Sofia RD, and French J (1994), Drug concentrations in human brain tissue samples from epileptic patients treated with felbamate, *Drug Metab Dispos*, 22(1): 168–70.

Meier KH, Olson KR, and Olson JL (2005), Acute felbamate overdose with crystalluria, *Clin Tox*, 43(3): 189–92.

Nagel TR and Schunk JE (1995), Felbamate overdose: A case report and discussion of a new antiepileptic drug, *Ped Emer Care*, 11(6): 369–71.

Rengstorff DS, Milstone AP, L Seger DL, and Meredith TJ (2000), Felbamate overdose complicated by massive crystalluria and acute renal failure, *J Tox Clin Tox*, 38(6): 667–9.

Richens A, Banfield CR, Salfi M, Nomeir A, Lin CC, Jensen P, Affrime MB, and Glue P (1997), Single and multiple dose pharmacokinetics of felbamate in the elderly, *Br J Clin Pharm*, 44(2): 129–34.

Sachdeo R, Narang-Sachdeo SK, Shumaker RC, Perhach JL, Lyness WH, and Rosenberg A (1997), Tolerability and pharmacokinetics of monotherapy felbamate doses of 1,200–6,000 mg/day in subjects with epilepsy, *Epilepsia*, 38(8): 887–92.

Fenfluramine

Brand names: Pondimin
Classification: anorectic
λ: 13–30 hrs
V_d: 12–16 L/kg
Usual dosage: 20 mg tid

Source	Therapeutic/ Nontoxic	Toxic	Lethal
Blood	0.04–0.2 mg/L	0.5–1 mg/L	6–16 mg/L
Urine			60–90 mg/L
Bile			64 mg/L
Liver			48–136 mg/kg
Kidney			27 mg/kg
Brain			42 mg/kg
Skeletal muscle			16 mg/kg
Cardiac muscle			20 mg/kg
Stomach contents			224 mg/L

Comments

- Not available in United States
- Associated with pulmonary hypertension

Selected Sources

Fleisher MR and Campbell DB (1969), Fenfluramine overdosage, *Lancet,* 2: 1306–7.

Gold RG, Gordon HE, da Costa RWD, Porteous IB, and Kimber KJ (1969), Fenfluramine overdosage, *Lancet,* 2: 1306.

Kintz, P and Mangin P (1992), Toxicological findings after fatal fenfluramine self-poisoning, *Hum Exp Tox,* 11(1): 51–2.

Namera A, Yashiki M, Liu J, Okajima K, Hara K, and Imamura T (2000), Simple and simultaneous analysis of fenfluramine, amphetamine and methamphetamine in whole blood by gas chromatography–mass spectrometry after headspace-solid phase microextraction and derivatization, *For Sci Intl,* 109(3): 215–23.

Fenoprofen

Brand names: Nalfon
Classification: NSAID
λ: 3 hrs
V_d: 0.06–0.12 L/kg
Usual dosage: 200–800 mg q 4–6 hrs

Source	Therapeutic/ Nontoxic	Toxic	Lethal
Blood	18–60 mg/L	No data available	

Selected Sources

Poggi JC, Barissa GR, Donadi EA, Foss MC, de Queiróz Cunha F, and Lanchote VL (2006), Pharmacodynamics, chiral pharmacokinetics and pharmacokinetic-pharmacodynamic modeling of fenoprofen in patients with diabetes mellitus, *J Clin Pharmacology*, 46(11): 1328–36.

Ruen A, Rodda BE, Warrick P, Ridolfo AS, and Gruber CM (1972), Physiological disposition of fenoprofen in man, *J Pharm Sci*, 61(5): 739–45.

Fentanyl

Brand names: Duragesic, Actiq, Ionsys, Sublimaze, Fentora
Street names: China Girl, King Ivory, Goodfellas
Classification: narcotic
λ: 3–12 hrs
V_d: 3–8 L/kg
Usual dosage: 25–100 μg/hr transdermal

Source	Therapeutic/ Nontoxic	Toxic	Lethal
Blood	0.0003–0.01 mg/L	0.003–0.02 mg/L	0.003–0.21 mg/L
Urine			0.0002–0.8 mg/L
Bile			0.05–0.06 mg/L
Liver			0.08–0.24 mg/kg
Kidney			0.01–0.09 mg/kg
Brain			0.03–0.05 mg/kg

Comments

- Tolerance can develop and should be considered when interpreting drug concentrations
- Metabolized by CYP 3A
- Concentrations for individuals on chronic pain therapy have been reported to be as high as 0.04 mg/L

Selected Sources

Bexar County Medical Examiner's Office data 1996–2007.
Chaturvedi AK, Rao NG, and Baird JR (1990), A death due to self-administered fentanyl, *J Anal Tox*, 14(6): 385–7.
Edinboro LE, Poklis A, Trautman D, Lowry S, Backer R, and Harvey CM (1997), Fatal fentanyl intoxication following excessive transdermal application, *J For Sci*, 42(4): 741–3.
Garriott JC, Rodriguez R, and Di Maio VJ (1984), A death from fentanyl overdose, *J Anal Tox*, 8(6): 288–9.
Henderson GL (1991), Fentanyl-related deaths: Demographics, circumstances and toxicology of 112 cases, *J For Sci*, 36(2): 422–33.
Jung BF, Reidenberg MM (2005), Interpretation of opioid levels: Comparison of levels during chronic pain therapy to levels from forensic autopsies, *Clin Pharm Ther*, 77(4): 324–34.
Kramer C and Tawney M (1998), A fatal overdose of transdermally administered fentanyl, *J Am Osteopath Assoc*, 98(7): 385–6.
Matejczyk RJ (1988), Fentanyl related overdose, *J Anal Tox*, 12(4): 236–8.

Pare EM, Monforte JR, Gault R, and Mirchandani H (1987), A death involving fentanyl, *J Anal Tox*, 11(6): 272–5.

Physicians' Desk Reference 61 Edition (2007), Thomson PDR, Montvale, NJ, p. 2373.

Reeves MD and Ginifer CJ (2002), Fatal intravenous misuse of transdermal fentanyl, *Med J Aust*, 177(10): 552–3.

Teske, J, Weller JP, Larsch K, Tröger HD, and Karst M (2007), Fatal outcome in a child after ingestion of a transdermal fentanyl patch, *Intl J Legal Med*, 121(2): 147–51.

Tharp AM, Winecker RE, and Winston DC (2004), Fatal intravenous fentanyl abuse: Four cases involving extraction of fentanyl from transdermal patches, *Am J For Med Path*, 25(2): 178–81.

Thompson JG, Baker AM, Bracey AH, Seningen J, Kloss JS, Quinn Strob AQ, and Apple FS (2007), Fentanyl concentrations in 23 postmortem cases from the Hennepin County medical examiner's office, *J For Sci*, 52(4): 978–81.

Fexofenadine

Brand names: Allegra
Classification: antihistamine
λ: 8–18 hrs
V_d: 5.2–6.5 L/kg
Usual dosage: 30–60 mg bid

Source	Therapeutic/ Nontoxic	Toxic	Lethal
Blood	0.05–0.3 mg/L	No data available	

Selected Sources

Russell T, Stoltz M, and Weir S (1998), Pharmacokinetics, pharmacodynamics, and tolerance of single- and multiple-dose fexofenadine hydrochloride in healthy male volunteers, *Clin Pharm Ther*, 64(6): 612–21.

Simons FER and Simons KJ (1999), Clinical pharmacology of new histamine H receptor antagonists, *Clin Pharmacokinetics*, 36(5): 329–52.

Flumazenil

Brand names: Anexate, Lanexat, Mazicon, Romazicon
Classification: benzodiazepine antagonist
λ: 21–75 min
V_d: 0.7–1.6 L/kg
Usual dosage: 0.2–1 mg iv/dose

Source	Therapeutic/ Nontoxic	Toxic	Lethal
Blood	0.004–0.1 mg/L	No data available	

Comments

- Used to treat benzodiazepine overdose

Selected Sources

Jones RD, Chan K, Roulson CJ, Brown AG, Smith ID, and Mya GH (1993), Pharmacokinetics of flumazenil and midazolam, *Br J Anaesth*, 70(3): 286–92.
Klotz U, Ziegler G, and Reimann IW (1984), Pharmacokinetics of the selective benzodiazepine antagonist Ro 15-1788 in man, *Eur J Clin Pharm*, 27(1): 115–7.

Flunitrazepam

Brand names: Rohypnol
Street names: Forget-Me-Not, Mexican valium, Roofies, Rope
Classification: benzodiazepine
λ: 9–24 hrs
V_d: 3.4–5.5 L/kg
Usual dosage: 1–2 mg/dose

Source	Therapeutic/ Nontoxic	Toxic	Lethal
Blood	0.001–0.015 mg/L	0.05 mg/L	0.07 mg/L
	0.02–0.05 mg/L 7-AF		0.12–1.6 mg/L 7-AF
Kidney			0.5 mg/kg

Comments

- Active metabolite: 7-aminoflunitrazepam (7-AF)
- Often not detected on routine (immunoassay) benzodiazepine screens

Selected Sources

Balmaceda-Harmelink U, Andresen H, and Tsokos M (2004), Suicidal monointoxication with flunitrazepam: Further comment on coloration phenomena of the upper gastrointestinal tract, *Archiv für Kriminologie*, 214(3–4): 93–8.

Boxenbaum HG, Posmanter HN, Macasieb T, Geitner KA, Weinfeld RE, and Moore JD (1978), Pharmacokinetics of flunitrazepam following single- and multiple-dose oral administration to healthy human subjects, *J Pharmacokinet Biopharm*, 6(4): 283–93.

Drummer OH, Syrjanen ML, and Cordner SM (1993), Deaths involving the benzodiazepine flunitrazepam, *Am J For Med Path*, 14(3): 238–43.

Heyndrickx B (1987), Fatal intoxication due to flunitrazepam, *J Anal Tox*, 11(6): 278.

Fluoride

Brand names: component of some insecticides/rodenticides
Classification: element
λ: 4–8 hrs
V_d: 0.75–1.8 L/kg
Usual dosage: not applicable

Source	Therapeutic/ Nontoxic	Toxic	Lethal
Blood	0.01–0.15 mg/L	1–2 mg/L	1.6–300 mg/L
Vitreous			2.5 mg/L
Urine	0.3–0.4 mg/L		3.2–670 mg/L
Bile			3.4 mg/L
Liver			4.4–81 mg/kg
Kidney			2.5–68 mg/kg
Brain			2.5–5 mg/kg
Stomach contents			260–1120 mg/L

Selected Sources

Adelson L (1974), Chapter XIII, Murder by poison, in *The Pathology of Homicide*, Charles C Thomas, Springfield, IL, pp. 725–875.

Ekstrand J, Alván G, Boréus LO, and Norlin A (1977), Pharmacokinetics of fluoride in man after single and multiple oral doses, *Eur J Clin Pharm*, 12(4): 311–7.

Kaa E, Selvig K, Dybdahl H, and Siboni A (1986), A case of fluoride poisoning, *Am J For Med Path*, 7(3): 266–7.

Martinez MA, Ballesteros S, Piga FJ, de la Torre CS, and Cubero C (2007), *The tissue distribution of fluoride in a fatal case of self-poisoning*, presented at the Society of Forensic Toxicologists meeting, Durham, North Carolina.

McBay AJ (1973), Toxicological findings in fatal poisonings, *Clin Chem*, 19(4): 361–5.

Menchel SM and Dunn WA (1984), Hydrofluoric acid poisoning, *Am J For Med Path*, 5(3): 245–8.

Poklis A and Mackell MA (1989), Disposition of fluoride in a fatal case of unsuspected sodium fluoride poisoning, *For Sci Intl*, 41(1–2): 55–9.

Speaker JH (1976), Determination of fluoride by specific ion electrode and report of a fatal case of fluoride poisoning, *J For Sci*, 21(1): 121–6.

Fluoxetine

Brand names: Prozac, Sarafem
Classification: antidepressant (SSRI)
λ: 1–3 dys
V_d: 20–45 L/kg
Usual dosage: 20–80 mg qd

Source	Therapeutic/ Nontoxic	Toxic	Lethal
Blood	0.02–0.45 mg/L	0.9–2 mg/L	1.3–7.0 mg/L
Urine	0.03–0.4 mg/L		5.5 mg/L
Bile	0.1–5.9 mg/L		13 mg/L
Liver	0.7–29 mg/kg		54 mg/kg
Kidney	0.2–8.7 mg/kg		
Brain	0.3–12 mg/kg		
Skeletal muscle	0.6–2.5 mg/kg		
Cardiac muscle	0.2–8.3 mg/kg		
Stomach contents			270 mg/L

Comments

- Metabolized by CYP 3A, 2C9, and 2C19
- Active metabolite: norfluoxetine
- Prolongs QT interval

Selected Sources

Bexar County Medical Examiner's Office data 1996–2007.
Compton R, Spiller HA, and Bosse GM (2005), Fatal fluoxetine ingestion with postmortem blood concentrations, *Clin Tox*, 43(4): 277–9.
Johnson RD, Lewis RJ, and Angier MK (2007), The distribution of fluoxetine in human fluids and tissues, *J Anal Tox*, 31(7): 409–14.
Kincaid RL, McMullin MM, Crookham SB, and Rieders F (1990), Report of a fluoxetine fatality, *J Anal Tox*, 14(5): 327–9.
Orsulak PJ, Kenney JT, Debus JR, Crowley G, and Wittman PD (1988), Determination of the antidepressant fluoxetine and its metabolite norfluoxetine in serum by reversed-phase HPLC with ultraviolet detection, *Clin Chem*, 34(9): 1875–8.
Roettger JR (1990), The importance of blood collection site for the determination of basic drugs: A case with fluoxetine and diphenhydramine overdose, *J Anal Tox*, 14(3): 191–2.

Fluphenazine

Brand names: Prolixin
Classification: antipsychotic
λ: 11–15 hrs (HCl); 7–10 d (decanoate)
V_d: 11 L/kg
Usual dosage: 2.5–10 mg tid/qd

Source	Therapeutic/ Nontoxic	Toxic	Lethal
Blood	0.002–0.02 mg/L	0.05–0.1 mg/L	See comments

Comments

- Fatalities reported are due to neuroleptic malignant syndrome
- May prolong QT interval

Selected Sources

Kratzsch C, Peters FT, Kraemer T, Weber AA, and Maurer HH (2003), Screening, library-assisted identification and validated quantification of fifteen neuroleptics and three of their metabolites in plasma by liquid chromatography/mass spectrometry with atmospheric pressure chemical ionization, *J Mass Spectrum*, 38(3): 283–95.

Roman M, Kronstrand R, Lindstedt D, and Josefsson M (2008), Quantitation of seven low-dosage antipsychotic drugs in human postmortem blood using LC-MS-MS, *J Anal Tox*, 32(2): 147–55.

Flurazepam

Brand names: Dalmane, Dalmadorm
Classification: benzodiazepine
λ: 1–3 hrs
V_d: 3–5 L/kg
Usual dosage: 15–30 mg qHS

Source	Therapeutic/ Nontoxic	Toxic	Lethal
Blood	0.0005–0.02 mg/L	0.15–0.2 mg/L	0.5–5.5 mg/L
Vitreous			1.3 mg/L
Urine			3.3–172 mg/L
Bile			33–323 mg/L
Liver			2.7–130 mg/kg
Kidney			0.9 mg/kg
Brain			0.8 mg/kg
Stomach contents			600 mg

Comments

- Active metabolite: *N*-1-desalkylflurazepam
- Tolerance can develop and should be considered when interpreting drug concentrations

Selected Sources

Ferrara SD, Tedeschi L, Marigo M, and Castagna F (1979), Concentrations of phenobarbital, flurazepam, and flurazepam metabolites in autopsy cases, *J For Sci*, 24(1): 61–9.

Martello S, Oliva A, De Giorgio F, and Chiarotti M (2006), Acute flurazepam intoxication: A case report, *Am J For Med Path*, 27(1): 55–7.

McIntyre IM, Syrjanen ML, Lawrence KL, Dow CA, and Drummer OH (1994), A fatality due to flurazepam, *J For Sci*, 39(6): 1571–4.

Physicians' Desk Reference 61 Edition (2007), Thomson PDR, Montvale, NJ, pp. 3342–3.

Fluvoxamine

Brand names: Luvox, Faverin, Dumyrox
Classification: antidepressant (SSRI)
λ: 9–28 hrs
V_d: 25 L/kg
Usual dosage: 50–100 mg qd

Source	Therapeutic/ Nontoxic	Toxic	Lethal
Blood	0.02–0.5 mg/L	0.65–1.9 mg/L	2.2–11 mg/L
Vitreous	0.16–0.28 mg/L		1.9 mg/L
Urine			4.1 mg/L
Bile	11 mg/L		68 mg/L
Stomach contents			28 mg/kg

Comments

- Metabolized by CYP 1A2 and 2D6

Selected Sources

Banerjee AK (1988), Recovery from prolonged cerebral depression after fluvoxamine overdose, *Br Med J (Clinical Research Ed.)*, 296: 1774.

Bexar County Medical Examiner's Office data 1996–2007.

DeVane CL and Gill HS (1997), Clinical pharmacokinetics of fluvoxamine: Applications to dosage regimen design, *J Clin Psychiatry*, 58(5): 7–14.

de Vries MH, Raghoebar M, Mathlener IS, and van Harten J (1992), Single and multiple oral dose fluvoxamine kinetics in young and elderly subjects, *Ther Drug Monit*, 14(6): 493–8.

Druid H and Holmgren P (1997), A compilation of fatal and control concentrations of drugs in postmortem femoral blood, *J For Sci*, 42(1): 79–87.

Garnier R, Azoyan P, Chataigner D, Taboulet P, Dellattre D, and Efthymiou ML (1993), Acute fluvoxamine poisoning, *J Int Med Res*, 21(4): 197–208.

Hahn I, Blancaflor G, Hoffman RS, Howland MA, and Nelson LS (2000), Fluvoxamine overdose producing status epilepticus, *Clin Tox*, 38(5): 573.

Kunsman GW, Rodriguez R, and Rodriguez P (1999), Fluvoxamine distribution in postmortem cases, *Am J For Med Path*, 20(1): 78–83.

Oka H, Shirakawa Y, Koyama K, Maekawa S, Hirota M, and Nishizaki O (2002), A case of fluvoxamine overdose, *Chudoku Kenkyu*, 15(1): 53–7.

Spigset O and Ohman R (1996), A case of fluvoxamine intoxication demonstrating nonlinear elimination pharmacokinetics, *J Clin Psychopharmacol*, 16(3): 254–5.

Wood, DM, Rajalingam Y, Greene SL, Morgan PE, Gerrie D, and Jones AL (2007), Status epilepticus following intentional overdose of fluvoxamine: A case report with serum fluvoxamine concentration, *Clin Tox*, 45(7): 791.

Formaldehyde

Brand names: not applicable
Classification: aldehyde
λ: 90 sec
V_d: unknown
Usual dosage: not applicable

Source	Therapeutic/ Nontoxic	Toxic	Lethal
Blood	2.7 mg/L FAH[a] 0.01–12 mg/L FA[b]	No data available	4.2–34 mg/L FAH[a] 210–1363 mg/L FA[b]
Liver			169 mg/kg FAH[a] 754 mg/kg FA[b]
Kidney			42 mg/kg FAH[a] 531 mg/kg FA[b]
Brain			45 mg/kg FAH[a] 248 mg/kg FA[b]
Cardiac muscle			49 mg/kg FAH[a] 534 mg/kg FA[b]
Stomach contents			6990 mg/kg FAH[a] None detected FA[b]

[a] FAH—formaldehyde; [b] FA—formic acid.

Comments

- Metabolized to formic acid

Selected Sources

Burkhart KK, Kulig KW, and McMartin KE (1990), Formate levels following a formalin ingestion, *Vet Hum Tox*, 32(2): 135–7.

Eells JT, McMartin KE, Black K, Virayotha V, Tisdell RH, and Tephly TR (1981), Formaldehyde poisoning. Rapid metabolism to formic acid, *JAMA*, 246(11): 1237–8.

Köppel C, Baudisch H, Schneider V, and Ibe K (1990), Suicidal ingestion of formalin with fatal complications, *Intensive Care Med*, 16(3): 212–4.

Nishi K, Yamada M, and Wakasugi C (1968), Formaldehyde poisoning: Report of an autopsy case, *Nihon Hoigaku Zasshi*, 42(1): 85–9.

Pandey CK, Agarwal A, Baronia A, and Singh N (2000), Toxicity of ingested formalin and its management, *Hum Exp Tox*, 19(6): 360–6.

Freon 11

Brand names: component of refrigerants, aerosol propellants
Alternate names: trichlorofluoromethane
Classification: volatile (fluorocarbon)
λ: 1–1.8 hrs
V_d: unknown
Usual dosage: not applicable

Source	Therapeutic/ Nontoxic	Toxic	Lethal
Blood	0.1–2.8 mg/L	No data available	0.6–63 mg/L
Urine	0.07–0.43 mg/L		< 0.1 mg/L
Liver			45–74 mg/kg
Kidney			50 mg/kg
Brain			61–109 mg/kg
Lung			32–149 mg/kg
Cardiac muscle			407 mg/kg

Comments

- Cardiotoxic: intoxication associated with arrhythmias

Selected Sources

Angerer J, Schröder B, and Heinrich R (1985), Exposure to fluorotrichloromethane (R-11), *Int Arch Occup Environ Health*, 56(1): 67–72.

Baselt RC and Cravey RH (1968), A fatal case involving trichloromonofluoromethane and dichlorodifluoromethane, *J For Sci*, 13(3): 407–10.

Christopoulos GN and Kirch ER (1974), Estimation of fluoroalkane propellants, *J For Sci*, 19(1): 168–71.

Goldermann L, Gellert J, and Teschke R (1983), Quantitative assessment of carbon tetrachloride levels in human blood by head-space gas chromatography: Application in a case of suicidal carbon tetrachloride intoxication, *Intensive Care Med*, 9(3): 131–5.

Groppi A, Polettini A, Lunetta P, Achille G, and Montagna M (1994), A fatal case of trichlorofluoromethane (Freon 11) poisoning. Tissue distribution study by gas chromatography-mass spectrometry, *J For Sci*, 39(3): 871–6.

Knight B (1991), *Forensic Pathology* Chapter 34, Deaths from organic solvents, Oxford University Press, New York, pp. 533–6.

Mergner GW, Blake DA, and Helrich M (1975), Biotransformation and elimination of 14C-trichlorofluoromethane (FC-11) and 14C-dichlorodifluoromethane (FC-12) in man, *Anesthesiology*, 42(3): 345–51.

Poklis A (1975), Determination of fluorocarbon 11 and fluorocarbon 12 in post-mortem tissues: A case report, *For Sci*, 5(1): 53–9.
Standefer JC (1975), Death associated with fluorocarbon inhalation: Report of a case, *J For Sci*, 20(3): 548–51.
Stephens BG (2004), Chapter XXII, Investigation of deaths from drug abuse, in *Spitz and Fisher's Medicolegal Investigation of Death Fourth Edition*, Spitz WU (Ed.), Charles C Thomas, Springfield, IL, pp. 1166–1217.

Freon 22

Brand names: component of refrigerants, aerosol propellants
Alternate names: chlorodifluoromethane
Classification: volatile (fluorocarbon)
λ: 1.9–4.6 hrs
V_d: unknown
Usual dosage: not applicable

Source	Therapeutic/ Nontoxic	Toxic	Lethal
Blood	0.25–1.4 mg/L	No data available	26–560 mg/L
Vitreous			0.7–1 mg/L
Urine	0.05–0.42 mg/L		0.9–1.7 mg/L
Bile			1.3 mg/L
Liver			4.4–381 mg/kg
Kidney			33–75 mg/kg
Brain			2.8–414 mg/kg
Lung			1.6–80 mg/kg

Comments

- Cardiotoxic: intoxication associated with arrhythmias

Selected Sources

Fitzgerald RL, Fishel CE, and Bush LL (1993), Fatality due to recreational use of chlorodifluoromethane and chloropentafluoroethane, *J For Sci*, 38(2): 477–83.

Kintz P, Baccino E, Tracqui A, and Mangin P (1996), Headspace GC/MS testing for chlorodifluoromethane in two fatal cases, *For Sci Intl*, 82(2): 171–5.

Koreeda A, Yonemitsu K, Mimasaka S, Ohtsu Y, and Tsunenari S (2007), An accidental death due to Freon 22 (monochlorodifluoromethane) inhalation in a fishing vessel, *For Sci Intl*, 168(2–3): 208–11.

Morita M, Miki A, Kazama H, and Sakata M (1977), Case report of deaths caused by freon gas, *For Sci*, 10(3): 253–60.

Stephens BG (2004), Chapter XXII, Investigation of deaths from drug abuse, in *Spitz and Fisher's Medicolegal Investigation of Death Fourth Edition*, Spitz WU (Ed.), Charles C Thomas, Springfield, IL, pp. 1166–217.

Woollen BH, Marsh JR, Mahler JD, Auton TR, Makepeace D, and Cocker J (1992), Human inhalation pharmacokinetics of chlorodifluoromethane (HCFC22), *Int Arch Occup Environ Health*, 64(5): 383–7.

Freon 113

Brand names: component of refrigerants, aerosol propellants
Alternate names: trichlorotrifluoroethane
Classification: volatile (fluorocarbon)
λ: 20–46 hrs
V_d: 4.2–10 L/kg
Usual dosage: not applicable

Source	Therapeutic/ Nontoxic	Toxic	Lethal
Blood	0.1–1.2 mg/L	No data available	0.4–32 mg/L
Liver			2.9–81 mg/kg
Kidney			476 mg/kg
Brain			0.5–1370 mg/kg
Lung			0.05–3.5 mg/kg
Skeletal muscle			8.8 mg/kg
Adipose tissue			5.4 mg/kg

Comments

- Cardiotoxic: intoxication associated with arrhythmias

Selected Sources

Clark MA, Jones JW, Robinson JJ, and Lord JT (1985), Multiple deaths resulting from shipboard exposure to trichlorotrifluoroethane, *J For Sci*, 30(4): 1256–9.
Knight B (1991), Chapter 34, Deaths from organic solvents, *Forensic Pathology*, Oxford University Press, New York, pp. 533–6.
May DC and Blotzer MJ (1984), A report of occupational deaths attributed to fluorocarbon-113, *Arch Environ Health*, 39(5): 352–4.
McGee MB, Meyer RF, and Jejurikar SG (1990), A death resulting from trichlorotrifluoroethane poisoning, *J For Sci*, 35(6): 1453–60.
Stephens BG (2004), Chapter XXII, Investigation of deaths from drug abuse, in *Spitz and Fisher's Medicolegal Investigation of Death Fourth Edition*, Spitz WU (Ed.), Charles C Thomas, Springfield, IL, pp. 1166–217.
Woollen BH, Guest EA, Howe W, Marsh JR, Wilson HK, and Auton TR (1990), Human inhalation pharmacokinetics of 1,1,2-trichloro-1,2,2-trifluoroethane (FC113), *Int Arch Occup Environ Health*, 62(1): 73–8.

Gabapentin

Brand names: Neurontin, Gabarone
Classification: anticonvulsant
λ: 5–7 hrs
V_d: 0.5–0.9 L/kg
Usual dosage: 300–600 mg tid

Source	Therapeutic/ Nontoxic	Toxic	Lethal
Blood	2.2–15 mg/L	23–104 mg/L	No data available

Selected Sources

Boyd RA, Türck D, Abel RB, Sedman AJ, and Bockbrader HN (1999), Effects of age and gender on single-dose pharmacokinetics of gabapentin, *Epilepsia,* 40(4): 474–9.

Gatti G, Ferrari AR, Guerrini R, Bonanni P, Bonomi I, and Perucca E (2003), Plasma gabapentin concentrations in children with epilepsy: Influence of age, relationship with dosage, and preliminary observations on correlation with clinical response, *Ther Drug Monit,* 25(1): 54–60.

Jones H, Aguila E, and Farber HW (2002), Gabapentin toxicity requiring intubation in a patient receiving long-term hemodialysis, *Ann Int Med,* 137(1): 74.

Spiller HA, Dunaway MD, and Cutino L (2002), Massive gabapentin and presumptive quetiapine overdose, *Vet Hum Tox,* 44(4): 243–4.

Verma A, St Clair EW, and Radtke RA (1999), A case of sustained massive gabapentin overdose without serious side effects, *Ther Drug Monit,* 21(6): 615–7.

Gamma-Hydroxybutyrate (GHB)

Brand names: not applicable
Street names: Liquid Ecstasy, Georgia Home Boy, Grievous Bodily Harm, Max (w/ amphetamine), Special K Lube (w/ ketamine and ETOH)
Classification: sedative/hypnotic
λ: 0.6–0.7 hrs
V_d: 0.4–1 L/kg
Usual dosage: 2–6 g/dose

Source	Endogenous	Therapeutic/ Nontoxic	Toxic	Lethal
Blood	0.04 mg/L	0.08–130 mg/L	130–295 mg/L	345–3385 mg/L
Vitreous				48–2856 mg/L
Urine	0–6.6 mg/L	5–840 mg/L	432–2407 mg/L	1665–33727 mg/L
Bile				1800 mg/L
Liver				52 mg/kg
Brain				102–221 mg/kg
Stomach contents				71 mg/L

Selected Sources

Abanades S, Farré M, Segura M, Pichini S, Barral D, Pacifici R, Pellegrini M, Fonseca F, Langohr K, and de la Torre R (2006), γ-Hydroxybutyrate (GHB) in humans, *Pharmacodynamics and Pharmacokinetics Annals of the New York Academy of Sciences*, 1074(1): 559–76.

Brenneisen R, Elsohly MA, Murphy TP, Passarelli J, Russmann S, and Salamone SJ (2004), Pharmacokinetics and excretion of gamma-hydroxybutyrate (GHB) in healthy subjects, *J Anal Tox*, 28(8): 625–30.

Caldicott DGE, Chow FY, Burns BJ, Felgate PD, and Byard RW (2004), Fatalities associated with the use of gamma-hydroxybutyrate and its analogues in Australasia, *Med J Aust*, 181(6): 310–3.

Couper FJ and Logan BK (2000), Determination of gamma-hydroxybutyrate (GHB) in biological specimens by gas chromatography–mass spectrometry, *J Anal Tox*, 24(1): 1–7.

Haller C, Thai D, Jacob P, and Dyer JE (2006), GHB urine concentrations after single-dose administration in humans, *J Anal Tox*, 30(6): 360–4.

Kalasinsky KS, Dixon MM, Schmunk GA, and Kish SJ (2001), Blood, brain and hair GHB concentrations following fatal ingestion, *J For Sci*, 46(3): 728–30.

Kintz P, Villain M, Pélissier AL, Cirimele V, and Leonetti G (2005), Unusually high concentrations in a fatal GHB case, *J Anal Tox*, 29(6): 582–5.

Mazarr-Proo S and Kerrigan S (2005), Distribution of GHB in tissues and fluids following a fatal overdose, *J Anal Tox*, 29(5): 398–400.

Sporer KA, Chin RL, Dyer JE, and Lamb R (2003), Gamma-hydroxybutyrate serum levels and clinical syndrome after severe overdose, *Ann Emer Med*, 42(1): 3–8.

Glutethimide

Brand names: Doriden
Street Names: Doors-and-Fours, Load, Pancakes (all w/ codeine)
Classification: sedative/hypnotic
λ: 4–12 hrs
V_d: 2–3 L/kg
Usual dosage: 500 mg qHS

Source	Therapeutic/ Nontoxic	Toxic	Lethal
Blood	1.3–7 mg/L	5–120 mg/L	20–97 mg/L
Urine	2.1–7.3 mg/L		5–20 mg/L
Liver			5–514 mg/kg
Kidney			10–40 mg/kg
Brain			3–61 mg/kg
Skeletal muscle			34 mg/kg

Comments

- Not available in United States
- Active metabolite: 4-hydroxyglutethimide

Selected Sources

Caplan YH, Ottinger WE, and Crooks CR (1983), Therapeutic and toxic drug concentrations in post mortem blood: A six year study in the State of Maryland, *J Anal Tox*, 7(5): 225–30.

Chazan JA and Garella S (1971), Glutethimide intoxication: A prospective study of 70 patients treated conservatively without hemodialysis, *Arch Int Med*, 128(2): 215–9.

Curry SH, Gordon JS, Riddall D, Simpson P, Binns TB, and Rondel RK (1971), Disposition of glutethimide in man, *Clin Pharm Ther*, 12(5): 849–57.

Gold M, Tassoni E, and Etzl E (1973), Comparison of glutethimide concentration in the serum and cerebrospinal fluid of humans in drug overdose, *Clin Chem*, 19(10): 1158–61.

Goldbaum LR, Williams M, and Johnston EH (1962), Determination and distribution of Doriden, *J For Sci*, 7: 499–503.

Greenblatt DJ, Allen MD, Harmatz JS, Noel BJ, and Shader RI (1979), Correlates of outcome following acute glutethimide overdosage, *J For Sci*, 24(1): 76–86.

Hansen AR, Kennedy KA, Ambre JJ, and Fischer LJ (1975), Glutethimide poisoning: A metabolite contributes to morbidity and mortality, *NEJM*, 292(5): 250–2.

Irey NS and Froede RC (1974), Evaluation of deaths from drug overdose: A clinicopathologic study, *Am J Clin Path*, 61(6): 778–84.

Parker KD, Elliott HW, Wright JA, Nomof H, and Hine CH (1970), Blood and urine concentrations of subjects receiving barbiturates, meprobamate, glutethimide, or diphenylhydantoin, *Clin Tox*, 3(1): 131–45.

Paterson SC (1985), Drug levels found in cases of fatal self-poisoning, *For Sci Intl,* 27(2): 129–33.

Wallace JE, Blum K, and Singh JM (1974), Determination of drugs in biological specimens—A review, *J Tox Clin Tox*, 7(5): 477–95.

Guaifenesin

Brand names: Hytuss, Organidin, Humibid, Mucinex
Classification: expectorant
λ: 1.4–5.3 hrs
V_d: 1 L/kg
Usual dosage: 200–400 mg q 4 hrs

Source	Therapeutic/ Nontoxic	Toxic	Lethal
Blood	0.1–1.4 mg/L	No data available	27 mg/L[a]

[a] Co-intoxicants diphenhydramine (8.8 mg/L) and chlorpheniramine (0.2 mg/L)

Selected Sources

Aluri JB and Stavchansky S (1993), Determination of guaifenesin in human plasma by liquid chromatography in the presence of pseudoephedrine, *J Pharma Biomed Anal*, 11(9): 803–8.

Eichhold TH, McCauley-Myers DL, Khambe DA, Thompson GA, and Hoke SH (2007), Simultaneous determination of dextromethorphan, dextrorphan and guaifenesin in human plasma using semi-automated liquid/liquid extraction and gradient liquid chromatography tandem mass spectrometry, *J Pharma Biomed Anal*, 43(2): 586–600.

Maynard WR and Bruce RB (1970), GLC determination of guaiacol glyceryl ether in blood, *J Pharma Sci*, 59(9): 1346–8.

Wogoman H, Steinberg M, and Jenkins AJ (1999), Acute intoxication with guaifenesin, diphenhydramine, and chlorpheniramine, *Am J For Med Path*, 20(2): 199–202.

Haloperidol

Brand names: Haldol
Classification: antipsychotic
λ: 13–23 hrs
V_d: 11–25 L/kg
Usual dosage: 0.5–2 mg bid/tid po; 2–5 mg/dose im

Source	Therapeutic/ Nontoxic	Toxic	Lethal
Blood	0.005–0.05 mg/L	0.05–0.5 mg/L	0.18–1.9 mg/L
Urine	0.4 mg/L		6.6 mg/L
Bile	0.4 mg/L		3.4 mg/L
Liver	5.0 mg/kg		44 mg/kg
Kidney	0.7 mg/kg		

Comments

- Associated with malignant neuroleptic syndrome
- Prolongs QT interval
- Metabolized by CYP 2D6, 3A, and 1A2

Selected Sources

Bexar County Medical Examiner's Office data 1996–2007.

Froemming JS, Lam YW, Jann MW, and Davis CM (1989), Pharmacokinetics of haloperidol, *Clin Pharmacokin*, 17(6): 396–423.

Kratzsch C, Peters FT, Kraemer T, Weber AA, and Maurer HH (2003), Screening, library-assisted identification and validated quantification of fifteen neuroleptics and three of their metabolites in plasma by liquid chromatography/mass spectrometry with atmospheric pressure chemical ionization, *J Mass Spectrum*, 38(3): 283–95.

Levine BS, Wu SC, Goldberger BA, and Caplan YH (1991), Two fatalities involving haloperidol, *J Anal Tox*, 15(5): 282–4.

Tonkin AL and Bochner F (1994), Therapeutic drug monitoring and patient outcome: A review of the issues, *Clin Pharmacokin*, 27(3): 169–74.

Tsujimoto A, Tsujimoto G, Ishizaki T, Nakazawa S, and Ichihashi Y (1982), Toxic haloperidol reactions with observation of serum haloperidol concentration in two children, *Dev Pharm Ther*, 4(1–2): 12–7.

Zaleon CR and Guthrie SK (1994), Antipsychotic drug use in older adults, *Am J Hosp Pharm*, 51(23): 2917–43.

Halothane

Brand names: Fluothane
Classification: halogenated anesthetic
λ: 40–45 min
V_d: 1 L/kg
Usual dosage: 0.5%–3% inhaled

Source	Therapeutic/ Nontoxic	Toxic	Lethal
Blood	7–310 mg/L	No data available	3.4–650 mg/L
Urine			0–20 mg/L
Bile			1.6–8.6 mg/L
Liver	630 mg/kg		1.7–880 mg/kg
Kidney			12–14 mg/kg
Brain			104–156 mg/kg

Comments

- Associated with malignant hyperthermia
- Hepatotoxic
- Therapeutic concentrations can be fatal if drug not administered in a monitored medical setting
- Metabolized by CYP 2E1

Selected Sources

Ardoin D, Hingson RA, Tomaro AJ, and Fike WW (1966), Chromatographic blood-gas studies of halothane in ambulatory oral surgical anesthesia, *Anesth Analg*, 45(3): 275–81.
Madea B and Musshoff F (1999), Homicidal poisoning with halothane, *Intl J Leg Med*, 113(1): 47–9.
Randall B and Corbett B (1982), Fatal halothane poisoning during anesthesia with other agents, *J For Sci*, 27(1): 225–30.

Heroin

Brand names: not applicable
Street names: Brown Sugar, H, Horse, Junk, Smack;
w/ cocaine: Belushi, Dynamite, Eightball, Speedball, Moonrock;
w/ cocaine and LSD: Frisco
Classification: narcotic
λ: 2–6 min (MAM 10–40 min)
V_d: 0.5–0.75 L/kg
Usual dosage: not applicable

	Chronic Use/Nontoxic		Lethal	
Source	Morphine	MAM	Morphine	MAM
Blood	0.01–0.23 mg/L	0–0.02 mg/L	0.01–1.7 mg/L	0–0.53 mg/L
Vitreous			0.01–0.2 mg/L	0.004–0.17 mg/L
Urine			0.01–12 mg/L	0.4 mg/L
Bile			0.002–40 mg/L	
Liver			0.04–10 mg/kg	
Kidney			0.7–1.9 mg/kg	
Brain			0.02–0.7 mg/kg	
Skeletal muscle	0.01–0.19 mg/kg	0–0.06 mg/kg	0.14–1 mg/kg	0.01–0.35 mg/kg

Comments

- Metabolized to morphine and 6-monoacetylmorphine (MAM)
- 6-MAM specific for heroin

Selected Sources

Bexar County Medical Examiner's Office data 1996–2007.
Girardin F, Rentsch KM, Schwab MA, Maggiorini M, Pauli-Magnus C, and Kullak-Ublick GA (2003), Pharmacokinetics of high doses of intramuscular and oral heroin in narcotic addicts, *Clin Pharm Thera*, 74(4): 341–52.
Moriya F and Hashimoto Y (1997), Distribution of free and conjugated morphine in body fluids and tissues in a fatal heroin overdose: Is conjugated morphine stable in postmortem specimens? *J For Sci*, 42(4): 736–40.
Nakamura GR (1978), Toxicologic assessments in acute heroin fatalities, *Clin Tox*, 13(1): 75–87.
Reed D, Spiehler VR, and Cravey RH (1977), Two cases of heroin-related suicide, *For Sci*, 9(1): 49–52.
Richards RG, Reed D, and Cravey RH (1976), Death from intravenously administered narcotics: A study of 114 cases, *J For Sci*, 21(3): 467–82.
Wyman J and Bultman S (2004), Postmortem distribution of heroin metabolites in femoral blood, liver, cerebrospinal fluid, and vitreous humor, *J Anal Tox*, 28(4): 260–3.

Hydrocodone

Brand names: component of Vicodin, Hycodan, Lortab, Norco, Hycotuss
Classification: narcotic
λ: 3.5–4.1 hrs
V_d: 3.3–4.7 L/kg
Usual dosage: 5–10 mg q 4–6 hrs

Source	Therapeutic/ Nontoxic	Toxic	Lethal
Blood	0.018–0.05 mg/L	0.1 mg/L	0.2–1.6 mg/L
Bile			0.12–14 mg/L
Skeletal muscle			0.27–0.92 mg/kg

Comments

- Active metabolites, hydromorphone and dihydrocodeine
- Metabolized by CYP 2D6
- Tolerance can develop and should be considered when interpreting drug concentrations

Selected Sources

Ackerman WE and Ahmad M (2007), Effect of cigarette smoking on serum hydrocodone levels in chronic pain patients, *J Ark Med Soc*, 104(1): 19–21.

Barnhart JW and Caldwell WJ (1977), Gas chromatographic determination of hydrocodone in serum, *J Chromatogr*, 130: 243–9.

Bexar County Medical Examiner's Office data 1996–2007.

Park JI, Nakamura GR, Griesemer EC, and Noguchi TT (1982), Hydromorphone detected in bile following hydrocodone ingestion, *J For Sci*, 27(1): 223–4.

Physicians' Desk Reference 61 Edition (2007), Thomson PDR, Montvale, NJ, pp. 535–6.

Spiller HA (2003), Postmortem oxycodone and hydrocodone blood concentrations, *J For Sci*, 48(2): 429–31.

Hydrogen Sulfide

Brand names: not applicable
Classification: gas
λ: unknown
V_d: unknown
Usual dosage: not applicable

	Nontoxic		Lethal	
Source	Sulfide	Thiosufide	Sulfide	Thiosufide
Blood	0–0.34 mg/L	0–0.05 mg/L	0.45–0.96 mg/L	2–16 mg/L
Urine				0.9–137 mg/L
Liver			38 mg/kg	
Kidney			34 mg/kg	
Lung			0.42 mg/kg	9.3 mg/kg
Brain			2.7–106 mg/kg	5 mg/kg
Skeletal muscle			0.16 mg/kg	

Comments

- Is a naturally occurring gas found in sewers and volcanic gas; is a component of natural gas
- Formed by the breakdown of organic material in the absence of oxygen
- Smells like rotten eggs
- Complexes with iron in mitochondrial enzymes, stopping cellular respiration
- Exposure can cause discoloration of coins in pockets

Selected Sources

Gerasimon G, Bennett S, Musser J, and Rinard J (2007), Acute hydrogen sulfide poisoning in a dairy farmer, *Clin Tox*, 45(4): 420–3.
Kage S, Kashimura S, Ikeda H, Kudo K, and Ikeda N (2002), Fatal and nonfatal poisoning by hydrogen sulfide at an industrial waste site, *J For Sci*, 47(3): 652–5.
Winek CL, Collom WD, and Wecht CH (1968), Death from hydrogen-sulphide fumes, *Lancet*, 1(7551): 1096.

Hydromorphone

Brand names: Dilaudid, Palladone
Classification: narcotic
λ: 1.7–3.5 hrs
V_d: 1.3–3.0 L/kg
Usual dosage: 1–4 mg q 4–6 hrs

Source	Therapeutic/ Nontoxic	Toxic	Lethal
Blood	0.001–0.05 mg/L	0.1 mg/L	0.08–2.7 mg/L
Vitreous			0.1 mg/L[a]
Urine			7.8 mg/L[a]
Liver			0.8 mg/kg[a]
Kidney			0.7 mg/kg[a]
Brain			0.5 mg/kg[a]

[a] ETOH co-intoxicant (BAC 0.09 g/dL)

Comments

- Is a metabolite of hydrocodone
- Tolerance can develop and should be considered when interpreting drug concentrations

Selected Sources

Bexar County Medical Examiner's Office data 1996–2007.
Levine B, Saady J, Fierro M, and Valentour J (1984), A hydromorphone and ethanol fatality, *J For Sci*, 29(2): 655–9.
Physicians' Desk Reference 61 Edition (2007), Thomson PDR, Montvale, NJ, pp. 440–6.
Wallage HR and Palmentier JPFP (2006), Hydromorphone-related fatalities in Ontario, *J Anal Tox*, 30(3): 202–9.

Hydroxyzine

Brand names: Vistaril, Atarax, Rezine
Classification: antihistamine/anxiolytic
λ: 5–24 hrs
V_d: 13–28 L/kg
Usual dosage: 25–100 mg qid

Source	Therapeutic/ Nontoxic	Toxic	Lethal
Blood	0.07–0.1 mg/L	0.1–1.4 mg/L	2.6–39 mg/L
Urine			1.4–19 mg/L
Bile			23–122 mg/L
Liver			15–414 mg/kg
Brain			0.5–163 mg/kg
Stomach contents			0.96–489 mg

Comments

- Metabolized by CYP 2D6
- May prolong QT interval

Selected Sources

Druid H and Holmgren P (1997), A compilation of fatal and control concentrations of drugs in postmortem femoral blood, *J For Sci*, 42(1): 79–87.
Johnson GR (1982), A fatal case involving hydroxyzine, *J Anal Tox*, 6(2): 69–70.
Kintz P, Godelar B, and Mangin P (1990), Gas chromatographic identification and quantification of hydroxyzine: Application in a fatal self-poisoning, *For Sci Intl* 48(2): 139–43.
Péhourcq F (2004), A simple high-performance liquid chromatographic method for detection of hydroxyzine in human plasma after overdose, *J Pharm Tox Methods*, 50(1): 41–4.
Spiehler VR and Fukumoto RI (1984), Another fatal case involving hydroxyzine, *J Anal Tox*, 8(5): 242–3.

Ibogaine

Brand names: not applicable
Classification: hallucinogen/stimulant
λ: 4–7 hrs
V_d: 13 L/kg
Usual dosage: 500–800 mg/dose

	Nontoxic		Lethal	
Source	Ibogaine	Noribogaine	Ibogaine	Noribogaine
Blood	0.03–1.3 mg/L	0.02–1.2 mg/L	0.36–11 mg/L	11–22 mg/L
Urine			7.1–83 mg/L	21–51 mg/L
Bile			21 mg/L	11 mg/L
Liver			1.7–40 mg/kg	6.2–50 mg/kg
Kidney			1.6–7.6 mg/kg	4.1–4.9 mg/kg
Brain			12 mg/kg	19 mg/kg
Skeletal muscle			7.7 mg/kg	3.4 mg/kg
Stomach contents			2.9 mg/L	1.2 mg/L

Comments

- Is an alkaloid from *Tabernanthe iboga*
- Used to treat opiate withdrawal
- Active metabolite: noribogaine
- Metabolized by CYP 2D6
- May be associated with sudden cardiac death at low concentrations

Selected Sources

Chèze M, Lenoan A, Deveaux M, Pépin G (2008), Determination of ibogaine and noribogaine in biological fluids and hair by LC-MS/MS after *Tabernanthe iboga* abuse iboga alkaloids distribution in a drowning death case, *For Sci Intl*, 176(1): 58–66.

Cienki J, Mash D, and Hearn W (2001), Ibogaine fatalities, *Clin Tox*, 39(5): 547.

Kontrimaviciūte V, Breton H, Mathieu O, Mathieu-Daudé J-C, and Bressolle FMM (2006), Liquid chromatography-electrospray mass spectrometry determination of ibogaine and noribogaine in human plasma and whole blood: Application to a poisoning involving *Tabernanthe iboga* root, *J Chromatogr B*, 843(2): 131–41.

Kontrimaviciūte V, Mathieu O, Mathieu-Daudé J-C, Vainauskas P, Casper T, and Baccino E (2006), Distribution of ibogaine and noribogaine in a man following a poisoning involving root bark of the *Tabernanthe iboga* shrub, *J Anal Tox*, 30(7): 434–40.

Maas U and Strubelt S (2006), Fatalities after taking ibogaine in addiction treatment could be related to sudden cardiac death caused by autonomic dysfunction, *Med Hypotheses*, 67(4): 960–4.

Mash DC, Kovera CA, Pablo J, Tyndale RF, Ervin FD, and Williams IC (2000), Ibogaine: Complex pharmacokinetics, concerns for safety and preliminary efficacy measures, *Ann NY Acad Sci*, 914: 394–401.

Ibuprofen

Brand names: Advil, Motrin
Classification: NSAID
λ: 1.5–2.5 hrs
V_d: 0.13–0.19 L/kg
Usual dosage: 200–800 mg q 4–6 hrs

Source	Therapeutic/ Nontoxic	Toxic	Lethal
Blood	10–50 mg/L	100–720 mg/L	81–1050 mg/L
Urine			264 mg/L
Liver			74–942 mg/kg
Brain			284 mg/kg
Stomach contents			116 mg/L; 131 mg total

Comments

- Metabolized by CYP 2C8 and 2C9

Selected Sources

Adams SS, Cliffe EE, Lessel B, and Nicholson JS (1967), Some biological properties of 2-(4-isobutylphenyl)-propionic acid, *J Pharm Sci*, 56:1686.
Greenblatt DJ, Abernethy DR, Maltis R, Harmatz JS, and Shader RI (1984), Absorption and disposition of ibuprofen in the elderly, *Arthritis Rheum*, 27(9): 1066–9.
Kunsman GW and Rohrig TP (1993), Tissue distribution of ibuprofen in a fatal overdose, *Am J For Med Path*, 14(1): 48–50.
Lee CY and Finkler A (1986), Acute intoxication due to ibuprofen overdose, *Arch Path Lab Med*, 110(8): 747–9.
Oker EE, Hermann L, Baum CR, Fentzke KM, Sigg T, and Leikin JB (2000), Serious toxicity in a young child due to ibuprofen, *Academic Emer Med*, 7(7): 821–3.
Seifert SA, Bronstein AC, and McGuire T (2000), Massive ibuprofen ingestion with survival, *J Tox Clin Tox*, 38(1): 55–7.
Wood DM, Monaghan J, Streete P, Jones AL, and Dargan PI (2006), Fatality after deliberate ingestion of sustained-release ibuprofen: A case report, *Crit Care*, 10(2): R44.

Imipramine

Brand names: Tofranil
Classification: antidepressant (TCA)
λ: 7–18 hrs
V_d: 16–20 L/kg
Usual dosage: 75–100 mg qd

Source	Therapeutic/ Nontoxic	Toxic	Lethal
Blood	0.1–0.3 mg/L	0.5–1.9 mg/L	1.2–28 mg/L
Vitreous			1.9 mg/L
Urine	0.5–20 mg/L		6.1–100 mg/L
Bile			72–97 mg/L
Liver	9.7–17 mg/kg		24–293 mg/kg
Kidney			37–55 mg/kg
Brain			28–67 mg/kg
Skeletal muscle			9.6–24 mg/kg
Cardiac muscle			19–65 mg/kg
Stomach contents			53–606 mg

Comments

- Active metabolite: desipramine
- May prolong QT interval
- Metabolized by CYP 2D6, 1A2, and 2C19

Selected Sources

Apple FS (1989), Postmortem tricyclic antidepressant concentrations: Assessing cause of death using parent drug to metabolite ratio, *J Anal Tox*, 13(4): 197–8.

Bexar County Medical Examiner's Office data 1996–2007.

Biggs JT, Spiker DG, Petit JM, and Ziegler VE (1977), Tricyclic antidepressant overdose: Incidence of symptoms, *JAMA*, 238(2): 135–8.

Hanzlick RL (1984), Postmortem blood concentrations of parent tricyclic antidepressant (TCA) drugs in 11 cases of suicide, *Am J For Med Path*, 5(1): 11–3.

Kinoshita H, Taniguchi T, Kubota A, Nishiguchi M, Ouchi H, and Minami T (2005), An autopsy case of imipramine poisoning, *Am J For Med Path*, 26(3), 271–4.

Oliver JS and Smith H (1977), A case of fatal imipramine poisoning in an infant, *Med Sci Law*, 17(3): 193–4.

Pounder DJ and Jones GR (1990), Post-mortem drug redistribution—A toxicological nightmare, *For Sci Intl*, 45(3): 253–63.

Quai I, Fagarasan M, Fagarasan E, and Usineviciu I (1985), Tricyclic antidepressants: Clinical considerations, tissue concentrations and morphopathologic changes in the acute intoxication in man, *Acta Medicinae Legalis et Socialis*, 35(1): 107–9.

Wallace JE, Blum K, and Singh JM (1974), Determination of drugs in biological specimens—A review, *J Tox Clin Tox*, 7(5): 477–95.

Insulin

Brand names: Novolog, Humalog, Lantus, Novolin, Humulin
Classification: hormone
λ: 1–1.5 hrs
V_d: 0.26–0.36 L/kg
Usual dosage: 0.3–1.5 units/kg/d sc in divided doses

Source	Therapeutic/ Nontoxic	Toxic	Lethal
Blood	6–26 µunit/mL	300–7390 µunit/mL	297–7500 µunit/mL
Bile	0–487 µunit/mL		768[a] µunit/mL
Adipose tissue			1–7.4 units/ g

[a] Nine days postinjection.

Comment

- Insulin is not found in significant concentrations in tissues (liver, brain, kidney, etc.)

Selected Sources

Batalis NI and Prahlow JA (2004), Accidental insulin overdose *J For Sci*, 49(5): 1117–20.
Bauman WA and Yalow RS (1981), Insulin as a lethal weapon, *J For Sci*, 26(3): 594–8.
Dickson SJ, Cairns ER, and Blazey ND (1977), The isolation and quantitation of insulin in post-mortem specimens—A case report, *For Sci*, 9(1): 37–42.
Lepore M, Pampanelli S, Fanelli C, Porcellati F, Bartocci L, and Di Vincenzo A (2000), Pharmacokinetics and pharmacodynamics of subcutaneous injection of long-acting human insulin analog glargine, NPH insulin, and ultralente human insulin and continuous subcutaneous infusion of insulin lispro, *Diabetes*, 49(12): 2142–8.
Martin FI, Hansen N, and Warne QL (1977), Attempted suicide by insulin overdose in insulin-requiring diabetics, *Med J Aust*, 1(3): 58–60.
Matsumura M, Nakashima A, and Tofuku Y (2000), Electrolyte disorders following massive insulin overdose in a patient with type 2 diabetes, *Int Med*, 39(1): 55–7.
Shibutani Y and Ogawa C (2000), Suicidal insulin overdose in a type 1 diabetic patient: relation of serum insulin concentrations to the duration of hypoglycemia, *J Diabetes Complications*, 14(1): 60–2.
Sturner WQ and Putnam RS (1972), Suicidal insulin poisoning with nine-day survival: Recovery in bile at autopsy by radioimmunoassay, *J For Sci*, 17(4): 514–21.
Velasco CA, Cole HS, and Camerini-Davalos RA (1974), Radioimmunoassay of insulin, with use of an immunosorbent, *Clin Chem*, 20(6): 700–2.

Iron

Brand names: not applicable
Classification: metal
λ: 5–6 hrs
V_d: 7.3 L/kg
Usual dosage: 15–60 mg qd

Source	Therapeutic/ Nontoxic[a]	Toxic[a]	Lethal[a]
Blood	0.35–1.5 mg/L	2.8–25.5 mg/L	5–50 mg/L
Liver	29–479 mg/kg		1504 mg/kg
Kidney	6.6–160 mg/kg		982 mg/kg
Brain	7.8–96 mg/kg		483 mg/kg
Skeletal muscle	11–59 mg/kg		
Cardiac muscle	5.8–73 mg/kg		

[a] All concentrations given are for serum

Selected Sources

Barr DG and Fraser DK (1968), Acute iron poisoning in children: Role of chelating agents, *Br Med J*, 1: 737–41.

Berman E (1980), *Toxic Metals and Their Analysis*. Heyden, Philadelphia.

Dale JC, Burritt MF, and Zinsmeister AR (2002), Diurnal variation of serum iron, iron-binding capacity, transferrin saturation, and ferritin levels, *Am J Clin Path*, 117(5): 802–8.

Danielson BG, Salmonson T, Derendorf H, and Geisser P (1996), Pharmacokinetics of iron(III)-hydroxide sucrose complex after a single intravenous dose in healthy volunteers, *Arzneimittel-Forschung*, 46(6): 615–21.

Greenblatt DJ, Allen MD, and Kock-Weser J (1976), Accidental iron poisoning in childhood: Six cases including one fatality, *Clin Pediatr*, 15(9): 835–8.

Jacobs J, Greene H, and Gendel BR (1965), Acute iron intoxication, *NEJM*, 273(21): 1124–7.

Mann KV, Picciotti MA, Spevack TA, and Durbin DR (1989), Management of acute iron overdose, *Clin Pharm*, 8(6): 428–40.

Peck MG, Rogers JF, and Rivenbark JF (1982), Use of high doses of deferoxamine (Desferal) in an adult patient with acute iron overdosage, *J Tox Clin Tox*, 19(8): 865–9.

Rahil-Khazen R, Bolann BJ, Myking A, and Ulvik RJ (2002), Multi-element analysis of trace element levels in human autopsy tissues by using inductively coupled atomic emission spectrometry technique (ICP-AES), *J Trace Elements in Med Bio*, 16(1): 15–25.

Sipahi T, Karakurt C, Bakirtas A, and Tavil B (2002), Acute iron ingestion, *Indian J Pediatr*, 69(11): 947–9.

Wu ML, Yang CC, Ger J, Deng JF (1998), A fatal case of acute ferric chloride poisoning, *Vet Hum Tox*, 40(1): 31–4.

Yukawa M, Amano K, Suzuki-Yasumoto M, and Terai M (1980), Distribution of trace elements in the human body determined by neutron activation analysis, *Arch Environ Health*, 35(1): 36–44.

Isoflurane

Brand names: Forane
Classification: halogenated anesthetic
λ: unknown
V_d: unknown
Usual dosage: 0.5%–3% inhaled

Source	Therapeutic/ Nontoxic	Toxic	Lethal
Blood	85–105 mg/L	No data available	46–48 mg/L
Urine			4.4 mg/L
Liver			97–1000 mg/kg
Kidney			27–53 mg/kg
Lung			34 mg/kg
Brain			307 mg/kg
Stomach contents			253 mg/kg

Comments

- Hepatotoxic
- Metabolized by CYP 2E1
- Therapeutic concentrations can be fatal if drug not administered in a monitored medical setting

Selected Sources

Kuhlman JJ, Magluilo J, Levine B, and Smith ML (1993), Two deaths involving isoflurane abuse, *J For Sci*, 38(4): 968–71.

Pavlic M, Haidekker A, Grubwieser P, and Rabl W (2002), Fatal accident caused by isoflurane abuse, *Int J Leg Med*, 116(6): 357–60.

Yang NC, Hwang KL, Hung DZ, Wuhh HH, and Ho WM (2000), Reliable gas chromatographic-mass spectrometric method combined with a headspace autosampler for isoflurane determination in blood, *J Chromatogr-B: Biomed Sci Appl*, 742(2): 277–82.

Isoniazid

Brand names: Rifamate (w/ rifampin), Nydrazid, Niazid
Alternate names: INH, isonicotinyl hydrazine
Classification: antituberculin
λ: 1–4 hrs
V_d: 0.5–0.8 L/kg
Usual dosage: 100–300 mg qd

Source	Therapeutic/ Nontoxic	Toxic	Lethal
Blood	0.9–12 mg/L	20–62 mg/L	43–184 mg/L
Urine			470 mg/L
Bile			900 mg/L
Liver			650 mg/kg
Kidney			110 mg/kg

Comments

- Hepatotoxic
- Intoxication treated with pyridoxine

Selected Sources

Brown CV (1972), Acute isoniazid poisoning, *Am J Resp Crit Care Med*, 105(2): 206–16.
Gurnani A, Chawla R, Kundra P, and Bhattacharya A (1992), Acute isoniazid poisoning, *Anaesthesia*, 47(9): 781–3.
Kinzig-Schippers M, Tomalik-Scharte D, Jetter A, Scheidel B, Jakob V, and Rodamer M (2005), Should we use N-acetyltransferase type 2 genotyping to personalize isoniazid doses? *Antimicrob Agents Chemother*, 49(5): 1733–8.

Isopropanol

Brand names: rubbing alcohol
Classification: solvent/disinfectant
λ: 2.6–3.7 hrs
V_d: 0.6 L/kg
Usual dosage: 60%–70% aqueous solution applied topically

Source	Therapeutic/ Nontoxic	Toxic	Lethal
Blood	No data available	150–5600 mg/L ISO[a] 1410–5850 mg/L acetone	1000–4780 mg/L ISO[a] 400–3000 mg/L acetone
Vitreous			1850 mg/L ISO[a] 1810 mg/L acetone
Liver			2660 mg/kg ISO[a] 120 mg/kg acetone

* ISO = isopropanolol

Comments

- Metabolized to acetone
- Can be a component of embalming fluid

Selected Sources

Alexander CB, McBay AJ, and Hudson RP (1982), Isopropanol and isopropanol deaths—Ten years' experience, *J For Sci*, 27(3): 541–8.

Bexar County Medical Examiner's Office data 1996–2007.

Pappas AA, Ackerman BH, Olsen KM, and Taylor EH (1991), Isopropanol ingestion: A report of six episodes with isopropanol and acetone serum concentration time data, *J Tox Clin Tox*, 29(1): 11–21.

Ketamine

Brand names: Ketalar, Ketanest, Ketaset
Street names: Jet, Special K, Vitamin K; Special K lube (w/ ETOH and GHB)
Classification: anesthetic
λ: 2.4–2.6 hrs
V_d: 2.8–3.3 L/kg
Usual dosage: 1–4.5 mg/kg/dose

Source	Therapeutic/ Nontoxic	Toxic	Lethal
Blood	1–6.3 mg/L	No data available	1.5–38 mg/L
Urine			1.2–8.5 mg/L
Bile			1.3–15 mg/L
Liver	0.8 mg/kg		4.9–6.6 mg/kg
Kidney	0.6 mg/kg		3.2–3.6 mg/kg
Brain	4 mg/kg		3.2–4.3 mg/kg
Cardiac muscle	3.5 mg/kg		2.4 mg/kg
Stomach contents			21 mg/L

Comments

- Therapeutic concentrations can be fatal if drug not administered in a monitored medical setting
- Metabolized by CYP 3A

Selected Sources

Bexar County Medical Examiner's Office data 1996–2007.

Geisslinger G, Hering W, Thomann P, Knoll R, Kamp HD, and Brune K (1993), Pharmacokinetics and pharmacodynamics of ketamine enantiomers in surgical patients using a stereoselective analytical method, *Br J Anaesth*, 70(6): 666–71.

Lalonde BR and Wallage HR (2004), Postmortem blood ketamine distribution in two fatalities, *J Anal Tox*, 28(1): 71–4.

Licata M, Pierini G, and Popoli G (1994), A fatal ketamine poisoning, *J For Sci*, 39(5): 1314–20.

Moore KA, Kilbane EM, Jones R, Kunsman GW, Levine B, and Smith M (1997), Tissue distribution of ketamine in a mixed drug fatality, *J For Sci*, 42(6): 1183–5.

Peyton SH, Couch AT, and Bos RO (1988), Tissue distribution of ketamine: Two case reports, *J Anal Tox*, 12(5): 268–9.

Tao Y, Chen XP, and Qin ZH (2005), A fatal chronic ketamine poisoning, *J For Sci*, 50(1): 173–6.

Lamotrigine

Brand names: Lamictal
Classification: anticonvulsant
λ: 12–74 hrs
V_d: 0.87–1.2 L/kg
Usual dosage: 25–200 mg qd

Source	Therapeutic/ Nontoxic	Toxic	Lethal
Blood	0.9–14 mg/L	16–47 mg/L	32–54 mg/L
Vitreous	0.3–1.8 mg/L		
Urine	3.3–9.4 mg/L		37 mg/L
Bile	11–59 mg/L		
Liver	16–36 mg/kg		220 mg/kg
Kidney			110 mg/kg

Comments

- Can cause hepatic necrosis

Selected Sources

Bexar County Medical Examiner's Office data 1996–2007.
Buckley NA, Whyte IM, and Dawson AH (1993), Self-poisoning with lamotrigine, *Lancet*, 342: 1552–3.
Dinnerstein E, Jobst BC, and Williamson PD (2007), Lamotrigine intoxication provoking status epilepticus in an adult with localization-related epilepsy, *Arch Neurol*, 64: 1344–1346.
Levine B, Jufer RA, and Smialek JE (2000), Lamotrigine distribution in two postmortem cases, *J Anal Tox*, 24(7): 635–7.
Physicians' Desk Reference 61 Edition (2007), Thomson PDR, Montvale, NJ, pp. 1481–90.
Pricone MG, King CV, Drummer OH, Opeskin K, and McIntyre IM (2000), Postmortem investigation of lamotrigine concentrations, *J For Sci*, 45(1): 11–5.

Lead

Brand names: not applicable
Classification: metal
λ: 1–2 mos (blood); 20–30 yrs (bone)
V_d: unknown
Usual dosage: not applicable

Source	Therapeutic/ Nontoxic	Toxic	Lethal
Blood	0.003–0.3 mg/L	0.4–1.5 mg/L	0.9–5.3 mg/L
Urine	0.008–0.19 mg/L		
Liver	0.16–3.1 mg/kg		8.4–34 mg/kg
Kidney	0.13–1.9 mg/kg		8.1–24 mg/kg
Brain	0.02–0.78 mg/kg		6.7–74 mg/kg
Skeletal muscle	0.02–0.52 mg/kg		
Cardiac muscle	0.01–0.98 mg/kg		
Bone	0.2 mg/kg		2–79 mg/kg

Comments

- Associated with basophilic stippling on blood smear
- Can see dental lead line
- Overdose treated with penacillamine, dimercaprol, and calcium disodium acetate

Selected Sources

Alexander FW and Delves HT (1972), Deaths from acute lead poisoning, *Arch Dis Child*, 47(253): 446–8.
Auyeung TW, Chang KKF, To CH, Mak A, and Szeto ML (2002), Three patients with lead poisoning following use of a Chinese herbal pill, *Hong Kong Med J*, 8(1): 60–2.
Barry PS (1975), A comparison of concentrations of lead in human tissues, *Br J Industrial Med*, 32(2): 119–39.
Berman E (1980), *Toxic Metals and Their Analysis*. Heyden, Philadelphia.
Chan H, Billmeier GJ, Evans WE, and Chan H (1977), Lead poisoning from ingestion of Chinese herbal medicine, *Clin Tox*, 10(3): 273–81.
Fung HT, Fung CW, and Kam CW (2003), Lead poisoning after ingestion of home-made Chinese medicines, *Emer Med*, 15(5–6): 518–20.
Sumino K, Hayakawa K, Shibata T, and Kitamura S (1975), Heavy metals in normal Japanese tissues. Amounts of 15 heavy metals in 30 subjects, *Arch Environ Health*, 30(10): 487–94.
Van Arsdale JL, Leiker RD, Kohn M, Merritt TA, and Horowitz BZ (2004), Lead poisoning from a toy necklace, *Pediatrics*, 114(4): 1096–9.

Levetiracetam

Brand names: Keppra
Classification: anticonvulsant
λ: 5–11 hrs
V_d: 0.5–0.7 L/kg
Usual dosage: 500–1500 mg bid

Source	Therapeutic/ Nontoxic	Toxic	Lethal
Blood	3.1–63 mg/L	72–400 mg/L	No data available

Selected Sources

Barrueto F, Williams K, Howland MA, Hoffman RS, and Nelson LS (2002), A case of levetiracetam (Keppra) poisoning with clinical and toxicokinetic data, *J Tox Clin Tox*, 40(7): 881–4.

Patsalos PN (2004), Clinical pharmacokinetics of levetiracetam, *Clin Pharmacokin*, 43(11): 707–24.

Physicians' Desk Reference 61 Edition (2007), Thomson PDR, Montvale, NJ, pp. 3314–20.

Levocetirizine

Brand names: Xyzal
Classification: antihistamine
λ: 7–8.5 hrs
V_d: 0.3–0.4 L/kg
Usual dosage: 2.5–5 mg qd

Source	Therapeutic/ Nontoxic	Toxic	Lethal
Blood	0.2–1 mg/L	No data available	

Comments

- Is the R-enantiomer of cetirizine

Selected Sources

Benedetti MS, Plisnier M, Kaise J, Maier L, Baltes E, and Arendt C (2001), Absorption, distribution, metabolism and excretion of [14C]levocetirizine, the R enantiomer of cetirizine, in healthy volunteers, *Eur J Clin Pharm*, 57(8): 571–82.
Physicians' Desk Reference 62 Edition (2008), Thomson PDR, Montvale, NJ, pp. 2898–901

Levorphanol

Brand names: Levo-Dromoran
Classification: narcotic
λ: 11–16 hrs
V_d: 10–13 L/kg
Usual dosage: 2–3 mg/dose

Source	Therapeutic/ Nontoxic	Toxic	Lethal
Blood	0.005–0.1 mg/L	0.1 mg/L	0.8–2.7 mg/L
Urine			2.3 mg/L
Bile			15–24 mg/L
Liver			5.4–11 mg/kg
Kidney			1–3.4 mg/kg
Brain			1.8 mg/kg
Stomach contents			47 mg

Comments

- Tolerance can develop and should be considered when interpreting drug concentrations

Selected Sources

Bednarczyk LR (1979), A death due to levorphanol, *J Anal Tox*, 3: 217–9.
Dixon R, Crews T, Inturrisi C, and Foley K (1983), Levorphanol: Pharmacokinetics and steady-state plasma concentrations in patients with pain, *Res Comm Chem Path Pharm*, 41(1): 3–17.
Turner JE and Richards RG (1977), A fatal case involving levorphanol, *J Anal Tox*, 1: 103–4, 564.

Lidocaine

Brand names: Xylocaine, Anestacon, Bactine
Classification: anesthetic/antiarrhythmic
λ: 0.7–1.8 hrs
V_d: 1.1–4.2 L/kg
Usual dosage: 0.5%–1.0% solution sc; 3–4.5 mg/kg/dose

Source	Therapeutic/ Nontoxic	Toxic	Lethal
Blood	0.9–5 mg/L	8–12 mg/L	11–92 mg/L
Vitreous	0.5 mg/L		
Urine	0.8 mg/L		9–49 mg/L
Bile	0.5 mg/L		6 mg/L
Liver	1.0 mg/kg		10–96 mg/kg
Kidney	0.25–0.4 mg/kg		12–204 mg/kg
Brain	0.3–1.5 mg/kg		6.6–135 mg/kg
Skeletal muscle	1.4–2.9 mg/kg		20 mg/kg
Cardiac muscle	0.8 mg/kg		9 mg/kg

Comments

- Metabolized by CYP 1A2 and 3A

Selected Sources

Bennett PN, Aarons LJ, Bending MR, Steiner JA, and Rowland M (1982), Pharmacokinetics of lidocaine and its deethylated metabolite: Dose and time dependency studies in man, *J Pharmacokine Biopharma*, 10(3): 265–81.

Centini F, Fiore C, Riezzo I, Rossi G, and Fineschi V (2007), Suicide due to oral ingestion of lidocaine: A case report and review of the literature, *For Sci Intl*, 171(1): 57–62.

Dawling S, Flanagan RJ, and Widdop B (1989), Fatal lignocaine poisoning: Report of two cases and review of the literature, *Hum Tox*, 8(5): 389–92.

Kudo K, Nishida N, Kiyoshima A, and Ikeda N (2004), A fatal case of poisoning by lidocaine overdosage—Analysis of lidocaine in formalin-fixed tissues: A case report, *Med Sci Law*, 44(3): 266–71.

Lee S, Lee S, In S, Choi H, Lim M, and Chung K (2003), Lidocaine intoxication: Two fatal cases, *Arch Pharm Res (Seoul)*, 26(4): 317–20.

Pounder DJ and Jones GR (1990), Post-mortem drug redistribution—A toxicological nightmare, *For Sci Intl*, 45(3): 253–63.

Sunshine I and Fike WW (1964), Value of thin-layer chromatography in two fatal cases of intoxication die to lidocaine and mepivacaine, *NEJM*, 271: 487–90.

Wu FL, Razzaghi A, and Souney PF (1993), Seizure after lidocaine for bronchoscopy: Case report and review of the use of lidocaine in airway anesthesia, *Pharmacotherapy*, 13(1): 72–8.

Lisdexamfetamine

Brand names: Vyvanse
Classification: stimulant
λ: 0.4–0.6 hrs
V_d: unknown
Usual dosage: 30–70 mg qd

Source	Therapeutic/ Nontoxic	Toxic	Lethal
Blood	0.03–0.05 mg/L LDA 0.02–0.15 mg/L amphetamine	See amphetamine	

Comments

- Prodrug of d-amphetamine
- Rapidly converted to amphetamine in the gastrointestinal tract

Selected Sources

Krishnan SM and Stark JG (2008), Multiple daily-dose pharmacokinetics of lisdexamfetamine dimesylate in healthy adult volunteers, *Curr Med Res Opin*, 24(1): 33–40.

Krishnan S and Zhang Y (2008), Relative bioavailability of lisdexamfetamine 70 mg capsules in fasted and fed healthy adult volunteers and in solution: A single-dose, crossover pharmacokinetic study, *J Clin Pharm*, 48(3): 293–302.

Physicians' Desk Reference 62 Edition (2008), Thomson PDR, Montvale, NJ, pp. 3115–8

Lithium

Brand names: Lithate, Lithobid, Eskalith
Classification: mood stabilizer (antimanic)
λ: 20–50 hrs
V_d: 0.3–1 L/kg
Usual dosage: 900–1200 mg qd

Source	Therapeutic/ Nontoxic	Toxic	Lethal
Blood	0.6–1.2 mEq/L	1.5–8.2 mEq/L	1.9–14 mEq/L
Urine			18 mEq/L
Bile			16 mEq/L
Liver			0.22–9.4 mEq/kg
Kidney			0.6–9.3 mEq/kg
Brain			0.35–6.5 mEq/kg
Skeletal muscle			0.38–2.2 mEq/kg
Cardiac muscle			0.42 mEq/kg

Comments

- To convert mEq/L to mg/L, multiply by 6.94; mEq/L = mmol/L (conversion factor specific for lithium)

Selected Sources

Achong MR, Fernandez PG, and McLeod PJ (1975), Fatal self-poisoning with lithium carbonate, *Can Med Assoc J*, 112(7): 868–70.
Amdisen A, Gottfries CG, Jacobsson L, and Winblad B (1974), Grave lithium intoxication with fatal outcome, *Acta Psychiatrica Scandinavica*, 255S: 25–33.
Chapman AJ and Lewis G (1972), Iatrogenic lithium poisoning: A case report with necropsy findings, *J Okla State Med Assoc*, 65(12): 491–4.
Giusti, GV and Chiarotti M (1981), Two cases of death associated with the use of lithium carbonate, *Am J For Med Path*, 2(1): 41–3.
Lum G (2007), Lithium self-intoxication treated with hemodialysis, *Lab Med*, 38(11): 667–8.
Physicians' Desk Reference 60 Edition (2006), Thomson PDR, Montvale, NJ, pp. 1670–2.
Winek CL, Bricker JD, and Fochtman FW (1980), Lithium intoxication: A case study, *For Sci Intl*, 15(3): 227–31.

Loratadine

Brand names: Claritin, Tavist
Classification: antihistamine
λ: 3.6–15 hrs
V_d: 119 L/kg
Usual dosage: 5–10 mg qd

Source	Therapeutic/ Nontoxic	Toxic	Lethal
Blood	0.007–0.03 mg/L	No data available	

Comments

- Active metabolite: descarboethoxyloratadine
- Metabolized by CYP 3A4 and 2D6
- May cause tachycardia and increased blood pressure
- May be hepatotoxic

Selected Sources

Cobb DB, Watson WA, and Fernández MC (2001), High-dose loratadine exposure in a six-year-old child, *Vet Hum Tox*, 43(3): 163–4.

Gokel Y, Satar S, and Sebe A (2000), Loratadine toxicity, *Am J Emer Med*, 18(5): 639–40.

Schiano TD, Bellary SV, Cassidy MJ, Thomas RM, and Black M (1996), Subfulminant liver failure and severe hepatotoxicity caused by loratadine use, *Ann Int Med*, 125(9): 738–40.

Simons FER and Simons KJ (1999), Clinical pharmacology of new histamine H receptor antagonists, *Clin Pharmacokine*, 36(5): 329–52.

Ten Eick AP, Blumer JL, and Reed MD (2001), Safety of antihistamines in children, *Drug Saf*, 24(2): 119–47.

Lorazepam

Brand names: Ativan
Classification: benzodiazepine
λ: 9–40 hrs
V_d: 1–1.5 L/kg
Usual dosage: 0.5–5 mg bid/tid

Source	Therapeutic/ Nontoxic	Toxic	Lethal
Blood	0.01–0.2 mg/L	0.3–0.6 mg/L	0.04–0.8 mg/L[a]
Skeletal muscle			0.36 mg/kg[b]

[a] All fatalities are mixed with other drugs; no pure fatalities reported.
0.04 mg/L mixed with morphine (0.06 mg/L), codeine (0.52 mg/L), sertraline (1.5 mg/L);
0.5 mg/L mixed with 0.278 g/dL BAC;
0.8 mg/L mixed with pseudoephedrine (2.8 mg/L), lamotrigine (17.4 mg/L), metoprolol (19.9 mg/L), citalopram (1.5 mg/L).

[b] Mixed with morphine (0.7 mg/L blood); blood lorazepam level = 0.2 mg/L.

Comments

- Tolerance can develop and should be considered when interpreting drug concentrations

Selected Sources

Allen MD, Greenblatt DJ, LaCasse Y, and Shader RI (1980), Pharmacokinetic study of lorazepam overdosage, *Am J Psychiatry*, 137(11): 1414–5.
Bexar County Medical Examiner's Office data 1996–2007.
Filter ER, Gorczynski L, and Fernandes JR (2007), Fatal intoxication with a selective serotonin reuptake inhibitor, lorazepam, and codeine, *Am J For Med Path*, 28(4): 361–3.
Kyriakopoulos AA, Greenblatt DJ, and Shader RI (1978), Clinical pharmacokinetics of lorazepam: A review, *J Clin Psychiatry*, 39(10 Pt 2): 16–23.

Loxapine

Brand names: Loxitane, Loxapac
Classification: antipsychotic
λ: 1–14 hrs
V_d: unknown
Usual dosage: 30–50 mg bid

Source	Therapeutic/ Nontoxic	Toxic	Lethal
Blood	0.01–0.06 mg/L	0.2–0.7 mg/L	1.2–9.5 mg/L
Vitreous			1.5 mg/L
Urine	0.01–0.05 mg/L		0.4–8 mg/L
Bile			29 mg/L
Liver	0.7 mg/kg		12–150 mg/kg
Brain	0.3 mg/kg		4.5 mg/kg

Comments

- Active metabolite: 8-hydroxyloxapine
- Can cause seizures

Selected Sources

Cooper TB, Bost R, and Sunshine I (1981), Postmortem blood and tissue levels of loxapine and its metabolites, *J Anal Tox*, 5(2): 99–100.
Lutz T, Jindal SP, and Cooper TB (1982), GLC/MS assay for loxapine in human biofluids and tissues with deuterium labeled analog as an internal standard, *J Anal Tox*, 6(6): 301–4.
Mazzola CD, Miron S, and Jenkins AJ (2000), Loxapine intoxication: Case report and literature review, *J Anal Tox*, 24(7): 638–41.
Reynolds PC, Som CW, and Hermann PW (1979), Loxapine fatalities, *Clin Tox*, 14(2): 181–5.
Simpson GM, Cooper TB, Lee JH, and Young MA (1978), Clinical and plasma level characteristics of intramuscular and oral loxapine, *Psychopharmacology*, 56(2): 225–32.
Vasiliades J, Sahawneh TM, and Owens C (1979), Determination of therapeutic and toxic concentrations of doxepin and loxapine using gas-liquid chromatography with a nitrogen-sensitive detector, and gas chromatography-mass spectrometry of loxapine, *J Chromatogr A*, 164(4): 457–70.

Lysergic Acid Diethylamide

Brand names: not applicable
Street names: LSD, Acid; w/ heroin: Frisco Special, Frisco Speedball
Classification: hallucinogen
λ: 3–5 hrs
V_d: 0.28 L/kg
Usual dosage: 100–500 mg/dose

Source	Therapeutic/ Nontoxic	Toxic	Lethal
Blood	0.001–0.005 mg/L	0.001–0.03 mg/L	0.005–0.01 mg/L
Urine	0.0003–0.18 mg/L		
Bile	0.03 mg/L		
Stomach contents			0.06–7 mg/L

Comments

- Fatalities are usually due to the injuries sustained while intoxicated rather than due to the drug itself

Selected Sources

Fysh RR, Oon MC, Robinson KN, Smith RN, White PC, and Whitehouse MJ (1985), A fatal poisoning with LSD, *For Sci Intl*, 28(2): 109–13.
Karch SB (Ed.) (1998), *Drug Abuse Handbook*, CRC Press, Boca Raton, FL, pp. 188–9
Klock JC, Boerner U, and Becker CE (1975), Coma, hyperthermia, and bleeding associated with massive LSD overdose: A report of eight cases, *Clin Tox*, 8(2): 191–203.
Smith RN and Robinson K (1985), Body fluid levels of lysergide (LSD), *For Sci Intl*, 28(3–4): 229–37.

Maprotiline

Brand names: Deprilept, Ludiomil, Psymion
Classification: antidepressant (tetracyclic)
λ: 27–105 hrs
V_d: 14–23 L/kg
Usual dosage: 50 mg tid

Source	Therapeutic/ Nontoxic	Toxic	Lethal
Blood	0.04–0.7 mg/L	0.5–1 mg/L	1.1–13 mg/L
Urine			11 mg/L
Bile			21 mg/L
Liver			16–228 mg/kg
Kidney			8.5–87 mg/kg
Brain			19–72 mg/kg
Skeletal muscle			1.5–10 mg/kg
Cardiac muscle			11–32 mg/kg

Comments

- Can cause seizures
- May prolong QT interval

Selected Sources

Curtis RA, Giacona N, Burrows D, Bauman JL, and Schaffer M (1984), Fatal maprotiline intoxication, *Drug Intell Clin Pharm*, 18(9): 716–20.

Fischbach R (1979), Maprotiline in adult depressed patients: A study of the relation between clinical efficacy and serum concentrations after repeated intravenous and peroral administration, *Drug Res/Arzneimittel-Forschung*, 29(2): 352–5.

Gupta RN, Molnar G, and Gupta ML (1977), Estimation of maprotiline in serum by gas-chromatography, with use of a nitrogen-specific detector, *Clin Chem*, 23(10): 1849–52.

Kasper S, Dötsch M, Kick H, Vieira A, and Möller HJ (1993), Plasma concentrations of fluvoxamine and maprotiline in major depression: Implications on therapeutic efficacy and side effects, *Eur Neuropsychopharm*, 3(1): 13–21.

Marks P, Anderson J, Vincent R, Hutchinson JT, and Rees HM (1979), Epileptiform seizures with maprotiline hydrochloride, *Postgrad Med J*, 55(648): 742.

Okoye MI, Stephens PL, Dummer DT, and Mueller WF (1985), A fatal maprotiline intoxication, *Am J For Med Path*, 6(1): 45–7.

Peverini R, Ashwal S, and Petry E (1988), Maprotiline poisoning in a child, *Am J Emer Med*, 6(3): 247–9.

Meclizine

Brand names: Antivert, Vertin-32
Classification: antihistamine
λ: 6 hrs
V_d: unknown
Usual dosage: 25–50 mg qd

Source	Therapeutic/ Nontoxic	Toxic	Lethal
Blood	0.005–1 mg/L	No data available	

Selected Sources

Bexar County Medical Examiner's Office data 1996–2007.

Fouda HG, Falkner FC, Hobbs DC, and Luther EW (1978), Selected ion monitoring assay for meclizine in human plasma, *Biomed Mass Spectrom*, 5(8): 491–4.

Melperone

Brand names: Buronil, Burnil, Eunerpan
Classification: antipsychotic
λ: 2.8–6.6 hrs
V_d: 7–10 L/kg
Usual dosage: 100–300 mg qd

Source	Therapeutic/ Nontoxic	Toxic	Lethal
Blood	0.01–0.4 mg/L	1.8 mg/L	1–23 mg/L
Urine			346 mg/L

Selected Sources

Borgström L, Larsson H, and Molander L (1982), Pharmacokinetics of parenteral and oral melperone in man, *Eur J Clin Pharm*, 23(2): 173–6.

Druid H and Holmgren P (1997), A compilation of fatal and control concentrations of drugs in postmortem femoral blood, *J For Sci*, 42(1):79–87.

Kratzsch C, Peters FT, Kraemer T, Weber AA, and Maurer HH (2003), Screening, library-assisted identification and validated quantification of fifteen neuroleptics and three of their metabolites in plasma by liquid chromatography/mass spectrometry with atmospheric pressure chemical ionization, *J Mass Spectrum*, 38(3): 283–95.

Stein S, Schmoldt A, and Schulz M (2000), Fatal intoxication with melperone, *For Sci Int*, 113(1–3): 409–13.

Meperidine

Brand names: Demerol, Pethidine
Classification: narcotic
λ: 3–8 hrs
V_d: 3.7–5.7 L/kg
Usual dosage: 50–150 mg q 3–4 hrs

Source	Therapeutic/ Nontoxic	Toxic	Lethal
Blood	0.2–0.5 mg/L	0.5–2.9 mg/L	6–20 mg/L
Urine	1–18 mg/L		2–150 mg/L
Bile	9 mg/L		
Liver	5 mg/kg		2–30 mg/kg
Brain			9.5–17 mg/kg
Skeletal muscle			19 mg/kg

Comments

- Active metabolite: normeperidine
- Tolerance can develop and should be considered when interpreting drug concentrations
- Metabolized by CYP 2B6

Selected Sources

Armstrong PJ and Bersten A (1986), Normeperidine toxicity, *Anesth Analg*, 65(5): 536–8.
Bexar County Medical Examiner's Office data 1996–2007.
Daldrup T (2004), A forensic toxicological dilemma: The interpretation of post-mortem concentrations of central acting analgesics, *For Sci Intl*, 142(2–3): 157–60.
Geller RJ (1993), Meperidine in patient-controlled analgesia: A near-fatal mishap, *Anesth Analg*, 76(3): 655–7.
Holmberg L, Odar-Cederlöf I, Boréus LO, Heyner L, and Ehrnebo M (1982), Comparative disposition of pethidine and norpethidine in old and young patients, *Eur J Clin Pharm*, 22(2): 175–9.
Siek TJ (1978), The analysis of meperidine and normeperidine in biological specimens, *J For Sci*, 23(1): 6–13.

Mepivacaine

Brand names: Carbocaine
Classification: local anesthetic
λ: 1.5–2 hrs
V_d: 0.5–4 L/kg
Usual dosage: 0.5%–1% solution sc

Source	Therapeutic/ Nontoxic	Toxic	Lethal
Blood	0.1–2.5 mg/L	5–6 mg/L	50 mg/L
Urine			100 mg/L
Bile			50 mg/L
Liver			75–88 mg/kg
Kidney			51–59 mg/kg
Brain			51–83 mg/kg

Selected Sources

Burm AG, Cohen IM, van Kleef JW, Vletter AA, Olieman W, and Groen K (1997), Pharmacokinetics of the enantiomers of mepivacaine after intravenous administration of the racemate in volunteers, *Anesth Analg*, 84(1): 85–9.

Dodson WE, Hillman RE, and Hillman LS (1975), Brain tissue levels in a fatal case of neonatal mepivacaine (carbocaine) poisoning, *J Pediat*, 86(4): 624–7.

Druid H and Holmgren P (1997), A compilation of fatal and control concentrations of drugs in postmortem femoral blood, *J For Sci*, 42(1): 79–87.

Nieddu M, Boatto G, Serra D, Soro A, Lorenzoni S, and Lubinu F (2007), HPLC-DAD determination of mepivacaine in cerebrospinal fluid from a fatal case, *J For Sci*, 52(5): 1223–4.

Popescu SM, Nechifor M, Baniceru M, Croitoru O, and Popescu F (2008), Effect of propranolol on mepivacaine serum concentrations in dental practice, *Oral Surg, Oral Med, Oral Pathol, Oral Radiol Endod*, 105(4): e19–23.

Schulz M and Schmoldt A (2003), Therapeutic and toxic blood concentrations of more than 800 drugs and other xenobiotics, *Pharmazie*, 58(7): 447–74.

Sunshine I and Fike WW (1964), Value of thin-layer chromatography in two fatal cases of intoxication due to lidocaine and mepivacaine, *NEJM*, 271: 487–90.

Meprobamate

Brand names: Miltown
Classification: sedative/anxiolytic
λ: 6–16 hrs
V_d: 0.7 L/kg
Usual dosage: 300–400 mg tid/qid

Source	Therapeutic/ Nontoxic	Toxic	Lethal
Blood	7–25 mg/L	30–177 mg/L	73–346 mg/L
Urine	24–176 mg/L		237–480 mg/L
Bile			220–697 mg/L
Liver			58–600 mg/kg
Kidney			285–550 mg/kg
Brain			118–140 mg/kg

Comments

- Is a metabolite of carisoprodol
- Tolerance can develop and should be considered when interpreting drug concentrations

Selected Sources

Bailey DN and Shaw RF (1983), Interpretation of blood glutethimide, meprobamate, and methyprylon concentrations in nonfatal and fatal intoxications involving a single drug, *J Tox Clin Tox*, 20(2): 133–45.

Felby S (1970), Concentrations of meprobamate in the blood and liver following fatal meprobamate poisoning, *Acta Pharmacologica et Toxicologica*, 28(5): 334–7.

Gaillard Y, Billault F, and Pépin G (1997), Meprobamate overdosage: A continuing problem sensitive GC-MS quantitation after solid phase extraction in 19 fatal cases, *For Sci Intl*, 86(3): 173–80.

Jenis EH, Payne RJ, and Goldbaum LR (1969), Acute meprobamate poisoning: A fatal case following a lucid interval, *JAMA*, 207(2): 361–2.

Kintz P, Tracqui A, Mangin P, and Lugnier AA (1988), Fatal meprobamate self-poisoning, *Am J For Med Path*, 9(2): 139–40.

Maes R, Hodnett N, Landesman H, Kananen G, Finkle B, and Sunshine I (1969), The gas chromatographic determination of selected sedatives (ethchlorvynol, paraldehyde, meprobamate, and carisoprodol) in biological material, *J For Sci*, 14(2): 235–54.

Parker KD, Elliott HW, Wright JA, Nomof H, and Hine CH (1970), Blood and urine concentrations of subjects receiving barbiturates, meprobamate, glutethimide, or diphenylhydantoin, *Clin Tox*, 3(1): 131–45.

Mercury

Brand names: not applicable
Classification: metal
λ: 3–45 dys
V_d: unknown
Usual dosage: not applicable

Source	Therapeutic/ Nontoxic	Toxic	Lethal
Blood	0.001–0.2 mg/L	0.18–0.62 mg/L	0.6–10 mg/L
Vitreous			0.07–0.14 mg/L
Urine	0.05–0.26 mg/L	0.5–8.3 mg/L	0.8 mg/L
Bile			0.5–2 mg/L
Liver	0.16–1.3 mg/kg		1.4–100 mg/kg
Kidney	0.18–2.6 mg/kg		2.4–200 mg/kg
Brain	0.04–0.17 mg/kg		1–100 mg/kg
Skeletal muscle	0.02–0.15 mg/kg		1.3–21 mg/kg
Cardiac muscle	0.02–0.13 mg/kg		
Hair		1.2–8 mg/kg	400–1600 mg/kg
Stomach contents			3–580 mg/L

Selected Sources

Al-saleem T (1976), Levels of mercury and pathological changes in patients with organomercury poisoning, *Bull World Health Organi*, 53 suppl: 99–104.

Gerstner HB and Huff JE (1977), Selected case histories and epidemiologic examples of human mercury poisoning, *Clin Tox*, 11(2): 131–50.

Klendshoj NC and Rejent TA (1966), Tissue levels of some poisoning agents less frequently encountered, *J For Sci*, 11(1): 75–80.

Magos L, Bakir F, Clarkson TW, Al-Jawad AM, and Al-Soffi MH (1976), Tissue levels of mercury in autopsy specimens of liver and kidney, *Bull World Health Organi*, 53 suppl: 93–7.

Sexton DJ, Powell KE, Liddle J, Smrek A, Smith JC, and Clarkson TW (1978), A nonoccupational outbreak of inorganic mercury vapor poisoning, *Arch Environ Health*, 33(4): 186–91.

Sumino K, Hayakawa K, Shibata T, and Kitamura S (1975), Heavy metals in normal Japanese tissues: Amounts of 15 heavy metals in 30 subjects, *Arch Environ Health*, 30(10): 487–94.

Mescaline

Brand names: not applicable
Alternate names: mescalito, peyote
Classification: psychodelic
λ: 6 hrs
V_d: unknown
Usual dosage: 100–500 mg/dose

Source	Intoxicated	Lethal
Blood	0.48–15 mg/L	See comments
Vitreous	2.4 mg/L	
Urine	61–1163 mg/L	
Liver	8.2–71 mg/kg	
Brain	2.2 mg/kg	

Comments

- Fatalities usually secondary to trauma while intoxicated
- From *Lophophora williamsii* (cactus)

Selected Sources

Henry JL, Epley J, and Rohrig TP (2003), The analysis and distribution of mescaline in post-mortem tissues, *J Anal Tox*, 27(6): 381–2.

Nolte KB and Zumwalt RE (1999), Fatal peyote ingestion associated with Mallory-Weiss lacerations, *West J Med*, 170(6): 328.

Metaxalone

Brand names: Skelaxin
Classification: muscle relaxant
λ: 1-15 hrs
V_d: unknown
Usual dosage: 800 mg tid/qid

Source	Therapeutic/ Nontoxic	Toxic	Lethal
Blood	0.7–2.8 mg/L	No data available	11–54 mg/L
Vitreous			3–12 mg/L
Urine	1.9 mg/L		7–14 mg/L
Bile			21–44 mg/L
Liver	9–14 mg/kg		45–195 mg/kg
Brain			163 mg/kg
Stomach contents			75 mg

Selected Sources

Gruszecki AC, Kloda S, Simmons GT, Daly TM, Hardy RW, and Robinson CA (2003), Polydrug fatality involving metaxalone, *J For Sci*, 48(2): 432–4.
Moore KA, Levine B, and Fowler D (2005), A fatality involving metaxalone, *For Sci Intl*, 149(2–3): 249–51.
Physicians' Desk Reference 60 Edition (2006), Thomson PDR, Montvale, NJ, pp. 1685–6.
Poklis JL, Ropero-Miller JD, Garside D, and Winecker RE (2004), Metaxalone (Skelaxin)-related death, *J Anal Tox*, 28(6): 537–41.

Methadone

Brand names: Dolophine, Methadose
Street name: Frizzies
Classification: narcotic
λ: 8–59 hrs
V_d: 3.6–5 L/kg
Usual dosage: 30–120 mg qd

Source	Therapeutic/ Nontoxic	Toxic	Lethal
Blood	0.03–0.75 mg/L	0.24–1 mg/L	0.2–4.5 mg/L
Vitreous			0.03–0.08 mg/L
Urine	0.2 mg/L	1 mg/L	17–132 mg/L
Bile			5.5–41 mg/L
Liver	0.53 mg/kg		0.8–50 mg/kg
Kidney			2.9–8 mg/kg
Brain	0.13 mg/kg		0.4–3.7 mg/kg
Skeletal muscle			0.55–1.7 mg/kg
Stomach contents			2.5–37 mg

Comments

- Tolerance can develop and should be considered when interpreting drug concentrations
- Metabolized by CYP 3A4, CYP 2B6, CYP 1A2, and CYP 2D6
- Prolongs QT interval
- Concentrations for individuals on chronic therapy have been reported to be as high as 1.1 mg/L

Selected Sources

Bastos ML and Galante L (1976), Toxicological findings in victims of traumatic deaths, *J For Sci*, 21(1): 176–86.

Bexar County Medical Examiner's Office data 1996–2007.

Caplan YH, Ottinger WE, Crooks CR (1983), Therapeutic and toxic drug concentrations in post-mortem blood: A six-year study in the state of Maryland, *J Anal Tox*, 7(5): 225–30.

Chugh SS, Socoteanu C, Reinier K, Walktz J, Jui J, and Gunson K (2008), A community-based evaluation of sudden death associated with therapeutic levels of methadone, *Am J Med* 121(1): 66–71.

Hantson P, Vanbinst R, and Wallemacq P (2003), Accidental methadone overdose in an opiate-naive elderly patient, *Intensive Care Med*, 29(11): 2105.

Irey NS and Froede RC (1974), Evaluation of deaths from drug overdose: A clinicopathologic study, *Am J Clin Path*, 61(6): 778–84.

Jung BF, Reidenberg MM (2005), Interpretation of opioid levels: Comparison of levels during chronic pain therapy to levels from forensic autopsies, *Clin Pharm Ther*, 77(4):324–34.

Li L, Levine B, and Smialek JE (2000), Fatal methadone poisoning in children: Maryland 1992–1996, *Subst Use Misuse*, 35(9): 1141–8.

Robinson AE and William FM (1971), The distribution of methadone in man, *J Pharm Pharmacol*, 23: 353–358.

Wolf BC, Lavezzi WA, Sullivan LM, and Flannagan LM (2004), Methadone-related deaths in Palm Beach County, *J For Sci*, 49(2): 375–8.

Worm K, Steentoft A, Kringsholm B (1993), Methadone and drug addicts, *Int J Legal Med*, 106: 119–23.

Ziminski KR, Wemyss CT, Bidanset JH, Manning TJ, and Lukash L (1984), Comparative study of postmortem barbiturates, methadone, and morphine in vitreous humor, blood, and tissue, *J For Sci*, 29(3): 903–9.

d-Methamphetamine

Brand names: Desoxyn
Street names: Chalk, Crystal, Ice, Meth, Speed, Crank
Classification: stimulant
λ: 6–15 hrs
V_d: 3–7 L/kg
Usual dosage: 5 mg tid/qid

Source	Therapeutic/ Nontoxic	Toxic	Lethal
Blood	0.02–0.05 mg/L	0.15–9.5 mg/L	0.1–69 mg/L
Urine			1–398 mg/L
Liver			0.2–206 mg/kg
Kidney			0.2–87 mg/kg
Brain			0.2–144 mg/kg
Skeletal muscle			0.5–48 mg/kg
Stomach contents			5.8–44 mg

Comments

- Active metabolite: amphetamine
- Deaths are due to cardiovascular and central nervous system effects
- May cross react on immunoassays with *l*-methamphetamine
- Metabolite of benzphetamine, famprofazone, and fencamfamine

Selected Sources

Bexar County Medical Examiner's Office data 1996–2007.

Cravey RH and Jain NC (1973), Testing for amphetamines: Medico-legal hazards, *Trauma*, 15(1): 49–94.

de la Torre R, Farré M, Navarro M, Pacifici R, Zuccaro P, and Pichini S (2004), Clinical pharmacokinetics of amfetamine and related substances: Monitoring in conventional and non-conventional matrices, *Clin Pharmacokine*, 43(3): 157–85.

Fukunaga T, Mizoi Y, Adachi J, Tatsuno Y, Fujiwara S, and Ueno Y (1987), Methamphetamine concentrations in blood, urine, and organs of fatal cases after abuse, *Nihon Hoigaku Zasshi*, 41(4): 328–34.

Inoue H, Ikeda N, Kudo K, Ishida T, Terada M, and Matoba R (2006), Methamphetamine-related sudden death with a concentration which was of a "toxic level," *Legal Med*, 8(3): 150–5.

Katsumata S, Sato K, Kashiwade H, Yamanami S, Zhou H, and Yonemura I (1993), Sudden death due presumably to internal use of methamphetamine, *For Sci Intl*, 62(3): 209–15.

Kojima T, Une I, and Yashiki M (1983), CI-Mass fragmentographic analysis of methamphetamine and amphetamine in human autopsy tissues after acute methamphetamine poisoning, *For Sci Intl*, 21(3): 253–8.

Lebish P, Finkle BS, and Brackett JW (1970), Determination of amphetamine, methamphetamine, and related amines in blood and urine by gas chromatography with hydrogen-flame ionization detector, *Clin Chem*, 16(3): 195–200.

Logan BK, Fligner CL, and Haddix T (1998), Cause and manner of death in fatalities involving methamphetamine, *J For Sci*, 43(1): 28–34.

l-Methamphetamine

Brand names: Vicks Inhaler
Classification: stimulant/decongestant
λ: 11–16 hrs
V_d: 3.7–4.6 L/kg
Usual dosage: ~3.3–4.2 μg/dose inhaled or 1.9–7.2 mg qd

Source	Therapeutic/Nontoxic	Toxic	Lethal
Blood	0.005–0.08 mg/L *l*-methamphetamine 0.0007–0.002 mg/L *l*-amphetamine	No data available	
Vitreous	0.02 mg/L *l*-methamphetamine		
Urine	0.31–6 mg/L *l*-methamphetamine		

Comments

- Active metabolite: *l*-amphetamine
- Metabolite of selegiline, famprofazone, and fencamfamine
- May cross react on immunoassays with d-methamphetamine

Selected Sources

Mendelson JE, McGlothlin D, Harris DS, Foster E, Everhart T, and Jacob P (2008), The clinical pharmacology of intranasal *l*-methamphetamine, *BMC Clin Pharm*, 8: 4.
Mendelson J, Uemura N, Harris D, Nath RP, Fernandez E, and Jacob P (2006), Human pharmacology of the methamphetamine stereoisomers, *Clin Pharm Thera*, 80(4): 403–20.
Wyman JF and Cody JT (2005), Determination of *l*-methamphetamine: A case history, *J Anal Tox*, 29(7): 759–61.

Methanol

Brand names: wood alcohol
Alternate names: methyl alcohol
Classification: solvent
λ: 2–24 hrs
V_d: 0.6 L/kg
Usual dosage: not applicable

Source	Therapeutic/ Nontoxic	Toxic	Lethal
Blood	No data available	200–1300 mg/L	230–4600 mg/L
Vitreous			120–1730 mg/L
Bile			1750 mg/L
Liver			56–4490 mg/kg
Kidney			67–1300 mg/kg
Brain			450–1590 mg/kg
Skeletal muscle			1120 mg/kg
Stomach contents			73 mg

Comments

- The presence of methanol and formaldehyde indicates embalming solution
- Formaldehyde is not part of methanol metabolism

Selected Sources

Bexar County Medical Examiner's Office data 1996–2007.

Hantson P, Haufroid V, and Mahieu P (2000), Determination of formic acid tissue and fluid concentrations in three fatalities due to methanol poisoning, *Am J For Med Path*, 21(4): 335–8.

Hashemy Tonkabony SE (1975), Post-mortem blood concentration of methanol in 17 cases of fatal poisoning from contraband vodka, *For Sci*, 6(1–2): 1–3.

Wallace JE, Blum K, and Singh JM (1974), Determination of drugs in biological specimens—A review, *J Tox ClinTox*, 7(5): 477–95.

Winek CL, Collom WD, and Davis ER (1973), Accidental solvent fatality, *Clin Tox*, 6(1): 23–7.

Wu Chen NB, Donoghue ER, and Schaffer MI (1985), Methanol intoxication: Distribution in postmortem tissues and fluids including vitreous humor, *J For Sci*, 30(1): 213–6.

Methaqualone

Brand names: not applicable
Street names: Quaaludes, Mandrax, Ludes
Classification: sedative/hypnotic
λ: 2.6–41 hrs
V_d: 5.4–7.7 L/kg
Usual dosage: 75–300 mg/dose

Source	Therapeutic/ Nontoxic	Toxic	Lethal
Blood	0.4–4 mg/L	2–22 mg/L	5–92 mg/L
Urine		0.5 mg/L	17 mg/L
Liver			26–89 mg/kg

Selected Sources

Alvan G, Ericsson O, Levander S, and Lindgren JE (1974), Plasma concentrations and effects of methaqualone after single and multiple oral doses in man, *Eur J Clin Pharm*, 7(6): 449–54.

Bailey DN and Jatlow PI (1973), Methaqualone overdose: Analytical methodology, and the significance of serum drug concentrations, *Clin Chem*, 19(6): 615–20.

Baselt RC and Cravey RH (1977), A compendium of therapeutic and toxic concentrations of toxicologically significant drugs in human biofluids, *J Anal Tox*, 1: 81–103.

Nayak RK, Smyth RD, Chamberlain JH, Polk A, and DeLong AF (1974), Methaqualone pharmacokinetics after single- and multiple-dose administration in man, *J Pharmacokin*, 2(2): 107–21.

Wetli CV (1983), Changing patterns of methaqualone abuse: A survey of 246 fatalities, *JAMA*, 249(5): 621–6.

Methocarbamol

Brand names: Robaxin
Classification: muscle relaxant
λ: 0.9–2.2 hrs
V_d: unknown
Usual dosage: 1500 mg qid

Source	Therapeutic/ Nontoxic	Toxic	Lethal[a]
Blood	16–40 mg/L	250 mg/L	257–525[a] mg/L
Bile			927 mg/L
Liver			459 mg/kg
Kidney			83 mg/kg

[a] Ethanol co-intoxicant (BAC 0.13 g/dL)

Selected Sources

Ferslew KE, Hagardorn AN, and McCormick WF (1990), A fatal interaction of methocarbamol and ethanol in an accidental poisoning, *J For Sci*, 35(2): 477–82.
Kemal M, Imami R, and Poklis A (1982), A fatal methocarbamol intoxication, *J For Sci*, 27(1): 217–22.
Schulz M and Schmoldt A (2003), Therapeutic and toxic blood concentrations of more than 800 drugs and other xenobiotics, *Pharmazie*, 58(7): 447–74.
Sica DA, Comstock TJ, Davis J, Manning L, Powell R, and Melikian A (1990), Pharmacokinetics and protein binding of methocarbamol in renal insufficiency and normals, *Eur J Clin Pharm*, 39(2): 193–4.

Methotrimeprazine

Brand names: Nosinan, Nozinan, Levoprome
Alternate names: levomepromazine
Classification: antipsychotic
λ: 15–30 hrs
V_d: 30 L/kg
Usual dosage: 25 mg bid/tid

Source	Therapeutic/ Nontoxic	Toxic	Lethal
Blood	0.02–0.14 mg/L	No data available	0.8–4.1 mg/L
Urine	0.08–0.5 mg/L		

Selected Sources

Avis SP and Holzbecher MD (1996), A fatal case of methotrimeprazine overdose, *J For Sci*, 41(6): 1080–1.

Dahl SG and Garle M (1977), Identification of nonpolar methotrimeprazine metabolites in plasma and urine by GLC-mass spectrometry, *J Pharm Sci*, 66(2): 190–3.

Druid H and Holmgren P (1997), A compilation of fatal and control concentrations of drugs in postmortem femoral blood, *J For Sci*, 42(1): 79–87.

Methsuximide

Brand names: Celontin
Classification: anticonvulsant
λ: 1–4 hrs
V_d: unknown
Usual dosage: 150–600 mg bid/tid/qid

Source	Therapeutic/ Nontoxic	Toxic	Lethal
Blood	0.01–0.1 mg/L 16–37 mg/L NDMS	0.02–1.1 mg/L 38–44 mg/L NDMS	No data available

Comments

- Active metabolite: *N*-desmethylmethsuximide (NDMS)

Selected Sources

Karch SB (1973), Methsuximide overdose: Delayed onset of profound coma, *JAMA*, 223(13): 1463–5.

Porter RJ, Penry JK, Lacy JR, Newmark ME, and Kupferberg HJ (1979), Plasma concentrations of phensuximide, methsuximide, and their metabolites in relation to clinical efficacy, *Neurology*, 29(11): 1509–13.

Strong JM, Abe T, Gibbs EL, and Atkinson AJ (1974), Plasma levels of methsuximide and *N*-desmethylmethsuximide during methsuximide therapy, *Neurology*, 24(3): 250–5.

Methylenedioxyamphetamine

Brand names: not applicable
Street names: MDA
Classification: hallucinogenic stimulant
λ: 6–10 hrs
V_d: unknown
Usual dosage: 80–160 mg/dose

Source	Therapeutic/ Nontoxic	Toxic	Lethal
Blood	0.01–0.3 mg/L	1.5–3.2 mg/L	2.3–26 mg/L
Urine			46–175 mg/L
Bile			5–9 mg/L
Liver			8–17 mg/kg
Kidney			18 mg/kg
Brain			10 mg/kg
Stomach contents			0.7–1.7 mg

Comments

- Metabolite of MDMA (methylenedioxymethamphetamine)

Selected Sources

Baselt RC and Cravey RH (1977), A compendium of therapeutic and toxic concentrations of toxicologically significant drugs in human biofluids, *J Anal Tox,* 1:81–103.
Cimbura G (1972), 3,4-Methylenedioxyamphetamine (MDA): Analytical and forensic aspects of fatal poisoning, *J For Sci,* 17(2): 329–33.
de la Torre R, Farré M, Navarro M, Pacifici R, Zuccaro P, and Pichini S (2004), Clinical pharmacokinetics of amfetamine and related substances: Monitoring in conventional and non-conventional matrices, *Clin Pharmacokine,* 43(3): 157–85.
Lukaszewski T (1979), 3,4-Methylenedioxyamphetamine overdose, *Clin Tox,* 15(4): 405–9.
Poklis A, Mackell MA, and Drake WK (1979), Fatal intoxication from 3,4-methylenedioxyamphetamine, *J For Sci,* 24(1): 70–5.
Reed D, Cravey RH, and Sedgwick PR (1972), A fatal case involving methylenedioxyamphetamine, *Clin Tox,* 5(1): 3–6.

Methylenedioxymethamphetamine

Brand names: not applicable
Street names: MDMA, XTC, Ectasy, Adam
Classification: hallucinogenic stimulant
λ: 6–9 hrs
V_d: 5.5–8.5 L/kg
Usual dosage: 50–150 mg/dose

Source	Therapeutic/ Nontoxic	Toxic	Lethal
Blood	0.1–0.25 mg/L	0.3–0.5 mg/L	0.4–11 mg/L
Vitreous			1.9–3.4 mg/L
Urine			14–171 mg/L
Bile			14–73 mg/L
Liver			5.1–26 mg/kg
Kidney			12–14 mg/kg
Brain			8.4–17 mg/kg
Skeletal muscle			4.5 mg/kg
Cardiac muscle			14 mg/kg
Stomach contents			118 mg/kg

Comments

- Active metabolite: MDA (methylenedioxyamphetamine)
- Metabolized by CYP 2D6

Selected Sources

de la Torre R, Farré M, Navarro M, Pacifici R, Zuccaro P, and Pichini S (2004), Clinical pharmacokinetics of amfetamine and related substances: Monitoring in conventional and non-conventional matrices, *Clin Pharmacokine*, 43(3): 157–85.

de Letter EA, Clauwaert KM, Lambert WE, van Bocxlaer JF, de Leenheer AP, and Piette MHA (2002), Distribution study of 3,4-methylenedioxymethamphetamine and 3,4-methylenedioxyamphetamine in a fatal overdose, *J Anal Tox*, 26(2): 113–8.

Duffy MR and Swart M (2006), Severe ecstasy poisoning in a toddler, *Anaesthesia*, 61(5): 498–501.

García-Repetto R, Moreno E, Soriano T, Jurado C, Giménez MP, and Menéndez M (2003), Tissue concentrations of MDMA and its metabolite MDA in three fatal cases of overdose, *For Sci Intl*, 135(2): 110–4.

Greene SL, Dargan PI, O'connor N, Jones AL, and Kerins M (2003), Multiple toxicity from 3,4-methylenedioxymethamphetamine ("ecstasy"), *Am J Emer Med*, 21(2): 121–4.

Rohrig TP and Prouty RW (1992), Tissue distribution of methylenedioxymethamphetamine, *J Anal Tox*, 16(1): 52–3.

Methylfentanyl

Brand names: not applicable
Alternate names: 3 MF, mefentanyl
Classification: narcotic
λ: unknown
V_d: unknown
Usual dosage: 5–10 μg/dose

Source	Therapeutic/ Nontoxic	Toxic	Lethal
Blood	No data available		0.002–0.05 mg/L
Bile			0.006 mg/L
Liver			0.08 mg/kg

Selected Sources

Gillespie TJ, Gandolfi AJ, Davis TP, and Morano RA (1982), Identification and quantification of alpha-methylfentanyl in post mortem specimens, *J Anal Tox*, 6(3): 139–42.
Ojanperä I, Gergov M, Rasanen I, Lunetta P, Toivonen S, and Tiainen E (2006), Blood levels of 3-methylfentanyl in 3 fatal poisoning cases, *Am J For Med Path*, 27(4): 328–31.

Methylphenidate

Brand names: Ritalin, Methylin
Street names: Uppers, West Coast
Classification: stimulant
λ: 2–4 hrs
V_d: 11–33 L/kg
Usual dosage: 5–20 mg bid/tid

Source	Therapeutic/ Nontoxic	Toxic	Lethal
Blood	0.01–0.06 mg/L	0.5–1 mg/L	2.3–2.8 mg/L
Urine	0.8–40 mg/L		
Bile			5.7 mg/L
Liver			2.1 mg/kg
Kidney			3.0 mg/kg

Selected Sources

de la Torre R, Farré M, Navarro M, Pacifici R, Zuccaro P, and Pichini S (2004), Clinical pharmacokinetics of amfetamine and related substances: Monitoring in conventional and non-conventional matrices, *Clin Pharmacokine*, 43(3): 157–85.

Levine B, Caplan YH, and Kauffman G (1986), Fatality resulting from methylphenidate overdose, *J Anal Tox*, 10(5): 209–10.

Schubert B (1970), Detection and identification of methylphenidate in human urine and blood samples, *Acta Chemica Scandinavica*, 24(2): 433–8.

Metoprolol

Brand names: Toprol, Lopressor
Classification: β-blocker
λ: 3–4 hrs
V_d: 2.5–5.6 L/kg
Usual dosage: 25–200 mg qd

Source	Therapeutic/ Nontoxic	Toxic	Lethal
Blood	0.07–0.5 mg/L	9.8–14 mg/L	3.5–75 mg/L
Vitreous			3.3–42 mg/L
Urine			1–194 mg/L
Bile			254 mg/L
Liver			6.3–230 mg/kg
Kidney			7.1 mg/kg
Stomach contents			80–215 mg

Comments

- Metabolized by CYP 2D6

Selected Sources

Bexar County Medical Examiner's Office data 1996–2007.
Moller BH (1976), Letter: Massive intoxication with metoprolol, *Br Med J*, 1(6003): 222.
Quarterman CP, Kendall MJ, and Jack DB (1981), The effect of age on the pharmacokinetics of metoprolol and its metabolites, *Br J Clin Pharm*, 11(3): 287–94.
Riker CD, Wright RK, Matusiak W, and de Tuscan BE (1987), Massive metoprolol ingestion associated with a fatality—A case report, *J For Sci*, 32(5): 1447–52.
Shore ET, Cepin D, and Davidson MJ (1981), Metoprolol overdose, *Ann Emer Med*, 10(10): 524–7.
Sire S (1976), Metoprolol intoxication, *Lancet*, 2(7995): 1137.
Stajić M, Granger RH, and Beyer JC (1984), Fatal metoprolol overdose, *J Anal Tox*, 8(5): 228–30.

Mianserin

Brand names: Tolvan, Bolvidon, Norval
Classification: antidepressant (tetracyclic)
λ: 28–38 hrs
V_d: 4–15 L/kg
Usual dosage: 20–60 mg qd

Source	Therapeutic/ Nontoxic	Toxic	Lethal
Blood	0.05–0.23 mg/L	0.3–0.8 mg/L	1.7–13 mg/L

Comments

- Prolongs QT interval

Selected Sources

Burgess CD, Turner P, and Wadsworth J (1978), Cardiovascular responses to mianserin hydrochloride: A comparison with tricyclic antidepressant drugs, *Br J Clin Pharm*, 5(Suppl 1): 21S–28S.

Coppen A and Kopera H (1978), Workshop on the clinical pharmacology and efficacy of mianserin, *Br J Clin Pharm*, 5(Suppl 1): 91S–99S.

Druid H and Holmgren P (1997), A compilation of fatal and control concentrations of drugs in postmortem femoral blood, *J For Sci*: 42(1):79–87.

Newman B and Crome P (1979), The clinical toxicology of mianserin hydrochloride, *Vet Hum Tox*, 21(Suppl): 60–2.

Shami M, Elliott HL, Kelman AW, and Whiting B (1983), The pharmacokinetics of mianserin, *Br J Clin Pharm*, 15(Suppl 2): 313S–322S.

Timmer CJ, Pourbaix S, Desager JP, Sclavons M, and Harvengt C (1985), Absolute bioavailability of mianserin tablets and solution in healthy humans, *Eur J Drug Metab Pharmacokine*, 10(4): 315–23.

Midazolam

Brand names: Versed
Classification: benzodiazepine
λ: 1–4 hrs
V_d: 1–6.6 L/kg
Usual dosage: 1–5 mg/dose

Source	Therapeutic/ Nontoxic	Toxic	Lethal
Blood	0.03–0.4 mg/L	0.2–2 mg/L	2.4–62 mg/L
Urine		1.8 mg/L	0.2–1.8 mg/L

Comments

- Tolerance can develop and should be considered when interpreting drug concentrations
- Metabolized by CYP 3A

Selected Sources

Bexar County Medical Examiner's Office data 1996–2007.

Blumer JL (1998), Clinical pharmacology of midazolam in infants and children, *Clin Pharmacokine*, 35(1): 37–47.

Druid H and Holmgren P (1997), A compilation of fatal and control concentrations of drugs in postmortem femoral blood, *J For Sci*, 42(1): 79–87.

Malinovsky JM, Populaire C, Cozian A, Lepage JY, Lejus C, and Pinaud M (1995), Premedication with midazolam in children: Effect of intranasal, rectal and oral routes on plasma midazolam concentrations, *Anaesthesia*, 50(4): 351–4.

Michalodimitrakis M, Christodoulou P, Tsatsakis AM, Askoxilakis I, Stiakakis I, and Mouzas I (1999), Death related to midazolam overdose during endoscopic retrograde cholangiopancreatography, *Am J For Med Path*, 20(1): 93–7.

Milnacipran

Brand names: Ixel
Classification: antidepressant (SNRI)
λ: 8 hrs
V_d: 3–8 L/kg
Usual dosage: 50–100 mg qd

Source	Therapeutic/ Nontoxic	Toxic	Lethal
Blood	0.1–0.3 mg/L	3.1 mg/L	No data available

Selected Sources

Puozzo C, Panconi E, and Deprez D (2002), Pharmacology and pharmacokinetics of milnacipran, *Intl Clin Psychopharmacology*, 17(1): S25–35.
Rop PP, Sournac MH, Burle J, Fornaris M, and Coiffait PE (2002), Blood concentration of milnacipran in a case of a fatal automobile accident, *J Anal Tox*, 26(2): 123–6.

Mirtazapine

Brand names: Remeron
Classification: antidepressant (tetracyclic)
λ: 12–20 hrs
V_d: 2.8–6.2 L/kg
Usual dosage: 15–45 mg qd

Source	Therapeutic/ Nontoxic	Toxic	Lethal[a]
Blood	0.02–0.23 mg/L	0.2–2.3 mg/L	0.1 mg/L[a]
Urine			0.6 mg/L[a]
Bile			2.9 mg/L[a]
Liver			2.2 mg/kg[a]
Kidney			1.8 mg/kg[a]
Brain			0.56 mg/kg[a]
Skeletal muscle			0.32 mg/kg[a]
Stomach contents			1.9 mg/L[a]

[a] Co-intoxicants sertraline (0.88 mg/L) and amitryptyline (0.04 mg/L)

Comments

- Metabolized by CYP 1A2 and 2D6

Selected Sources

Gerritsen AW (1997), Safety in overdose of mirtazapine: A case report, *J Clin Psych*, 58(6): 271.

Holzbach R, Jahn H, Pajonk FG, and Mähne C (1998), Suicide attempts with mirtazapine overdose without complications, *Biol Psychiatry*, 44(9): 925–6.

Retz W, Maier S, Maris F, and Rösler M (1998), Non-fatal mirtazapine overdose, *Int Clin Psychopharmacol*, 13(6): 277–9.

Timmer CJ, Sitsen JM, and Delbressine LP (2000), Clinical pharmacokinetics of mirtazapine, *Clin Pharmacokine*, 38(6): 461–74.

Wenzel S, Aderjan R, Mattern R, Pedal I, and Skopp G (2006), Tissue distribution of mirtazapine and desmethylmirtazapine in a case of mirtazapine poisoning, *For Sci Intl*, 156(2–3): 229–36.

Mizolastine

Brand names: Mizollen, Mistamine
Classification: antihistamine
λ: 5.6–17 hrs
V_d: 1–1.4 L/kg
Usual dosage: 10 mg qd

Source	Therapeutic/ Nontoxic	Toxic	Lethal
Blood	0.05–2.5 mg/L	No data available	

Selected Sources

Lebrun-Vignes B, Diquet B, and Chosidow O (2001), Clinical pharmacokinetics of mizolastine, *Clin Pharmacokine,* 40(7): 501–7.

Rosenzweig P, Thebault JJ, Caplain H, Dubruc C, Bianchetti G, and Fuseau E (1992), Pharmacodynamics and pharmacokinetics of mizolastine (SL 85.0324), a new nonsedative H1 antihistamine, *Ann Allergy,* 69(2): 135–9.

Simons FER and Simons KJ (1999), Clinical pharmacology of new histamine H receptor antagonists, *Clin Pharmacokine,* 36(5): 329–52.

Moclobemide

Brand names: Aurorix, Manerix
Classification: antidepressant (MAOI)
λ: 1–4 hrs
V_d: 0.8–1.3 L/kg
Usual dosage: 100–200 mg bid/tid

Source	Therapeutic/ Nontoxic	Toxic	Lethal
Blood	0.22–1.6 mg/L	2.8–61 mg/L	15–498 mg/L
Urine			96–324 mg/L
Liver			45–432 mg/kg
Kidney			57 mg/kg
Cardiac muscle			21 mg/kg

Comments

- Not available in United States
- Metabolized by CYP 2C18, CYP 2D6, and CYP 1A2

Selected Sources

Caccia S (1998), Metabolism of the newer antidepressants. An overview of the pharmacological and pharmacokinetic implications, *Clin Pharmacokine*, 34(4): 281–302.

Camaris C and Little D (1997), A fatality due to moclobemide, *J For Sci*, 42(5): 954–5.

Gaillard Y and Pépin G (1997) Moclobemide fatalities: Report of two cases and analytical determinations by GC-MS and HPLC-PDA after solid-phase extraction, *For Sci Intl*, 87(3): 239–48.

Giroud C, Horisberger B, Eap C, Augsburger M, Ménétrey A, and Baumann P (2004), Death following acute poisoning by moclobemide, *For Sci Intl*, 140(1): 101–7.

Iwersen S and Schmoldt A (1996), Three suicide attempts with moclobemide, *J Tox Clin Tox*, 34(2): 223–5.

Raaflaub J, Haefelfinger P, and Trautmann KH (1984), Single-dose pharmacokinetics of the MAO-inhibitor moclobemide in man, *Drug Res/Arzneimittel-Forschung*, 34(1): 80–2.

Rogde S, Hilberg T, and Teige B (1999), Fatal combined intoxication with new antidepressants: Human cases and an experimental study of postmortem moclobemide redistribution, *For Sci Intl*, 100(1–2): 109–16.

Modafinil

Brand names: Provigil
Classification: stimulant
λ: 10–17 hrs
V_d: 0.8 L/kg
Usual dosage: 200–400 mg qd

Source	Therapeutic/ Nontoxic	Toxic	Lethal
Blood	3.7–17 mg/L	No data available	

Selected Sources

Hellriegel ET, Arora S, Nelson M, and Robertson P (2002), Steady-state pharmacokinetics and tolerability of modafinil administered alone or in combination with dextroamphetamine in healthy volunteers, *J Clin Pharm*, 42(4): 450–60.

Robertson P and Hellriegel ET (2003), Clinical pharmacokinetic profile of modafinil, *Clin Pharmacokine*, 42(2): 123–37.

Molindone

Brand names: Moban
Classification: antipsychotic
λ: 2 hrs
V_d: 3–6 L/kg
Usual dosage: 5–50 mg tid/qid

Source	Therapeutic/ Nontoxic	Toxic	Lethal
Blood	0.007–0.4 mg/L	0.15 mg/L	6–19 mg/L
Urine			37–247 mg/L
Bile			23 mg/L
Liver			26–69 mg/kg
Stomach contents			23–1200 mg/L

Selected Sources

Bexar County Medical Examiner's Office data 1996–2007.

Flammia DD, Bateman HR, Saady JJ, and Christensen ED (2004), Tissue distribution of molidone in a multidrug overdose, *J Anal Tox*, 28(6): 533–6.

Johnson SB, Alvarez WA, and Freinhar JP (1986), A case of massive rhabdomyolysis following molindone administration, *J Clin Psychiatry*, 47(12): 607–8.

Zetin M, Cramer M, Garber D, Plon L, Paulshock M, and Hoffman HE (1985), Bioavailability of oral and intramuscular molindone hydrochloride in schizophrenic patients, *Clin Ther*, 7(2): 169–75.

Morphine

Brand names: MS Contin, Roxanol, Kadian, Avinza, Oramorph
Street names: Dreamer, Hows, M, Miss Emma
Classification: narcotic
λ: 1.3–6.7 hrs
V_d: 2–5 L/kg
Usual dosage: 5–30 mg q 4–8 hrs

Source	Therapeutic/ Nontoxic	Toxic	Lethal
Blood	0.001–0.2 mg/L	0.3–2.5 mg/L	0.2–7.2 mg/L
Vitreous			0.03–0.8 mg/L
Urine	0.5–20 mg/L		11–323 mg/L
Bile			0.05–248 mg/L
Liver			0.05–18 mg/kg
Kidney			0.05–7 mg/kg
Brain			0.05–1 mg/kg
Skeletal muscle			0.1–2 mg/kg

Comments

- Tolerance can develop and should be considered when interpreting drug concentrations
- Concentrations for individuals on chronic pain therapy have been reported to routinely be as high as 0.7 mg/L; two studies report values >2 mg/L
- Metabolite of heroin
- Active metabolites, morphine-3-glucoronide and normorphine

Selected Sources

Chan SC, Chan EM, and Kaliciak HA (1986), Distribution of morphine in body fluids and tissues in fatal overdose, *J For Sci*, 31(4): 1487–91.

Felby S, Christensen H, and Lund A (1974), Morphine concentrations in blood and organs in cases of fatal poisoning, *For Sci*, 3(1): 77–81.

Jung BF, Reidenberg MM (2005), Interpretation of opioid levels: Comparison of levels during chronic pain therapy to levels from forensic autopsies, *Clin Pharm Ther*, 77(4):324–34.

Shelly MP and Park GR (1984), Morphine toxicity with dilated pupils, *Br Med J (Clin Res Ed.)*, 289(6451): 1071–2.

Stanski DR, Greenblatt DJ, Lappas DG, Koch-Weser J, and Lowenstein E (1976), Kinetics of high-dose intravenous morphine in cardiac surgery patients, *Clin Pharmacol Ther*, 19(6): 752–6.

Wallace JE, Blum K, and Singh JM (1974), Determination of drugs in biological specimens—A review, *J Tox Clin Tox*, 7(5): 477–95.

Ziminski KR, Wemyss CT, Bidanset JH, Manning TJ, and Lukash L (1984), Comparative study of postmortem barbiturates, methadone, and morphine in vitreous humor, blood, and tissue, *J For Sci*, 29(3): 903–9.

Nalbuphine

Brand names: Nubain
Classification: narcotic agonist–antagonist
λ: 2.5–5 hrs
V_d: 2.3–7 L/kg
Usual dosage: 10–20 mg q 3–6 hrs

Source	Therapeutic/ Nontoxic	Toxic	Lethal
Blood	0.04–1.6 mg/L	No data available	

Selected Sources

Aitkenhead AR, Lin ES, and Achola KJ (1988), The pharmacokinetics of oral and intravenous nalbuphine in healthy volunteers, *Br J Clin Pharm*, 25(2): 264–8.
Miller RR (1980), Evaluation of nalbuphine hydrochloride, *Am J Hosp Pharm*, 37(7): 942–9.

Naloxone

Brand names: Narcan
Classification: narcotic antagonist
λ: 30–80 min
V_d: 0.8–2.6 L/kg
Usual dosage: 0.4–2 mg/dose

Source	Therapeutic/ Nontoxic	Toxic	Lethal
Blood	0.004–0.08 mg/L	No data available	

Comments

- Used to treat narcotic overdose

Selected Sources

Ngai SH, Berkowitz BA, Yang JC, Hempstead J, and Spector S (1976), Pharmacokinetics of naloxone in rats and in man: Basis for its potency and short duration of action, *Anesthesiology*, 44(5): 398–401.

Reid RW, Deakin A, and Leehey DJ (1993), Measurement of naloxone in plasma using high-performance liquid chromatography with electrochemical detection, *J Chromatogr A*, 614(1): 117–22.

Naltrexone

Brand names: Depade, Revia
Classification: narcotic antagonist
λ: 1–10 hrs
V_d: 14–16 L/kg
Usual dosage: 50 mg qd

Source	Therapeutic/ Nontoxic	Toxic	Lethal
Blood	0.002–0.05 mg/L	No data available	

Comments

- Used to treat narcotic overdose

Selected Sources

Verebey K and Mulé SJ (1979), Naltrexone, 6 beta-naltrexol and 2-hydroxy-3-methoxy-6 beta-naltrexol plasma levels in schizophrenic patients after large oral doses of naltrexone, *NIDA Res Monogr*, 27: 296–301.

Verebey K, Volavka J, Mulé SJ, and Resnick RB (1976), Naltrexone: disposition, metabolism, and effects after acute and chronic dosing, *Clin Pharmacol Ther*, 20(3): 315–28.

Naproxen

Brand names: Naprosyn, Aleve, Anaprox
Classification: NSAID
λ: 10–18 hrs
V_d: 0.14–0.18 L/kg
Usual dosage: 250–500 mg bid/tid

Source	Therapeutic/ Nontoxic	Toxic	Lethal
Blood	20–110 mg/L	414–840 mg/L	No data available

Comments

- Metabolized by CYP 1A2 and 2C9

Selected Sources

Anttila M, Haataja M, and Kasanen A (1980), Pharmacokinetics of naproxen in subjects with normal and impaired renal function, *Eur J Clin Pharm*, 18(3): 263–8.

Bexar County Medical Examiner's Office data 1996–2007.

Fredell EW and Strand LJ (1977), Naproxen overdose, *JAMA*, 238(9): 938.

Mullen WM, Meier KM, Hagar SM, and Olson KR (2003), Severe naproxen overdose with elevated serum levels, *J Tox Clin Tox*, 41(5): 655.

Physicians' Desk Reference 60 Edition (2006), Thomson PDR, Montvale, NJ, p. 2769.

van den Ouweland FA, Franssen MJ, van de Putte LB, Tan Y, van Ginneken CA, and Gribnau FW (1987), Naproxen pharmacokinetics in patients with rheumatoid arthritis during active polyarticular inflammation, *Br J Clin Pharm*, 23(2): 189–93.

Nefazodone

Brand names: Serzone
Classification: antidepressant
λ: 6–8 hrs
V_d: 0.22–0.87 L/kg
Usual dosage: 100–300 mg bid

Source	Therapeutic/ Nontoxic	Toxic	Lethal
Blood	0.4–3.9 mg/L	5.5 mg/L	No data available

Comments

- Active metabolite: hydroxynefazodone
- Metabolized by CYP 3A

Selected Sources

Barbhaiya RH, Buch AB, and Greene DS (1996), A study of the effect of age and gender on the pharmacokinetics of nefazodone after single and multiple doses, *J Clin Psychopharmacol*, 16(1): 19–25.

Gaffney PN, Schuckman HA, and Beeson MS (1998), Nefazodone overdose, *Ann Pharmacother*, 32(11): 1249–50.

Nicotine

Brand names: Nicorette, Nicotrol, Nicoderm, Habitrol, Prostep
Classification: alkaloid
λ: 24–84 min
V_d: 1 L/kg
Usual dosage: 0.2–4 mg/dose

Source	Therapeutic/ Nontoxic	Toxic	Lethal
Blood	0.003–0.17 mg/L	0.2–1 mg/L	3.7–5800 mg/L
Urine		1.1 mg/L	7–10 mg/L
Liver	0.01–0.33 mg/kg		4–2270 mg/kg
Kidney	0.007–0.16 mg/kg		10–1128 mg/kg
Brain	0.001–0.09 mg/kg		8–1910 mg/kg
Skeletal muscle	0.003–0.05 mg/kg		12 mg/kg

Comments

- Metabolized by CYP 2B6

Selected Sources

Davies P, Levy S, Pahari A, and Martinez D (2001), Acute nicotine poisoning associated with a traditional remedy for eczema, *Arch Dis Child*, 85(6): 500–2.

Grusz-Harday E (1967), Fatal nicotine poisoning, *Archiv für Toxikologie*, 23(1): 35–41.

Krauland W, Schneider V, and Klug E (1973), Fatal nicotine poisoning due to miscalculated nicotine test, *Zeitschrift für Rechtsmedizin*, 72(4): 269–77.

Lavoie FW and Harris TM (1991), Fatal nicotine ingestion, *J Emer Med*, 9(3): 133–6.

Sanchez P, Ducassé JL, Lapeyre-Mestre M, Martinet O, Rougé P, and Jorda MF (1996), Nicotine poisoning as a cause of cardiac arrest? *J Tox Clin Tox*, 34(4): 475–6.

Urakawa N, Nagata T, Kudo K, Kimura K, and Imamura T (1994), Simultaneous determination of nicotine and cotinine in various human tissues using capillary gas chromatography/mass, *Int J Legal Med*, 106(5): 232–6.

Woolf A, Burkhart K, Caraccio T, and Litovitz T (1996), Self-poisoning among adults using multiple transdermal nicotine patches, *J Tox Clin Tox*, 34(6): 691–8.

Nifedipine

Brand names: Adalat, Nifediac, Afeditab
Classification: calcium channel blocker
λ: 2–8 hrs
V_d: 1.2–1.4 L/kg
Usual dosage: 30–120 mg qd

Source	Therapeutic/ Nontoxic	Toxic	Lethal
Blood	0.02–0.05 mg/L	0.13–0.6 mg/L	0.21–0.54 mg/L
Urine			0.97 mg/L
Liver			0.26–1.1 mg/kg
Kidney			0.95 mg/kg
Brain			1.9 mg/kg

Comments

- Metabolized by CYP 3A

Selected Sources

Bexar County Medical Examiner's Office data 1996–2007.
Debbas NM, Jackson SH, Shah K, Abrams SM, Johnston A, and Turner P (1986), The bioavailability and pharmacokinetics of slow release nifedipine during chronic dosing in volunteers, *Br J Clin Pharmacol*, 21(4): 385–8.
Ferner RE, Monkman S, Riley J, Cholerton S, Idle JR, and Bateman DN (1990), Pharmacokinetics and toxic effects of nifedipine in massive overdose, *Hum Exper Tox*, 9(5): 309–11.
Kleinbloesem CH, van Brummelen P, Faber H, and Breimer DD (1987), Pharmacokinetics and hemodynamic effects of long-term nifedipine treatment in hypertensive patients, *J Cardiovasc Pharmacol*, 9(2): 202–8.
Kleinbloesem CH, van Brummelen P, van de Linde JA, Voogd PJ, and Breimer DD (1984), Nifedipine: Kinetics and dynamics in healthy subjects, *Clin Pharmacol Ther*, 35(6): 742–9.
Lee DC, Greene T, Dougherty T, and Pearigen P (2000), Fatal nifedipine ingestions in children, *J Emer Med*, 19(4): 359–61.
Miller MA, Masneri DA, and Herold T (2007), Delayed clinical decompensation and death after pediatric nifedipine overdose, *Am J Emer Med*, 25(2): 197–8.
Schiffl H, Ziupa J, and Schollmeyer P (1984), Clinical features and management of nifedipine overdosage in a patient with renal insufficiency, *J Tox Clin Tox*, 22(4): 387–95.

Nitrazepam

Brand names: Mogadon
Classification: benzodiazepine
λ: 17–48 hrs
V_d: 2–5 L/kg
Usual dosage: 2.5–10 mg qd

Source	Therapeutic/ Nontoxic	Toxic	Lethal
Blood	0.01–0.06 mg/L	0.2 mg/L	0.5–9 mg/L
Urine			6–10 mg/L
Liver			0.06–4 mg/kg
Kidney			0.08–0.7 mg/kg
Brain			0.4 mg/kg
Skeletal muscle			2.1 mg/kg

Comments

- Tolerance can develop and should be considered when interpreting drug concentrations

Selected Sources

Brødsgaard I, Hansen AC, and Vesterby A (1995), Two cases of lethal nitrazepam poisoning, *Am J For Med Path*, 16(2): 151–3.

Druid H and Holmgren P (1997), A compilation of fatal and control concentrations of drugs in postmortem femoral blood, *J For Sci*, 42(1):79–87.

Drummer OH and Ranson DL (1996), Sudden death and benzodiazepines, *Am J For Med Path*, 17(4): 336–42.

Giusti GV and Chiarotti M (1979), Lethal nitrazepam intoxications, report of two cases, *Zeitschrift für Rechtsmedizin*, 84(1): 75–8.

Kangas L, Iisalo E, Kanto J, Lehtinen V, Pynnönen S, and Ruikka I (1979), Human pharmacokinetics of nitrazepam: Effect of age and diseases, *Eur J Clin Pharmacol*, 15(3): 163–70.

Moriya F and Hashimoto Y (2003), Tissue distribution of nitrazepam and 7-aminonitrazepam in a case of nitrazepam intoxication, *For Sci Intl*, 131(2–3): 108–12.

Oliver JS and Smith H (1974), Determination of nitrazepam in poisoning cases, *For Sci*, 4(2): 183–6.

Nitrous Oxide

Brand names: Inomax
Street names: Laughing gas, Whippets, Buzz Bomb, Hippie Crack
Classification: inhaled anesthetic
λ: ~5 min
V_d: unknown
Usual dosage: 5%–40% inhaled

Source	Therapeutic/ Nontoxic	Toxic	Lethal
Blood	10–407 mg/L	146 mg/L	123–930 mg/L
Lung			2420 mg/kg
Brain			2200 mg/kg

Comments

- Therapeutic concentrations can be fatal if drug not administered in a monitored medical setting

Selected Sources

Chadly A, Marc B, Barres D, and Durigon M (1989), Suicide by nitrous oxide poisoning, *Am J For Med Path*, 10(4): 330–1.
DiMaio VJ and Garriott J (1978), Four deaths resulting from abuse of nitrous oxide, *J For Sci*, 23(1): 169–72.
Luskus LJ, Kilian HJ, Lackey WW, and Biggs JD (1977), Gases released from tissue and analyzed by infrared and gas chromatography/mass spectroscopy techniques, *J For Sci*, 22(3): 500–7.
Sher AM, Braude BM, Cleaton-Jones PE, Moyes DG, and Mallett J (1984), Nitrous oxide sedation in dentistry: A comparison between rotameter settings, pharyngeal concentrations and blood levels of nitrous oxide, *Anaesthesia*, 39(3): 236–9.
Wagner SA, Clark MA, Wesche DL, Doedens DJ, and Lloyd AW (1992), Asphyxial deaths from the recreational use of nitrous oxide, *J For Sci*, 37(4): 1008–15.

Nortriptyline

Brand names: Pamelor, Aventyl
Classification: antidepressant (TCA)
λ: 15–90 hrs
V_d: 20–57 L/kg
Usual dosage: 20–50 mg bid/tid

Source	Therapeutic/ Nontoxic	Toxic	Lethal
Blood	0.01–0.28 mg/L	0.47–1.3 mg/L	0.87–86 mg/L
Vitreous			1.4 mg/L
Bile			28 mg/L
Liver			50–664 mg/kg
Kidney			904 mg/kg
Brain			97–202 mg/kg
Skeletal muscle			2.6–3.9 mg/kg
Stomach contents			9.4–81 mg

Comments

- Metabolite of amitriptyline
- Metabolized by CYP 2D6
- May prolong QT interval

Selected Sources

Bexar County Medical Examiner's Office data 1996–2007.

Furlanut M, Benetello P, and Spina E (1993), Pharmacokinetic optimisation of tricyclic antidepressant therapy, *Clin Pharmacokinet*, 24(4): 301–18.

Iversen BM, Willassen YW, and Bakke OM (1978), Charcoal haemoperfusion in nortriptyline poisoning, *Lancet*, 1(8060): 388–9.

Robinson AE, Coffer AI, and McDowall RD (1974), Toxicology of some autopsy cases involving tricyclic antidepressant drugs, *Zeitschrift für Rechtsmedizin*, 74(4): 261–6.

Rohrig TP and Prouty RW (1989), A nortriptyline death with unusually high tissue concentrations, *J Anal Tox*, 13(5): 303–4.

Rudorfer MV and Robins E (1981), Fatal nortriptyline overdose, plasma levels, and in vivo methylation of tricyclic antidepressants, *Am J Psych*, 138(7): 982–3.

Olanzapine

Brand names: Zyprexa
Classification: antipsychotic
λ: 21–54 hrs
V_d: 10–26 L/kg
Usual dosage: 5–20 mg qd

Source	Therapeutic/ Nontoxic	Toxic	Lethal
Blood	0.009–0.1 mg/L	0.05–1 mg/L	0.24–5.2 mg/L
Vitreous			2.3 mg/L
Urine			0.35–6.9 mg/L
Liver			0.61 mg/kg
Brain			0.16–0.86 mg/kg
Stomach contents			0.2–41 mg/L

Comments

- Metabolized by CYP 1A2

Selected Sources

Bexar County Medical Examiner's Office data 1996–2007.
Cohen LG, Fatalo A, Thompson BT, Di Centes Bergeron G, Flood JG, and Poupolo PR (1999), Olanzapine overdose with serum concentrations, *Ann Emer Med*, 34(2): 275–8.
Elian AA (1998), Fatal overdose of olanzepine, *For Sci Intl*, 91(3): 231–5.
Gerber JE and Cawthon B (2000), Overdose and death with olanzapine: Two case reports, *Am J For Med Path*, 21(3): 249–51.
Kratzsch C, Peters FT, Kraemer T, Weber AA, and Maurer HH (2003), Screening, library-assisted identification and validated quantification of fifteen neuroleptics and three of their metabolites in plasma by liquid chromatography/mass spectrometry with atmospheric pressure chemical ionization, *J Mass Spectrum*, 38(3): 283–95.
Merrick TC, Felo JA, and Jenkins AJ (2001), Tissue distribution of olanzapine in a postmortem case, *Am J For Med Path*, 22(3): 270–4.
O'Malley GF, Seifert S, Heard K, Daly F, and Dart RC (1999), Olanzapine overdose mimicking opioid intoxication, *Ann Emer Med*, 34(2): 279–81.
Stephens BG, Coleman DE, and Baselt RC (1998), Olanzapine-related fatality, *J For Sci*, 43(6): 1252–3.
Yip L, Dart RC, and Graham K (1998), Olanzapine toxicity in a toddler, *Pediatrics*, 102(6): 1494.

Oleandrin

Brand names: Anvirzel (oleandrin extract)
Classification: cardiac glycoside
λ: unknown
V_d: unknown
Usual dosage: 15 mg qd

Source	Therapeutic/ Nontoxic	Toxic	Lethal
Blood	0.001–0.007 mg/L	0.008–0.03 mg/L	12 mg/L
Urine		0.001 mg/L	
Liver			30 mg/kg
Kidney			39 mg/kg
Brain			10 mg/kg
Cardiac muscle			1.1–23 mg/kg
Stomach contents			182 mg/L

Comments

- From *Nerium oleander*
- Cross reacts with digoxin RIA

Selected Sources

Ansford AJ and Morris H (1981), Fatal oleander poisoning, *Med J Aust*, 1(7): 360–1.
Arao T, Fuke C, Takaesu H, Nakamoto M, Morinaga Y, and Miyazaki T (2002), Simultaneous determination of cardenolides by sonic spray ionization liquid chromatography-ion trap mass spectrometry—A fatal case of oleander poisoning, *J Anal Tox*, 26(4): 222–7.
Blum LM and Rieders F (1987), Oleandrin distribution in a fatality from rectal and oral *Nerium oleander* extract administration, *J Anal Tox*, 11(5): 219–21.
Dasgupta A and Datta P (2004), Rapid detection of oleander poisoning using digoxin immunoassays: Comparison of five assays, *Ther Drug Monit*, 26(6): 658–63.
Gechtman C, Guidugli F, Marocchi A, Masarin A, and Zoppi F (2006), Unexpectedly dangerous escargot stew: Oleandrin poisoning through the alimentary chain, *J Anal Tox*, 30(9): 683–6.
Pietsch J, Oertel R, Trautmann S, Schulz K, Kopp B, and Dressler J (2005), A non-fatal oleander poisoning, *Int J Legal Med*, 119(4): 236–40.
Wang X, Plomley JB, Newman RA, and Cisneros A (2000), LC/MS/MS analyses of an oleander extract for cancer treatment, *Anal Chem*, 72(15): 3547–52.

Ondansetron

Brand names: Zofran
Classification: antiemetic
λ: 5–7 hrs
V_d: 1.4–3 L/kg
Usual dosage: 8 mg q 8 hrs

Source	Therapeutic/ Nontoxic	Toxic	Lethal
Blood	0.03–0.14 mg/L	No data available	

Comments

- Metabolized by CYP 1A2, 2D6, 3A
- May prolong QT interval

Selected Sources

Colthup PV, Felgate CC, Palmer JL, and Scully NL (1991), Determination of ondansetron in plasma and its pharmacokinetics in the young and elderly, *J Pharma Sci*, 80(9): 868–71.

Colthup PV and Palmer JL (1989), The determination in plasma and pharmacokinetics of ondansetron, *Eur J Cancer Clin Oncol*, 25(Suppl. 1): S71–4.

Hsyu PH, Pritchard JF, Bozigian HP, Lloyd TL, Griffin RH, and Shamburek R (1994), Comparison of the pharmacokinetics of an ondansetron solution (8 mg) when administered intravenously, orally, to the colon, and to the rectum, *Pharma Res*, 11(1): 156–9.

Orphenadrine

Brand names: Norflex, Norgesic (w/ aceta and caffeine)
Classification: anti-Parkinson/muscle relaxant
λ: 13–20 hrs
V_d: 4.3–7.8 L/kg
Usual dosage: 25–100 mg bid

Source	Therapeutic/ Nontoxic	Toxic	Lethal
Blood	0.1–0.85 mg/L	2–3.6 mg/L	4–368 mg/L
Urine			3–122 mg/L
Bile			85–234 mg/L
Liver			7–23 mg/kg
Kidney			9.8–105 mg/kg
Brain			3.3–20 mg/kg
Stomach contents			11–7500 mg

Selected Sources

Bozza-Marrubini M, Frigerio A, Ghezzi R, Parelli L, Restelli L, and Selenati A (1977), Two cases of severe orphenadrine poisoning with atypical features, *Acta Pharmacologica et Toxicologica*, 41(Suppl. 2): 137–52.

Furlanut M, Bettio D, Bertin I, Colombo G, and Benetello P (1985), Orphenadrine serum levels in a poisoned patient, *Hum Tox*, 4(3): 331–3.

Labout JJ, Thijssen CT, Keijser GG, and Hespe W (1982), Difference between single and multiple dose pharmacokinetics of orphenadrine hydrochloride in man, *Eur J Clin Pharm*, 21(4): 343–50.

Paterson SC (1985), Drug levels found in cases of fatal self-poisoning, *For Sci Intl*, 27(2): 129–33.

Robinson AE, Holder AT, McDowall RD, Powell R, and Sattar H (1977), Forensic toxicology of some orphenadrine-related deaths, *For Sci*, 9(1): 53–62.

Van Herreweghe I, Mertens K, Maes V, and Ramet J (1999), Orphenadrine poisoning in a child: Clinical and analytical data, *Intensive Care Med*, 25(10): 1134–6.

Wilkinson LF, Thomson BM, and Pannell LK (1983), A report on the analysis of orphenadrine in post mortem specimens, *J Anal Tox*, 7(2): 72–5.

Oxazepam

Brand names: Serax
Classification: benzodiazepine
λ: 5–15 hrs
V_d: 0.6–2 L/kg
Usual dosage: 15–30 mg tid/qid

Source	Therapeutic/ Nontoxic	Toxic	Lethal
Blood	0.1–1.4 mg/L	0.5–4 mg/L	4.6–6.3 mg/L
Urine		1.3 mg/L	

Comments

- Metabolite of temazepam and nordiazepam
- Tolerance can develop and should be considered when interpreting drug concentrations

Selected Sources

Druid H and Holmgren P (1997), A compilation of fatal and control concentrations of drugs in postmortem femoral blood, *J For Sci*, 42(1): 79–87.

Greenblatt DJ (1981), Clinical pharmacokinetics of oxazepam and lorazepam, *Clin Pharmacokinet*, 6(2): 89–105.

Knowles JA and Ruelius HW (1972), Absorption and excretion of 7-chloro-1,3-dihydro-3-hydroxy-5-phenyl-2H-1,4-benzodiazepin-2-one (oxazepam) in humans: Determination of the drug by gas-liquid chromatography with electron capture detection, *Drug Res/ Arzneimittel-Forschung*, 22(4): 687–92.

Moshkowitz M, Pines A, Finkelstein A, Hershkowitz R, and Levo Y (1990), Skin blisters as a manifestation of oxazepam toxicity, *J Tox Clin Tox*, 28(3): 383–6.

Shimkin PM and Shaivitz SA (1966), Oxazepam poisoning in a child, *JAMA*, 196(7): 662–3.

Oxcarbazepine

Brand names: Trileptal
Classification: anticonvulsant
λ: 1–5 hrs
V_d: 3.9–12 L/kg
Usual dosage: 300–1200 mg bid

Source	Therapeutic/ Nontoxic	Toxic	Lethal
Blood	0.01–5 mg/L OX[a]		No data available
	8–35 mg/L 10-OHC[b]	32–45 mg/L 10-OHC	

[a] OX= oxcarbazepine; [b]10-OHC= 10-hydroxycarbazepine

Comments

- Active metabolite: 10-hydroxycarbazepine (λ 7–20 hrs)
- Tolerance can develop and should be considered when interpreting drug concentrations

Selected Sources

Jolliff HA, Fehrenbacher N, and Dart RC (2001), Bradycardia, hypotension and tinnitus after accidental oxcarbazepine overdose, *J Tox Clin Tox*, 39(3): 316–7.

May TW, Korn-Merker E, and Rambeck B (2003), Clinical pharmacokinetics of oxcarbazepine, *Clin Pharmacokinet*, 42(12): 1023–42.

van Opstal JM, Janknegt R, Cilissen J, L'Ortije WH M, Nel JE, and De Heer F (2004), Severe overdosage with the antiepileptic drug oxcarbazepine, *Br J Clin Pharmacol*, 58(3): 329–31.

Oxycodone

Brand names: Roxicodone, Oxycontin; Percocet, Endocet, Roxicet (w/ aceta); Percodan (w/ ASA)
Classification: narcotic
λ: 3–8 hrs
V_d: 1.8–3.7 L/kg
Usual dosage: 5–30 mg q 4–6 hrs

Source	Therapeutic/ Nontoxic	Toxic	Lethal
Blood	0.01–0.1 mg/L	0.2–2.4 mg/L	0.5–8 mg/L
Vitreous			0.25 mg/L
Urine			47 mg/L
Bile			23 mg/L
Liver			0.2–1.6 mg/kg
Stomach contents			9–740 mg

Comments

- Active metabolite: oxymorphone
- Tolerance can develop and should be considered when interpreting drug concentrations
- Concentrations for individuals on chronic pain therapy have been reported to be as high as 0.5 mg/L

Selected Sources

Anderson DT, Fritz KL, and Muto JJ (2002), Oxycontin: The concept of a "ghost pill" and the postmortem tissue distribution of oxycodone in 36 cases, *J Anal Tox*, 26(7): 448–59.

Armstrong EJ, Jenkins AJ, Sebrosky GF, and Balraj EK (2004), An unusual fatality in a child due to oxycodone, *Am J For Med Path*, 25(4): 338–41.

Bexar County Medical Examiner's Office data 1996–2007.

Jung BF, Reidenberg MM (2005), Interpretation of opioid levels: Comparison of levels during chronic pain therapy to levels from forensic autopsies, *Clin Pharm Ther*, 77(4):324–34.

Lalovic B, Kharasch E, Hoffer C, Risler L, Liu-Chen LY, and Shen DD (2006), Pharmacokinetics and pharmacodynamics of oral oxycodone in healthy human subjects: Role of circulating active metabolites, *Clin Pharm Thera*, 79(5): 461–79.

Leow KP, Smith MT, Williams B, and Cramond T (1992), Single-dose and steady-state pharmacokinetics and pharmacodynamics of oxycodone in patients with cancer, *Clin Pharm Thera*, 52(5): 487–95.

Levine B, Moore KA, Aronica-Pollak P, and Fowler DF (2004), Oxycodone intoxication in an infant: Accidental or intentional exposure? *J For Sci*, 49(6): 1358–60.

Schneir AB, Vadeboncoeur TF, Offerman SR, Barry JD, Ly BT, and Williams SR (2002), Massive OxyContin ingestion refractory to naloxone therapy, *Ann Emer Med*, 40(4): 425–8.

Spiller HA (2003), Postmortem oxycodone and hydrocodone blood concentrations, *J For Sci*, 48(2): 429–31.

Wolf BC, Lavezzi WA, Sullivan LM, and Flannagan LM (2005), One hundred seventy two deaths involving the use of oxycodone in Palm Beach County, *J For Sci*, 50(1): 192–5.

Oxymorphone

Brand names: Opana, Numorphan
Classification: narcotic
λ: 7.2–11.3 hrs
V_d: 3 L/kg
Usual dosage: 5–20 mg q 4–6 hrs

Source	Therapeutic/ Nontoxic	Toxic	Lethal
Blood	0.0003–0.007 mg/L	No data available	

Comments

- Metabolite of oxycodone
- Active metabolite: 6-hydroxyoxymorphone
- Tolerance can develop and should be considered when interpreting drug concentrations

Selected Sources

Adams MP and Ahdieh H (2005), Single- and multiple-dose pharmacokinetic and dose-proportionality study of oxymorphone immediate-release tablets, *Drugs R D*, 6(2): 91–9.
Guay DRP (2007), Use of oral oxymorphone in the elderly, *Consult Pharm*, 22(5): 417–30.

Pancuronium

Brand names: Pavulon
Classification: neuromuscular blocker
λ: 1.9–2.2 hrs
V_d: 0.28 L/kg
Usual dosage: 0.04–0.1 mg/kg/dose

Source	Therapeutic/ Nontoxic	Toxic	Lethal
Blood	1–1.5 mg/L	0.4 mg/L	1.6 mg/L
Urine			1.5 mg/L
Liver			25 mg/kg

Comments

- Therapeutic concentrations can be fatal if drug not administered in a monitored medical setting

Selected Sources

Poklis A and Melanson EG (1980), A suicide by pancuronium bromide injection: Evaluation of the fluorometric determination of pancuronium in postmortem blood, serum and urine, *J Anal Tox*, 4(6): 275–80.
Vandenbrom RH and Wierda JM (1988), Pancuronium bromide in the intensive care unit: A case of overdose, *Anesthesiology*, 69(6): 996–7.

Papaverine

Brand names: Para-Time
Classification: vasodilator
λ: 1.1–1.5 hrs
V_d: 0.4–1.5 L/kg
Usual dosage: 150–300 mg bid

Source	Therapeutic/ Nontoxic	Postmortem Procurement	Toxic	Lethal
Blood	0.2–4 mg/L	0.04–42 mg/L	No data available	

Comments

- Often used postmortem to dilate veins for procurement procedures
- Overdose may result in hepatotoxicity or lactic acidosis

Selected Sources

Bexar County Medical Examiner's Office data 1996–2007.

Guttman DE, Kostenbauder HB, Wilkinson GR, and Dubé PH (1974), GLC determination of papaverine in biological fluids, *J Pharmacol Sci*, 63(10): 1625–6.

Lee BY, Sakamoto H, Trainor F, Brody G, and Cho YW (1978), Comparison of soft gelatin capsule vs. sustained release formulation of papaverine HCl: Vasodilation and plasma levels, *Int J Clin Pharmacol Biopharm*, 16(1): 32–9.

Ronnov-Jessen V and Tjernlund A (1969), Hepatotoxicity due to treatment with papaverine: Report of four cases, *NEJM*, 281(24): 1333–5.

Vaziri ND, Stokes J, and Treadwell TR (1981), Lactic acidosis, a complication of papaverine overdose, *Clin Tox*, 18(4): 417–23.

Paraldehyde

Brand names: Paral
Classification: sedative/hypnotic
λ: 3–10 hrs
V_d: 0.9 L/kg
Usual dosage: 5–10 mL/dose

Source	Therapeutic/ Nontoxic	Toxic	Lethal
Blood	15–100 mg/L	200–1744 mg/L	490–1600 mg/L
Urine		570 mg/L	210 mg/L
Bile			500 mg/L
Liver			1850 mg/kg
Kidney			700 mg/kg
Brain			590 mg/kg
Stomach contents			12–14 mg/L

Selected Sources

Bostrom B (1982), Paraldehyde toxicity during treatment of status epilepticus, *Am J Dis Child*, 136(5): 414–5.

DiMaio VJM and Garriott JC (1974), A fatal overdose of paraldehyde during treatment of a case of delirium tremens, *J For Sci*, 19(4): 755–9

Figot PP, Hine CH, and Way EL (1952), The estimation and significance of paraldehyde levels in blood and brain, *Acta Pharmacologica et Toxicologica*, 8(3): 290–304.

Hayward JN and Boshell BR (1957), Paraldehyde intoxication with metabolic acidosis; report of two cases, experimental data and a critical review of the literature, *Am J Med*, 23(6): 965–76.

Maes R, Hodnett N, Landesman H, Kananen G, Finkle B, and Sunshine I (1969), The gas chromatographic determination of selected sedatives (ethchlorvynol, paraldehyde, meprobamate, and carisoprodol) in biological material, *J For Sci*, 14(2): 235–54.

Niyogi SK (1973), Drug levels in cases of poisoning, *For Sci*, 2:67–98.

Paroxetine

Brand names: Paxil, Pexeva
Classification: antidepressant (SSRI)
λ: 7–65 hrs
V_d: 3–28 L/kg
Usual dosage: 20–40 mg qd

Source	Therapeutic/ Nontoxic	Toxic	Lethal
Blood	0.002–0.06 mg/L	0.35–1.8 mg/L	1–16 mg/L
Urine			10–11 mg/L
Liver			110–113 mg/kg
Stomach contents			8.7–100 mg

Comments

- Prolongs QT interval

Selected Sources

Bexar County Medical Examiner's Office data 1996–2007.
DeVane CL (2003), Pharmacokinetics, drug interactions, and tolerability of paroxetine and paroxetine CR, *Psychopharmacol Bull*, 37(Suppl. 1). 29–41.
Goeringer KE, Raymon L, Christian GD, and Logan BK (2000), Postmortem forensic toxicology of selective serotonin reuptake inhibitors: A review of pharmacology and report of 168 cases, *J For Sci*, 45(3): 633–48.
Velez LI, Shepherd G, Roth BA, and Benitez FL (2004), Serotonin syndrome with elevated paroxetine concentrations, *Ann Pharmacother*, 38(2): 269–72.
Vermeulen T (1998), Distribution of paroxetine in three postmortem cases, *J Anal Tox*, 22(6): 541–4.
Wagstaff AJ, Cheer SM, Matheson AJ, Ormrod D, and Goa KL (2002), Paroxetine: An update of its use in psychiatric disorders in adults, *Drugs*, 62(4): 655–703.

Pemoline

Brand names: Cylert
Classification: stimulant
λ: 2–12 hrs
V_d: 0.2–0.6 L/kg
Usual dosage: 37.5–75 mg qd

Source	Therapeutic/ Nontoxic	Toxic	Lethal
Blood	1.7–7 mg/L	No data available	

Selected Sources

Collier CP, Soldin SJ, Swanson JM, MacLeod SM, Weinberg F, and Rochefort JG (1985), Pemoline pharmacokinetics and long term therapy in children with attention deficit disorder and hyperactivity, *Clin Pharmacokinet*, 10(3): 269–78.

Sallee F, Stiller R, Perel J, and Bates T (1985), Oral pemoline kinetics in hyperactive children, *Clin Pharmacol Ther*, 37(6): 606–9.

Pentazocine

Brand names: Talwin, Talacen (w/ aceta)
Classification: narcotic
λ: 2–3.5 hrs
V_d: 4.4–7.8 L/kg
Usual dosage: 50–100 mg q 3–4 hrs

Source	Therapeutic/ Nontoxic	Toxic	Lethal
Blood	0.05–0.24 mg/L	0.5–2 mg/L	1–9.2 mg/L
Urine	1 mg/L		3–13 mg/L
Liver			34–43 mg/kg

Comments

- Tolerance can develop and should be considered when interpreting drug concentrations

Selected Sources

Berkowitz BA, Asling JH, Shnider SM, and Way EL (1969), Relationship of pentazocine plasma levels to pharmacological activity in man, *Clin Pharmacol Ther*, 10(3): 320–8.
Bexar County Medical Examiner's Office data 1996–2007.
Poklis A and Mackell MA (1982), Toxicological findings in deaths due to ingestion of pentazocine: A report of two cases, *For Sci Intl*, 20(1): 89–95.
Stahl SM and Kasser IS (1983), Pentazocine overdose, *Ann Emer Med*, 12(1): 28–31.

Pentobarbital

Brand names: Nembutal
Classification: barbiturate
λ: 15–50 hrs
V_d: 0.5–1 L/kg
Usual dosage: 50–200 mg/dose

Source	Therapeutic/ Nontoxic	Toxic	Lethal
Blood	1–5 mg/L	8–24 mg/L	15–241 mg/L
Vitreous			7–27 mg/L
Urine			5–97 mg/L
Bile			59–152 mg/L
Liver			8–980 mg/kg
Kidney			7–72 mg/kg
Brain			4–48 mg/kg
Stomach contents			74–550 mg

Comments

- Tolerance can develop and should be considered when interpreting drug concentrations

Selected Sources

Bexar County Medical Examiner's Office data 1996–2007.

Broughton PM, Higgins G, O'Brien JR (1956), Acute barbiturate poisoning, *Lancet*, 270: 180–4.

Caplan YH, Ottinger WE, and Crooks CR (1983), Therapeutic and toxic drug concentrations in post mortem blood: A six year study in the State of Maryland, *J Anal Tox*, 7(5): 225–30.

Koyama K, Suzuki R, Yoshida T, and Kikuno T (2007), Usefulness of serum concentration measurement for acute pentobarbital intoxication in patients, *Chudoku Kenkyu*, 20(1): 45–53.

Parker KD, Elliott HW, Wright JA, Nomof H, and Hine CH (1970), Blood and urine concentrations of subjects receiving barbiturates, meprobamate, glutethimide, or diphenylhydantoin, *Clin Tox*, 3(1): 131–45.

Robinson AE and McDowall RD (1979), The distribution of amylobarbitone, butobarbitone, pentobarbitone and quinalbarbitone and the hydroxylated metabolites in man, *J Pharm Pharmacol*, 31(6): 357–65.

Romain N, Giroud C, Michaud K, and Mangin P (2003), Suicide by injection of a veterinarian barbiturate euthanasia agent: Report of a case and toxicological analysis, *For Sci Intl*, 131(2–3): 103–7.

Ziminski KR, Wemyss CT, Bidanset JH, Manning TJ, and Lukash L (1984), Comparative study of postmortem barbiturates, methadone, and morphine in vitreous humor, blood, and tissue, *J For Sci*, 29(3): 903–9.

Perphenazine

Brand names: Trilafon, Etrafon (w/ amitryptiline), Decentan
Classification: antipsychotic
λ: 8–12 hrs
V_d: 10–35 L/kg
Usual dosage: 4–16 mg tid/bid/qd

Source	Therapeutic/ Nontoxic	Toxic	Lethal
Blood	0.0003–0.03 mg/L	0.8–1.2 mg/L	No data available

Comments

- Metabolized by CYP 2D6

Selected Sources

Hansen LB and Larsen NE (1977), Plasma concentrations of perphenazine and its sulphoxide metabolite during continuous oral treatment, *Psychopharmacology*, 53(2): 127–30.

Larsen NE (1998), Oral intake of perphenazine decanoate, *Ther Drug Monit*, 20(6): 724.

Linnet K (1997), An evaluation of linearity of kinetics for the neuroleptics perphenazine and zuclopenthixol, *Eur J Clin Pharmacol*, 52(4): 317–8.

Phencyclidine

Brand names: not applicable
Street names: PCP, Angel Dust, Peter Pan, Killer Weed, Wack, Ozone, Lovely; w/ Crack: Spaceball, Parachute, Space Base, Tragic Magic; w/ Marijuana: Happy Stick, Love Boat, Supergrass
Classification: psychotropic
λ: 7–46 hrs
V_d: 5.3–7.5 L/kg
Usual dosage: 5–10 mg/dose

Source	Therapeutic/ Nontoxic	Toxic	Lethal
Blood	0.3–1.1 mg/L	0.09–0.5 mg/L	0.3–25 mg/L
Urine	0.6–11 mg/L	0.1–69 mg/L	4.3–120 mg/L
Bile			3.5 mg/L
Liver	0.3–2.2 mg/kg		0.9–170 mg/kg
Stomach contents			4.2–185 mg/L

Selected Sources

Bexar County Medical Examiner's Office data 1996–2007.

Caplan YH, Orloff KG, Thompson BC, and Fisher RS (1979), Detection of phencyclidine in medical examiner's cases, *J Anal Tox*, 3: 47–52.

Marshman JA, Ramsay MP, and Sellers EM (1976), Quantitation of phencyclidine in biological fluids and application to human overdose, *Tox Applied Pharm*, 35(1): 129–36.

Noguchi TT and Nakamura GR (1978), Phencyclidine-related deaths in Los Angeles County, 1976, *J For Sci*, 23(3): 503–7.

Reynolds PC (1976), Clinical and forensic experiences with phencyclidine, *Clin Tox*, 9(4): 547–52.

Phendimetrazine

Brand names: Bontril, Obex
Classification: stimulant/anorectic
λ: 2–9 hrs
V_d: unknown
Usual dosage: 35 mg tid

Source	Therapeutic/ Nontoxic	Toxic	Lethal
Blood	0.07–0.2 mg/L	No data available	0.3–0.7 mg/L
Urine			0.32 mg/L
Bile			2 mg/L
Stomach contents			24 mg/L

Selected Sources

Beckett AH and Raisi A (1976), Bioavailability in man of phendimetrazine from various dosage forms, *J Pharm Pharmacol*, 28 Suppl: 40P.

Hood I, Monforte J, Gault R, and Mirchandani H (1988), Fatality from illicit phendimetrazine use, *J Tox Clin Tox*, 26(3–4): 249–55.

Kintz P, Tracqui A, Mangin P, Lugnier AA, and Chaumont AJ (1989), A simple gas chromatographic identification and determination of 11 CNS stimulants in biological samples. Application on a fatality involving phendimetrazine, *For Sci Intl*, 40(2): 153–9.

Rudolph GR, Miksic JR, and Levitt MJ (1983), GLC determination of phendimetrazine in human plasma, serum, or urine, *J Pharmacol Sci*, 72(5): 519–21.

Phenelzine

Brand names: Nardil
Classification: antidepressant (MAOI)
λ: 1.5–6 hrs
V_d: unknown
Usual dosage: 15 mg tid/ qd

Source	Therapeutic/ Nontoxic	Toxic	Lethal
Blood	0.05–0.18 mg/L	0.5 mg/L	1.3–2 mg/L
Urine			58 mg/L

Selected Sources

Caddy BA and Stead AH (1978), Three cases of poisoning involving the drug phenelzine, *For Sci Soc J*, 18(3–4): 207–8.

Georgotas A, McCue RE, Cooper TB, Nagachandran N, and Friedhoff A (1989), Factors affecting the delay of antidepressant effect in responders to nortriptyline and phenelzine, *Psychiatry Res*, 28(1): 1–9.

Waring WS and Wallace WAH (2007), Acute myocarditis after massive phenelzine overdose, *Eur J Clin Pharmacol*, 63(11): 1007–9.

Pheniramine

Brand names: Avil; ingredient in many OTC cold medicines
Classification: antihistamine
λ: 8–19 hrs
V_d: 1.5–3 L/kg
Usual dosage: 25–50 mg q 8 hrs

Source	Therapeutic/ Nontoxic	Toxic	Lethal
Blood	0.17–0.89 mg/L	No data available	1.9–30 mg/L
Urine			149 mg/L
Liver			6.6–115 mg/kg
Kidney			4.0 mg/kg
Brain			5.3 mg/kg

Selected Sources

Queree EA, Dickson SJ, and Missen AW (1979), Therapeutic and toxic levels of pheniramine in biological specimens, *J Anal Tox*, 3: 253–5.

Witte PU, Irmisch R, and Hajdú P (1985), Pharmacokinetics of pheniramine (Avil) and metabolites in healthy subjects after oral and intravenous administration, *Int J Clin Pharmacol Ther Tox*, 23(1): 59–62.

Phenobarbital

Brand names: Luminal, Solfoton
Classification: barbiturate
λ: 2–6 dys
V_d: 0.5–0.6 L/kg
Usual dosage: 30–100 mg bid/qd

Source	Therapeutic/ Nontoxic	Toxic	Lethal
Blood	4–40 mg/L	35–253 mg/L	48–348 mg/L
Vitreous			2–22 mg/L
Urine	6.4–22 mg/L		38 mg/L
Bile			75 mg/L
Liver	2.4–5.2 mg/kg		17–275 mg/kg
Kidney	1.7–4.9 mg/kg		12–84 mg/kg
Brain	0.01–3.6 mg/kg		5–75 mg/kg
Skeletal muscle			35 mg/kg

Comments

- Metabolized by CYP 2C9 and 2C19
- Tolerance can develop and should be considered when interpreting drug concentrations

Selected Sources

Amitai Y and Degani Y (1990), Treatment of phenobarbital poisoning with multiple dose activated charcoal in an infant, *J Emer Med*, 8(4): 449–50.

Bexar County Medical Examiner's Office data 1996–2007.

Bruce AM and Smith H (1977), The investigation of phenobarbitone, phenytoin and primidone in the death of epileptics, *Med Sci Law*, 17(3): 195–9.

Caplan YH, Ottinger WE, and Crooks CR (1983), Therapeutic and toxic drug concentrations in post mortem blood: A six year study in the State of Maryland, *J Anal Tox*, 7(5): 225–30.

Costello JB and Poklis A (1981), Treatment of massive phenobarbital overdose with dopamine diuresis, *Arch Int Med*, 141(7): 938–40.

Flanagan RJ (1998), Guidelines for the interpretation of analytical toxicology results and unit of measurement conversion factors, *Ann Clin Biochem*, 35: 261–7.

Lal R, Faiz S, Garg RK, Baweja KS, Guntupalli J, and Finkel KW (2006), Use of continuous venovenous hemodiafiltration in a case of severe phenobarbital poisoning, *Am J Kidney Dis*, 48(2): e13–15.

Lindberg MC, Cunningham A, and Lindberg NH (1992), Acute phenobarbital intoxication, *South Med J*, 85(8): 803–7.

Parker KD, Elliott HW, Wright JA, Nomof H, and Hine CH (1970), Blood and urine concentrations of subjects receiving barbiturates, meprobamate, glutethimide, or diphenylhydantoin, *Clin Tox*, 3(1): 131–45.

Paterson SC (1985), Drug levels found in cases of fatal self-poisoning, *For Sci Intl*, 27(2): 129–33.

Sunshine I and Hackett E (1957), Chemical findings in cases of fatal barbiturate intoxications, *J For Sci*, 2(2): 149–58.

Ziminski KR, Wemyss CT, Bidanset JH, Manning TJ, and Lukash L (1984), Comparative study of postmortem barbiturates, methadone, and morphine in vitreous humor, blood, and tissue, *J For Sci*, 29(3): 903–9.

Phentermine

Brand names: Pro-Fast, Adipex
Classification: stimulant/anorectic
λ: 19–24 hrs
V_d: 3–4 L/kg
Usual dosage: 37.5 mg qd

Source	Therapeutic/ Nontoxic	Toxic	Lethal
Blood	0.07–0.1 mg/L	0.2–0.9 mg/L	1.5–7.6 mg/L
Urine	5–25 mg/L		70–150 mg/L
Bile			7 mg/L
Liver			14–15 mg/kg
Kidney			12–16 mg/kg
Stomach contents			16 mg

Selected Sources

Bexar County Medical Examiner's Office data 1996–2007.

Groenewoud G, Schall R, Hundt HK, Müller FO, and van Dyk M (1993), Steady-state pharmacokinetics of phentermine extended-release capsules, *Int J Clin Pharmacol Ther Tox*, 31(8): 368–72.

Levine B, Caplan YH, and Dixon AM (1984), A fatality involving phentermine, *J For Sci*, 29(4): 1242–5.

Phenylephrine

Brand names: Sudafed PE, Neo-Synephrine; ingredient in OTC cold medicines
Classification: α-adrenergic agonist
λ: 0.5–3 hrs
V_d: 3.5–4.9 L/kg
Usual dosage: 10 mg q 4 hrs

Source	Therapeutic/ Nontoxic	Toxic	Lethal
Blood	0.0002–0.04 mg/L	No data available	

Selected Sources

Hengstmann JH and Goronzy J (1982), Pharmacokinetics of 3H-phenylephrine in man, *Eur J Clin Pharmacol*, 21(4): 335–41.
Ptácek P, J Klíma J, and Macek J (2007), Development and validation of a liquid chromatography tandem mass spectrometry method for the determination of phenylephrine in human plasma and its application to a pharmacokinetic study, *J Chromatogr B*, 858(1–2): 263–8.

Phenylpropanolamine (PPA)

Brand names: Accutrim, Dexatrim
Classification: α-adrenergic agonist
λ: 3–4.5 hrs
V_d: 4.5 L/kg
Usual dosage: 25–75 mg q 6–8 hrs

Source	Therapeutic/ Nontoxic	Toxic	Lethal
Blood	0.05–0.3 mg/L	2 mg/L	0.63–48 mg/L

Comments

- Associated with arrhythmias and hemorrhagic cerebrovascular accidents

Selected Sources

Augenstein WL, Bakerman P, and Radetsky M (1988), PPA overdose resulting in pulmonary edema and death, *Vet Hum Tox*, 30: 365.
Bexar County Medical Examiner's Office data 1996–2007.
Druid H and Holmgren P (1997), A compilation of fatal and control concentrations of drugs in postmortem femoral blood, *J For Sci*, 42(1): 79–87.
Lake CR, Gallant S, Masson E, and Miller P (1990), Adverse drug effects attributed to phenylpropanolamine: A review of 142 case reports, *Am J Med*, 89(2): 195–208.
Scherzinger SS, Dowse R, and Kanfer I (1990), Steady state pharmacokinetics and dose-proportionality of phenylpropanolamine in healthy subjects, *J Clin Pharmacol*, 30(4): 372–7.

Phenytoin

Brand names: Dilantin
Classification: anticonvulsant
λ: 7–60 hrs
V_d: 0.6–0.7 L/kg
Usual dosage: 100–200 mg tid

Source	Therapeutic/ Nontoxic	Toxic	Lethal
Blood	2–20 mg/L	20–101 mg/L	45–94 mg/L
Liver			14–272 mg/kg
Kidney			5.2–112 mg/kg
Brain			15–78 mg/kg

Comments

- Metabolized by CYP 2C9, 2C8, and 2C19

Selected Sources

Brandolese R, Scordo MG, Spina E, Gusella M, and Padrini R (2001), Severe phenytoin intoxication in a subject homozygous for CYP2C9*3, *Clin Pharmacol Ther*, 70(4): 391–4.

Bruce AM and Smith H (1977), The investigation of phenobarbitone, phenytoin and primidone in the death of epileptics, *Med Sci Law*, 17(3): 195–9.

Coutselinis A, Dimopoulos G, and Varsami P (1975), Fatal intoxication with diphenylhydantoin: Report of two cases, *For Sci*, 6(3): 131–3.

Craig S (2004), Phenytoin overdose complicated by prolonged intoxication and residual neurological deficits, *Emer Med Australasia*, 16(4): 361–5.

Flanagan RJ (1998), Guidelines for the interpretation of analytical toxicology results and unit of measurement conversion factors, *Ann Clin Biochem*, 35: 261–7.

Jenkins A (2006), A case of phenytoin toxicity in a patient with advanced lung cancer, *Palliat Med*, 20(4): 479–80.

Laubscher FA (1966), Fatal diphenylhydantoin poisoning. A case report, *JAMA*, 198(10): 1120–1.

Levine M and Jones MW (1983), Toxic reaction to phenytoin following a viral infection, *Can Med Assoc J*, 128(11): 1270–1.

Mellick LB, Morgan JA, and Mellick GA (1989), Presentations of acute phenytoin overdose, *Am J Emer Med*, 7(1): 61–7.

Murphy JM, Motiwala R, and Devinsky O (1991), Phenytoin intoxication, *South Med J*, 84(10): 1199–204.

Pholcodine

Brand names: Galenphol
Classification: antitussive
λ: 35–50 hrs
V_d: 30–40 L/kg
Usual dosage: 20–60 mg q 4 hrs

Source	Therapeutic/ Nontoxic	Toxic	Lethal
Blood	0.009–0.06 mg/L	No data available	

Selected Sources

Chen ZR, Bochner F, and Somogyi A (1988), Pharmacokinetics of pholcodine in healthy volunteers: Single and chronic dosing studies, *Br J Clin Pharmacol*, 26(4): 445–53.

Laine K, Kivistö KT, Ojala-Karlsson P, and Neuvonen PJ (1997), Effect of activated charcoal on the pharmacokinetics of pholcodine, with special reference to delayed charcoal ingestion, *Ther Drug Monit*, 19(1): 46–50.

Pimozide

Brand names: Orap
Classification: antipsychotic
λ: 55–111 hrs
V_d: 13–37 L/kg
Usual dosage: 1–5 mg bid

Source	Therapeutic/ Nontoxic	Toxic	Lethal
Blood	0.003–0.01 mg/L	0.02 mg/L	No data available
Urine		0.09 mg/L	

Comments

- Prolongs QT interval

Selected Sources

Desta Z, Kerbusch T, and Flockhart DA (1999), Effect of clarithromycin on the pharmacokinetics and pharmacodynamics of pimozide in healthy poor and extensive metabolizers of cytochrome P450 2D6 (CYP2D6), *Clin Pharmacol Ther*, 65(1): 10–20.

Sallee FR, Pollock BG, Stiller RL, Stull S, Everett G, and Perel JM (1987), Pharmacokinetics of pimozide in adults and children with Tourette's syndrome, *J Clin Pharmacol*, 27(10): 776–81.

Salness RA, Goetz CM, and Gorman RL (1992), Two cases of pimozide ingestion, *Vet Hum Tox*, 34: 1.

Prazepam

Brand names: Centrax, Lysanxia, Demetrin
Classification: benzodiazepine
λ: 1–2 hrs
V_d: 12–14 L/kg
Usual dosage: 30 mg bid/tid

Source	Therapeutic/ Nontoxic	Toxic	Lethal
Blood	0.008–0.3 mg/L	1–5 mg/L	No data available

Comments

- Active metabolite: nordiazepam (λ 38–135 hrs)
- Tolerance can develop and should be considered when interpreting drug concentrations

Selected Sources

Repetto MR and Repetto M (1997), Habitual, toxic, and lethal concentrations of 103 drugs of abuse in humans, *J Tox Clin Tox*, 35(1):1–9.

Schulz M and Schmoldt A (2003), Therapeutic and toxic blood concentrations of more than 800 drugs and other xenobiotics, *Pharmazie*, 58(7): 447–74.

Smith MT, Evans LE, Eadie MJ, and Tyrer JH (1979), Pharmacokinetics of prazepam in man, *Eur J Clin Pharmacol*, 16(2): 141–7.

Pregabalin

Brand names: Lyrica
Classification: anticonvulsant
λ: 4.6–6.8 hrs
V_d: 0.5 L/kg
Usual dosage: 150–600 mg qd

Source	Therapeutic/ Nontoxic	Toxic	Lethal
Blood	2.8–11 mg/L	7.7–60[a] mg/L	No data available

[a] Co-intoxicant lamotrigine (45 mg/L)

Selected Sources

Berry D and Millington C (2005), Analysis of pregabalin at therapeutic concentrations in human plasma/serum by reversed-phase HPLC, *Ther Drug Monit*, 27(4): 451–6.

Braga AJ and Chidley K (2007), Self-poisoning with lamotrigine and pregabalin, *Anaesthesia*, 62(5): 524–7.

Olaizola I, Ellger T, Young P, Bösebeck F, Evers S, and Kellinghaus C (2006), Pregabalin-associated acute psychosis and epileptiform EEG-changes, *Seizure*, 15(3): 208–10.

Physicians' Desk Reference 62 Edition (2008), Thomson PDR, Montvale, NJ, pp. 2517–24.

Randinitis EJ, Posvar EL, Alvey CW, Sedman AJ, Cook JA, and Bockbrader HN (2003), Pharmacokinetics of pregabalin in subjects with various degrees of renal function, *J Clin Pharmacol*, 43(3): 277–83.

Primidone

Brand names: Mysoline, Myidone, Sertan
Classification: barbiturate
λ: 10–21 hrs
V_d: 0.6–1 L/kg
Usual dosage: 250 mg tid/qid

Source	Therapeutic/ Nontoxic	Toxic	Lethal
Blood	5–19 mg/L	80–209 mg/L	65 mg/L
Urine		1570 mg/L	

Comments

- Active metabolite: phenobarbital

Selected Sources

Bailey DN and Jatlow PI (1972), Chemical analysis of massive crystalluria following primidone overdose, *Am J Clin Path*, 58(5): 583–9.

Baselt RC and Cravey RH (1977), A compendium of therapeutic and toxic concentrations of toxicologically significant drugs in human biofluids, *J Anal Tox*, 1:81–103.

Booker HE, Hososkowa K, Burdette RD, Darcey B, and Tassinari CA (1970), A clinical study of serum primidone levels, *Epilepsia*,11(4): 395–402.

Cate JC and Tenser R (1975), Acute primidone overdosage with massive crystalluria, *Clin Tox*, 8(4): 385–9.

Lehmann DF (1987), Primidone crystalluria following overdose: A report of a case and an analysis of the literature, *Med Tox*, 2(5): 383–7.

Martines C, Gatti G, Sasso E, Calzetti S, and Perucca E (1990), The disposition of primidone in elderly patients, *Br J Clin Pharmacol*, 30(4): 607–11.

van Heist AN, de Jung W, Seldenrijk R, and van Dijk A (1983), Coma and crystalluria: A massive primidone intoxication treated with haemoperfusion, *J Tox Clin Tox*, 20(4): 307–18.

Procainamide

Brand names: Pronestyl
Classification: antiarrhythmic
λ: 2.5–4.7 hrs
V_d: 1.3–2.2 L/kg
Usual dosage: 250–500 mg q 3–6 hrs

Source	Therapeutic/ Nontoxic	Toxic	Lethal
Blood	4–8 mg/L	8–63 mg/L	30 mg/L

Comments

- Active metabolite: *N*-acetylprocainamide (NAPA)
- Prolongs QT interval

Selected Sources

Bizjak ED, Nolan PE, Brody EA, and Galloway JM (1999), Procainamide-induced psychosis: A case report and review of the literature, *Ann Pharmacother*, 33(9): 948–51.

Koch-Weser J and Klein SW (1971), Procainamide dosage schedules, plasma concentrations, and clinical effects, *JAMA*, 215(9): 1454–60.

Villalba-Pimentel L, Epstein LM, Sellers EM, Foster JR, Bennion LJ, and Nadler LM (1973), Survival after massive procainamide ingestion, *Am J Cardiol*, 32(5): 727–30.

White SR, Dy G, and Wilson JM (2002), The case of the slandered Halloween cupcake: Survival after massive pediatric procainamide overdose, *Pediat Emerg Care*, 18(3): 185–8.

Prochlorperazine

Brand names: Compazine
Classification: antipsychotic/antiemetic
λ: 7–21 hrs
V_d: 13–32 L/kg
Usual dosage: 5–10 mg tid/qid

Source	Therapeutic/ Nontoxic	Toxic	Lethal
Blood	0.002–0.05 mg/L	0.2–1.6 mg/L	5 mg/L

Comment

- May prolong QT interval

Selected Sources

Isah AO, Rawlins MD, and Bateman DN (1991), Clinical pharmacology of prochlorperazine in healthy young males, *Br J Clin Pharmacol*, 32(6): 677–84.

Schulz M and Schmoldt A (2003), Therapeutic and toxic blood concentrations of more than 800 drugs and other xenobiotics, *Pharmazie*, 58(7): 447–74.

Taylor WB and Bateman DN (1987), Preliminary studies of the pharmacokinetics and pharmacodynamics of prochlorperazine in healthy volunteers, *Br J Clin Pharmacol*, 23(2): 137–42.

Tompsett SL (1968), The spectrofluorimetric determination of phenothiazine drugs in blood serum, *Acta Pharmacologica et Toxicologica*, 26(4): 298–302.

Procyclidine

Brand names: Kemadrin
Classification: anti-Parkinson's
λ: 8–18 hrs
V_d: 0.7–1.3 L/kg
Usual dosage: 2.5–5 mg tid/qid

Source	Therapeutic/ Nontoxic	Toxic	Lethal
Blood	0.11–0.74 mg/L	1–2 mg/L	7.8 mg/L

Selected Sources

Missen AW, Dickson SJ, and Cleary WT (1978), Analysis of procylidine in blood by gas-liquid chromatography with nitrogen-phosphorus detector, *J Anal Tox*, 2: 238–40.
Schulz M and Schmoldt A (2003), Therapeutic and toxic blood concentrations of more than 800 drugs and other xenobiotics, *Pharmazie*, 58(7): 447–74.
Whiteman PD, Fowle AS, Hamilton MJ, Peck AW, Bye A, and Dean K (1985), Pharmacokinetics and pharmacodynamics of procyclidine in man, *Eur J Clin Pharmacol*, 28(1): 73–8.

Promazine

Brand names: Sparine
Classification: antipsychotic
λ: 9–40 hrs
V_d: 23–43 L/kg
Usual dosage: 50–150 mg im q 4–6 hrs

Source	Therapeutic/ Nontoxic	Toxic	Lethal
Blood	0.003–0.14 mg/L	1–1.8 mg/L	5 mg/L

Selected Sources

Hu OY, Tang HS, Sheeng TY, Chen SC, Lee SK, and Chung PH (1990), Pharmacokinetics of promazine: I. Disposition in patients with acute viral hepatitis B, *Biopharma Drug Dispos*, 11(7): 557–68.

Larsimont V, Meins J, Fieger-Büschges H, and Blume H (1998), Validated high-performance liquid chromatographic assay for the determination of promazine in human plasma: Application to pharmacokinetic studies, *J Chromatogr–B*, 719 (1–2): 222–6.

Schulz M and Schmoldt A (2003), Therapeutic and toxic blood concentrations of more than 800 drugs and other xenobiotics, *Pharmazie*, 58(7): 447–74.

Tompsett SL (1968), The spectrofluorimetric determination of phenothiazine drugs in blood serum, *Acta Pharmacologica et Toxicologica*, 26(4): 298–302.

Promethazine

Brand names: Phenergan
Classification: antiemetic
λ: 9–16 hrs
V_d: 9–19 L/kg
Usual dosage: 12.5–50 mg q 4–6 hrs

Source	Therapeutic/ Nontoxic	Toxic	Lethal
Blood	0.004–0.2 mg/L	0.14[a]–2 mg/L	1.9–8 mg/L
Urine		0.08 mg/L	50 mg/L
Liver	9–12 mg/kg		50–180 mg/kg
Kidney	7 mg/kg		26–92 mg/kg

[a] Concentration obtained 5 hrs postexposure

Selected Sources

Bonnichsen R, Geertinger P, and Maehly AC (1970), Toxicological data on phenothiazine drugs in autopsy cases, *Zeitschrift für Rechtsmedizin*, 67(3): 158–69.

Druid H and Holmgren P (1997), A compilation of fatal and control concentrations of drugs in postmortem femoral blood, *J For Sci*, 42(1):79–87.

Pan CV, Quintela AG, Anuncibay PG, and Vic JM (1989), Topical promethazine intoxication, *DICP*, 23(1): 89.

Strenkoski-Nix LC, Ermer J, DeCleene S, Cevallos W, and Mayer PR (2000), Pharmacokinetics of promethazine hydrochloride after administration of rectal suppositories and oral syrup to healthy subjects, *Am J Health Syst Pharm*, 57(16): 1499–505.

Propane

Brand names: component of aerosol propellants and fuel sources
Classification: volatile (aliphatic hydrocarbon)
λ: unknown
V_d: unknown
Usual dosage: not applicable

Source	Therapeutic/ Nontoxic	Toxic	Lethal
Blood	No data available		0.2–69 mg/L
Urine			0.5–2 mg/L
Liver			0.3–33 mg/kg
Kidney			0.2–75 mg/kg
Brain			1–128 mg/kg
Lung			0.2–55 mg/kg
Spleen			0.3–26 mg/kg
Skeletal muscle			0.3–213 mg/kg
Cardiac muscle			1.7–34 mg/kg
Adipose tissue			0.9–1276 mg/kg

Comments

- Cardiotoxic: intoxication associated with arrhythmias

Selected Sources

Broussard L (2002), Chapter 19, Inhalants, in *Principles of Forensic Toxicology*, Levine B (Ed.), American Association for Clinical Chemistry, Washington, DC, USA, pp. 345–53.

Fukunaga T, Yamamoto H, Tanegashima A, Yamamoto Y, and Nishi K (1996), Liquefied petroleum gas (LPG) poisoning: Report of two cases and review of the literature, *For Sci Intl*, 82(3): 193–200.

Stephens BG (2004), Chapter XXII, Investigation of deaths from drug abuse, in *Spitz and Fisher's Medicolegal Investigation of Death Fourth Edition*, Spitz WU (Ed.), Charles C Thomas, Springfield, IL, pp. 1166–217.

Propofol

Brand names: Diprivan
Classification: anesthetic
λ: 1.5–8 hrs
V_d: 1.8–25 L/kg
Usual dosage: 5–50 μg/kg/min

Source	Therapeutic/ Nontoxic	Toxic	Lethal
Blood	0.78–15 mg/L	No data available	0.22–5.5 mg/L
Urine			5.4–94 mg/L
Bile			0.25 mg/L
Liver			1.4–27 mg/kg
Kidney			1.8–5.5 mg/kg
Brain			2.9–17 mg/kg
Skeletal muscle			222 mg/kg

Comments

- Therapeutic concentrations can be fatal if drug not administered in a monitored medical setting

Selected Sources

Addison J, Vorce SP, Levine B, and Mallak C (2007), *Distribution of propofol in two cases of self-administration deaths.* Presented at the Society of Forensic Toxicologists meeting, Durham, North Carolina.

Albanese J, Martin C, Lacarelle B, Saux P, Durand A, and Gouin F (1990), Pharmacokinetics of long-term propofol infusion used for sedation in ICU patients, *Anesthesiology*, 73(2): 214–7.

Bexar County Medical Examiner's Office data 1996–2007.

Chao TC, Lo DS, Chui PP, and Koh TH (1994), The first fatal 2,6-di-isopropylphenol (propofol) poisoning in Singapore: A case report, *For Sci Intl*, 66(1): 1–7.

Drummer OH (1992), A fatality due to propofol poisoning, *J For Sci*, 37(4): 1186–9.

Iwersen-Bergmann S, Rösner P, Kühnau HC, Junge M, and Schmoldt A (2001), Death after excessive propofol abuse, *Int J Legal Med*, 114(4–5): 248–51.

Roussin A, Mirepoix M, Lassabe G, Dumestre-Toulet V, Gardette V, and Montastruc J-L (2006), Death related to a recreational abuse of propofol at therapeutic dose range, *Br J Anaesth*, 97(2): 268.

Propoxyphene

Brand names: Darvon; Wygesic, Darvocet, Propacet (w/ aceta)
Classification: narcotic
λ: 6–12 hrs
V_d: 16 L/kg
Usual dosage: 65 mg q 4 hrs

Source	Therapeutic/ Nontoxic	Toxic	Lethal
Blood	0.01–0.8 mg/L	0.8–1 mg/L	0.9–60 mg/L
Urine	0.05–0.07 mg/L		0.7–75 mg/L
Bile			43 mg/L
Liver	0.05–0.16 mg/kg		2.1–550 mg/kg
Kidney			3–58 mg/kg
Brain			20 mg/kg
Skeletal muscle			1.3–8.4 mg/kg
Stomach contents			2.1–759 mg

Comments

- Active metabolite: norpropoxyphene
- Parent to metabolite ratio can be used to determine acute versus chronic use
- Tolerance can develop and should be considered when interpreting drug concentrations

Selected Sources

Baselt RC and Wright JA (1975), Propoxyphene and norpropoxyphene tissue concentrations in fatalities associated with propoxyphene hydrochloride and propoxyphene napsylate, *Arch Tox*, 34(2): 145–52.

Bexar County Medical Examiner's Office data 1996–2007.

Christensen H (1977), Dextropropoxyphene and norpropoxyphene in blood, muscle, liver and urine in fatal poisoning, *Acta Pharmacologica et Toxicologica*, 40(2): 298–309.

Cravey RH, Shaw RF, Nakamura GR (1974), Incidence of propoxyphene poisoning: A report of fatal cases, *J For Sci*, 19(1): 72–80.

Druid H and Holmgren P (1997), A compilation of fatal and control concentrations of drugs in postmortem femoral blood, *J For Sci*, 42(1): 79–87.

Irey NS and Froede RC (1974), Evaluation of deaths from drug overdose: A clinicopathologic study, *Am J Clin Path*, 61(6): 778–84.

Langford AM, Taylor KK, and Pounder DJ (1998), Drug concentration in selected skeletal muscles, *J For Sci*, 43(1): 22–7.

Ogbuihi S, Bohn G, and Audick W (1980), Fatal case of propoxyphene overdose: Morphological and toxicological findings, *Zeitschrift für Rechtsmedizin*, 84(2): 161–6.
Rios JF (1973), Propoxyphene: Two fatalities due to overdose, *Virginia Medical Monthly*, 100(1): 47–9.
Robinson AE, Sattar H, McDowall RD, Holder AT, and Powell R (1977), Forensic toxicology of some deaths associated with the combined use of propoxyphene and acetaminophen (paracetamol), *J For Sci*, 22(4): 708–17.
Sturner WQ and Garriott JC (1973), Deaths involving propoxyphene: A study of 41 cases over a two-year period, *JAMA*, 223(10): 1125–30.
Wetli CV and Bednarczyk LR (1980), Deaths related to propoxyphene overdose: A ten-year assessment, *South Med J*, 73(9): 1205–9.

Propranolol

Brand names: Inderal
Classification: β-blocker
λ: 2–6 hrs
V_d: 3–5 L/kg
Usual dosage: 40–180 mg bid/tid

Source	Therapeutic/ Nontoxic	Toxic	Lethal
Blood	0.03–0.3 mg/L	2–12 mg/L	4–167 mg/L
Urine			0.3–0.9 mg/L
Liver			10–170 mg/kg
Kidney			26–119 mg/kg
Brain			6–67 mg/kg
Stomach contents			130–23000 mg/kg

Comments

- Metabolized by CYP 1A2, 2D6, and 2C19

Selected Sources

Fucci N and Offidani C (2000), An unusual death by propranolol ingestion, *Am J For Med Path*, 21(1): 56–8.

Gault R, Monforte JR, and Khasnabis S (1977), A death involving propranolol (Inderal), *Clin Tox*, 11(3): 295–9.

Hong CY, Yang WC, and Chiang BN (1983), Importance of membrane stabilizing effect in massive overdose of propranolol: Plasma level study in a fatal case, *Hum Tox*, 2(3): 511–7.

Jones JW, Clark MA, and Mullen BL (1982), Suicide by ingestion of propranolol, *J For Sci*, 27(1): 213–6.

Kristinsson J and Jóhannesson T (1977), A case of fatal propranolol intoxication, *Acta Pharmacologica et Toxicologica*, 41(2): 190–2.

Leahey WJ, Neill JD, Varma MP, and Shanks RG (1980), Comparison of the efficacy and pharmacokinetics of conventional propranolol and a long acting preparation of propranolol, *Br J Clin Pharmacol*, 9(1): 33–40.

McVey FK and Corke CF (1991), Extracorporeal circulation in the management of massive propranolol overdose, *Anaesthesia*, 46(9): 744–6.

Paterson SC (1985), Drug levels found in cases of fatal self-poisoning, *For Sci Intl* 27(2):129–33.

Suarez RV, Greenwald MS, and Geraghty E (1988), Intentional overdosage with propranolol: A report of two cases, *Am J For Med Path*, 9(1): 45–7.

Pseudoephedrine

Brand names: Sudafed; component of many OTC cold medicines
Classification: α and β adrenergic agonist
λ: 3–20 hrs
V_d: 2–3 L/kg
Usual dosage: 60 mg q 4–6 hrs

Source	Therapeutic/ Nontoxic	Toxic	Lethal
Blood	0.32–0.63 mg/L	1.4 mg/L	12–33 mg/L

Selected Sources

Bexar County Medical Examiner's Office data 1996–2007.

Bye C, Hill HM, Hughes DT, and Peck AW (1975), A comparison of plasma levels of L(+) pseudoephedrine following different formulations, and their relation to cardiovascular and subjective effects in man, *Eur J Clin Pharmacol*, 8(1): 47–53.

Hanzlick R (1995), National Association of Medical Examiners Pediatric Toxicology (PedTox) Registry Report 3. Case submission summary and data for acetaminophen, benzene, carboxyhemoglobin, dextromethorphan, ethanol, phenobarbital, and pseudoephedrine, *Am J For Med Path*, 16(4): 270–7.

Sica DA and Comstock TJ (1989), Pseudoephedrine accumulation in renal failure, *Am J Med Sci*, 298(4): 261–3.

Psilocybin

Brand names: not applicable
Street names: Magic Mushrooms, Shrooms
Classification: hallucinogen
λ: unknown
V_d: unknown
Usual dosage: 10–20 mg/dose

Source	Therapeutic/ Nontoxic	Toxic	Lethal
Blood	0.005–0.02 mg/L PI	No data available	
Urine	0.23 mg/L		

Comments

- Active metabolite: psilocin (PI) (λ 1.5–4.5 hrs; V_d 2.5–5 L/kg)
- From *Psilocybe* mushrooms

Selected Sources

Hasler F, Bourquin D, Brenneisen R, Bär T, and Vollenweider FX (1997), Determination of psilocin and 4-hydroxyindole-3-acetic acid in plasma by HPLC-ECD and pharmacokinetic profiles of oral and intravenous psilocybin in man, *Pharmaceutica Acta Helvetiae*, 72(3): 175–84.

Sticht G and Käferstein H Detection of psilocin in body fluids, (2000), *For Sci Intl*, 113(1–3): 403–7.

Pyridostigmine

Brand names: Mestinon
Classification: cholinesterase inhibitor
λ: 1–3 hrs
V_d: 0.5–1.7 L/kg
Usual dosage: 30–120 mg q 6–8 hrs

Source	Therapeutic/ Nontoxic	Toxic	Lethal
Blood	0.01–1.2 mg/L	No data available	

Selected Sources

Aquilonius SM and Hartvig P (1986), Clinical pharmacokinetics of cholinesterase inhibitors, *Clin Pharmacokinetics*, 11(3): 236–49.

Stone JG, Matteo RS, Ornstein E, Schwartz AE, Ostapkovich N, and Jamdar SC (1995), Aging alters the pharmacokinetics of pyridostigmine, *Anesth Analg*, 81(4): 773–6.

Pyrilamine

Brand names: Pyrlex: component of many OTC cold medicines
Classification: antihistamine
λ: unknown
V_d: unknown
Usual dosage: 25–50 mg bid

Source	Therapeutic/ Nontoxic	Toxic	Lethal
Blood	No data available	0.12 mg/L	11 mg/L
Liver			18 mg/kg
Brain			71 mg/kg
Stomach contents			578 mg

Selected Sources

Freedberg RS, Friedman GR, Palu RN, and Feit F (1987), Cardiogenic shock due to antihistamine overdose: Reversal with intra-aortic balloon counterpulsation, *JAMA*, 257(5): 660–1.

Johnson GR (1981), A fatal case involving pyrilamine, *Clin Tox*, 18(8): 907–9.

Quazepam

Brand names: Doral
Classification: benzodiazepine
λ: 25–41 hrs
V_d: 5–8.6 L/kg
Usual dosage: 7.5–15 mg qHS

Source	Therapeutic/ Nontoxic	Toxic	Lethal
Blood	0.03–0.15 mg/L	No data available	

Comments

- Active metabolites, 2-oxoquazepam and *N*-desalkyl-2-oxoquazepam
- Tolerance can develop and should be considered when interpreting drug concentrations

Selected Sources

Chung M, Hilbert JM, Gural RP, Radwanski E, Symchowicz S, and Zampaglione N (1984), Multiple-dose quazepam kinetics, *Clin Pharmacol Ther*, 35(4): 520–4.

Yasui-Furukori N, Takahata T, Kondo T, Mihara K, Kaneko S, and Tateishi T (2003), Time effects of food intake on the pharmacokinetics and pharmacodynamics of quazepam, *Br J Clin Pharmacol*, 55(4): 382–8.

Zampaglione N, Hilbert JM, Ning J, Chung M, Gural R, and Symchowicz S (1985), Disposition and metabolic fate of 14C-quazepam in man, *Drug Metab Dispos*, 13(1): 25–9.

Quetiapine

Brand names: Seroquel
Classification: antipsychotic
λ: 5–7 hrs
V_d: 6–14 L/kg
Usual dosage: 50–300 mg bid/qd

Source	Therapeutic/ Nontoxic	Toxic	Lethal
Blood	0.04–0.6 mg/L	1.8–13 mg/L	4–21 mg/L
Vitreous			0.9–5 mg/L
Urine			3–151 mg/L
Bile			12–158 mg/L
Liver			1.1–120 mg/kg
Kidney			4.2 mg/kg
Brain			1.2 mg/kg
Skeletal muscle			5.9 mg/kg
Cardiac muscle			5.3 mg/kg
Stomach contents			64–1600 mg/L

Comments

- Metabolized by CYP 3A4
- Prolongs QT interval

Selected Sources

Beelen AP, Yeo KT, and Lewis LD (2001), Asymptomatic QTc prolongation associated with quetiapine fumarate overdose in a patient being treated with risperidone, *Hum Exper Tox*, 20(4): 215–9.

Bexar County Medical Examiner's Office data 1996–2007.

Davis PC, Wong J, and Gefvert O (1999), Analysis and pharmacokinetics of quetiapine and two metabolites in human plasma using reversed-phase HPLC with ultraviolet and electrochemical detection, *J Pharm Biomed Anal*, 20(1–2): 271–82.

Flammia DD, Valouch T, and Venuti S (2006), Tissue distribution of quetiapine in 20 cases in Virginia, *J Anal Tox*, 30(4): 287–92.

Harmon TJ, Benitez JG, Krenzelok EP, and Cortes-Belen E (1998), Loss of consciousness from acute quetiapine overdosage, *J Tox Clin Tox*, 36(6): 599–602.

Hunfeld NGM, Westerman EM, Boswijk DJ, de Haas JAM, van Putten MJAM, and Touw DJ (2006), Quetiapine in overdosage: A clinical and pharmacokinetic analysis of 14 cases, *Ther Drug Monit*, 28(2): 185–9.

Langman LJ, Kaliciak HA, and Carlyle S (2004), Fatal overdoses associated with quetiapine, *J Anal Tox*, 28(6): 520–5.

Nudelman E, Vinuela LM, and Cohen CI (1998), Safety in overdose of quetiapine: A case report, *J Clin Psychiatry*, 59(8): 433.

Parker DR and McIntyre IM (2005), Case studies of postmortem quetiapine: Therapeutic or toxic concentrations? *J Anal Tox*, 29(5): 407–12.

Wise S and Jenkins AJ (2005), Disposition of quetiapine in biological specimens from postmortem cases, *J For Sci*, 50(1): 209–14.

Quinidine

Brand names: Cardioquin, Conchinin, Duraquin, Quinalan, Quinate, Quinidex
Classification: antiarrhythmic/antimalarial
λ: 3–16 hrs
V_d: 1.5–4 L/kg
Usual dosage: 324–648 mg bid/tid

Source	Therapeutic/ Nontoxic	Toxic	Lethal
Blood	2–5 mg/L	8.5–28 mg/L	19–45 mg/L
Liver			220 mg/kg

Comments

- Metabolized by CYP 3A
- Prolongs QT interval

Selected Sources

Baselt RC and Cravey RH (1977), A compendium of therapeutic and toxic concentrations of toxicologically significant drugs in human biofluids, *J Anal Tox,* 1:81–103.
Bexar County Medical Examiner's Office data 1996–2007.
El-Eraky H and Thomas SHL (2003), Effects of sex on the pharmacokinetic and pharmacodynamic properties of quinidine, *Br J Clin Pharm*, 56(2): 198–204.
Flanagan RJ (1998), Guidelines for the interpretation of analytical toxicology results and unit of measurement conversion factors, *Ann Clin Biochem*, 35: 261–7.
Haapanen EJ and Pellinen TJ (1981), Hemoperfusion in quinidine intoxication, *Acta Medica Scandinavica*, 210(6): 515–6.
Kerr F, Kenoyer G, and Bilitch M (1971), Quinidine overdose: Neurological and cardiovascular toxicity in a normal person, *Br Heart J*, 33(4): 629–31.
Reimold EW, Reynolds WJ, Fixler DE, and McElroy L (1973), Use of hemodialysis in the treatment of quinidine poisoning, *Pediatrics*, 52(1): 95–9.
Shub C, Gau GT, Sidell PM, and Brennan LA (1978), The management of acute quinidine intoxication, *Chest,* 73(2): 173–8.
Woie L and Oyri A (1974), Quinidine intoxication treated with hemodialysis, *Acta Medica Scandinavica*, 195(3): 237–9.

Quinine

Brand names: Qualaquin, Quinerva, Quinite
Classification: antimalarial
λ: 9–18 hrs
V_d: 1–2.2 L/kg
Usual dosage: 650 mg tid

Source	Therapeutic/ Nontoxic	Toxic	Lethal
Blood	2–5 mg/L	6–16 mg/L	11–58 mg/L
Liver			52–350 mg/kg
Kidney			72–370 mg/kg
Brain			63–72 mg/kg

Comments

- Metabolized by CYP 3A4 and 2C19
- Active metabolite: 3-hydroxyquinine
- Prolongs QT interval

Selected Sources

Auprayoon P, Sukontason K, Na-Bangchang K, Banmairuroi V, Molunto P, and Karbwang J (1995), Pharmacokinetics of quinine in chronic liver disease, *Br J Clin Pharmacol*, 40(5). 494–7.

Bodenhamer JE and Smilkstein MJ (1993), Delayed cardiotoxicity following quinine overdose: A case report, *J Emer Med*, 11(3): 279–85.

Coutselinis A and Boukis D (1977), Quinine concentrations in blood and viscera in a case of acute fatal intoxication, *Clin Chem*, 23(5): 914.

Dyson EH, Proudfoot AT, Prescott LF, and Heyworth R (1985), Death and blindness due to overdose of quinine, *Br Med J*, 291: 31–3.

Floyd M, Hill AV, Ormston BJ, Menzies R, and Porter R (1974), Quinine amblyopia treated by hemodialysis, *Clin Nephrol*, 2(1): 44–6.

Jamaludin A, Mohamad M, Navaratnam V, Selliah K, Tan SC, and Wernsdorfer WH (1988), Relative bioavailability of the hydrochloride, sulphate and ethyl carbonate salts of quinine, *Br J Clin Pharmacol*, 25(2): 261–3.

Markham TN, Dodson VN, and Eckberg DL (1967), Peritoneal dialysis in quinine sulfate intoxication, *JAMA*, 202(12): 1102–3.

Morrison LD, Velez LI, Shepherd G, Bey T, and Benitez FL (2003), Death by quinine, *Vet Hum Tox*, 45(6): 303–6.

Townend BS, Sturm JW, and Whyte S (2004), Quinine associated blindness, *Aust Fam Physician*, 33(8): 627–8.

Wenstone R, Bell M, and Mostafa SM (1989), Fatal adult respiratory distress syndrome after quinine overdose, *Lancet*, 1: 1143–4.

Winek CL, Davis ER, Collom WD, and Shanor SP (1974), Quinine fatality—case report, *Clin Tox*, 7(2): 129–32.

Reboxetine

Brand names: Edronax, Vestra
Classification: antidepressant (NRI)
λ: 12–15 hrs
V_d: 0.7–2.4 L/kg
Usual dosage: 2–4 mg bid

Source	Therapeutic/ Nontoxic	Toxic	Lethal
Blood	0.03–0.27 mg/L	No data available	

Selected Sources

Bergmann JF, Laneury JP, Duchene P, Fleishaker JC, Houin G, and Ségrestaa JM (2000), Pharmacokinetics of reboxetine in healthy, elderly volunteers, *Eur J Drug Metab Pharmacokinet*, 25(3–4): 195–8.

Hendershot PE, Fleishaker JC, Lin KM, Nuccio ID, and Poland RE (2001), Pharmacokinetics of reboxetine in healthy volunteers with different ethnic descents, *Psychopharmacology*, 155(2): 148–53.

Pellizzoni C, Poggesi I, Jørgensen NP, Edwards DM, Paus E, and Benedetti MS (1996), Pharmacokinetics of reboxetine in healthy volunteers: Single against repeated oral doses and lack of enzymatic alterations, *Biopharm Drug Dispos*, 17(7): 623–33.

Remifentanil

Brand names: Ultiva
Classification: narcotic
λ: 0.1–0.3 hrs
V_d: 0.1–0.4 L/kg
Usual dosage: 0.05–2 μg/kg/min iv

Source	Therapeutic/ Nontoxic	Toxic	Lethal
Blood	0.0001–0.1 mg/L	No data available	

Selected Sources

Egan TD, Lemmens HJ, Fiset P, Hermann DJ, Muir KT, and Stanski DR (1993), The pharmacokinetics of the new short-acting opioid remifentanil (GI87084B) in healthy adult male volunteers, *Anesthesiology*, 79(5): 881–92.

Westmoreland CL, Hoke JF, Sebel PS, Hug CC, and Muir KT (1993), Pharmacokinetics of remifentanil (GI87084B) and its major metabolite (GI90291) in patients undergoing elective inpatient surgery, *Anesthesiology*, 79(5): 893–903.

Ricin

Brand names: not applicable
Classification: plant lectin
λ: unknown
V_d: unknown
Usual dosage: not applicable

Source	Therapeutic/ Nontoxic[a]	Toxic[a]	Lethal[a]
Blood	0.25–26 ng/mL	0.3–1.5 ng/mL	
Urine	None detected ricin		0.3 ng/mL ricin
	None detected ricinine		0.08–10 ng/mL ricinine

[a] Note units are in ng/mL

Comments

- From *Ricinus communis* (castor bean)
- Inhibits protein synthesis
- Lethal dose 1–20 mg/kg (~8 beans)
- Death usually occurs 48–72 hrs postexposure

Selected Sources

Audi J, Belson M, Patel M, Schier J, and Osterloh J (2005), Ricin poisoning: A comprehensive review, *JAMA*, 294(18): 2342–51.

Fodstad O, Kvalheim G, Godal A, Lotsberg J, Aamdal S, and Høst H (1984), Phase I study of the plant protein ricin, *Cancer Res*, 44(2): 862–5.

Godal A, Fodstad O, Ingebrigtsen K, and Pihl A (1984), Pharmacological studies of ricin in mice and humans, *Cancer Chemother Pharmacol*, 13(3): 157–63.

Godal A, Olsnes S, and Pihl A (1981), Radioimmunoassays of abrin and ricin in blood, *J Tox Environ Health*, 8(3): 409–17.

Johnson RC, Lemire SW, Woolfitt AR, Ospina M, Preston KP, and Olson CT (2005), Quantification of ricinine in rat and human urine: A biomarker for ricin exposure, *J Anal Tox*, 29(3): 149–55.

Kopferschmitt J, Flesch F, Lugnier A, Sauder P, Jaeger A, and Mantz JM (1983), Acute voluntary intoxication by ricin, *Hum Tox*, 2(2): 239–42.

Risperidone

Brand names: Risperdal
Classification: antipsychotic
λ: 2.5–23 hrs
V_d: 0.9–2 L/kg
Usual dosage: 2–8 mg bid/qd

Source	Therapeutic/ Nontoxic	Toxic	Lethal
Blood	0.009–0.1 mg/L	1.1 mg/L	1.8 mg/L
Urine		5.6 mg/L	14 mg/L
Stomach contents			35 mg/L

Comments

- Active metabolite: 9-hydroxyrisperdone
- Metabolized by CYP 2D6 and 3A
- Prolongs QT interval

Selected Sources

Brown K, Levy H, Brenner C, Leffler S, and Hamburg EL (1993), Overdose of risperidone, *Ann Emer Med*, 22(12): 1908–10.
Lee HS, Tan CH, Au LS, and Khoo YM (1997), Serum and urine risperidone concentrations in an acute overdose, *J Clin Psychopharmacol*, 17(4): 325–6.
Springfield AC and Bodiford E (1996), An overdose of risperidone, *J Anal Tox*, 20(3): 202–3.
van Schaick EA, Lechat P, Remmerie BMM, Ko G, Lasseter KC, and Mannaert E (2003), Pharmacokinetic comparison of fast-disintegrating and conventional tablet formulations of risperidone in healthy volunteers, *Clin Thera*, 25(6): 1687–99.
Zhou Z-L, Li X, Peng H-Y, Yu X-Y, Yang M, and Su F-L (2006), Multiple dose pharmacokinetics of risperidone and 9-hydroxyrisperidone in Chinese female patients with schizophrenia, *Acta Pharmacologica Sinica*, 27(3): 381–6.

Rocuronium

Brand names: Zemuron
Classification: neuromuscular blocker
λ: 1–2 hrs
V_d: 0.1–0.5 L/kg
Usual dosage: 0.6–1.2 mg/kg/dose

Source	Therapeutic/ Nontoxic	Toxic	Lethal[a]
Blood	0.06–10 mg/L	No data available	1.5 mg/L
Urine			2.1 mg/L

[a] Co-intoxicant laudanosine (8.9 mg/L blood); rocuronium thought to have caused death

Comments

- Therapeutic concentrations can be fatal if drug not administered in a monitored medical setting

Selected Sources

Fuchs-Buder T, Strowitzki M, Rentsch K, Schreiber JU, Philipp-Osterman S, and Kleinschmidt S (2004), Concentration of rocuronium in cerebrospinal fluid of patients undergoing cerebral aneurysm clipping, *Br J Anaesth,* 92(3): 419–21.

McCoy EP, Mirakhur RK, Maddineni VR, Wierda JM, and Proost JH (1996), Pharmacokinetics of rocuronium after bolus and continuous infusion during halothane anaesthesia, *Br J Anaesth,* 76(1): 29–33.

Sayer H, Quintela O, Marquet P, Dupuy J-L, Gaulier JM, and Lachâtre G (2004), Identification and quantitation of six non-depolarizing neuromuscular blocking agents by LC-MS in biological fluids, *J Anal Tox,* 28(2): 105–10.

van Miert MM, Eastwood NB, Boyd AH, Parker CJ, and Hunter JM (1997), The pharmacokinetics and pharmacodynamics of rocuronium in patients with hepatic cirrhosis, *Br J Clin Pharmacol,* 44(2): 139–44.

Rotigotine

Brand names: Neupro
Classification: dopamine agonist (anti-Parkinson's)
λ: 5–7 hrs
V_d: 84 L/kg
Usual dosage: 2–6 mg qd transdermal patch

Source	Therapeutic/ Nontoxic	Toxic	Lethal
Blood	0.0001–0.006 mg/L	No data available	

Comments

- Recalled in Europe and United States due to delivery system

Selected Sources

Babic T, Boothmann B, Polivka J, Rektor I, Boroojerdi B, and Häck HJ (2006), Rotigotine transdermal patch enables rapid titration to effective doses in advanced-stage idiopathic Parkinson disease: Subanalysis of a parallel group, open-label, dose-escalation study, *Clinical Neuropharmacol*, 29(4): 238–42.

Cawello W, Wolff HM, Meuling WJA, Horstmann R, and Braun M (2007), Transdermal administration of radiolabelled [14C] rotigotine by a patch formulation: A mass balance trial, *Clin Pharmacokinetics*, 46(10): 851–7.

Physicians' Desk Reference 62 Edition (2008), Thomson PDR, Montvale, NJ, pp. 3038–42.

Scopolamine

Brand names: Scopace, Hyoscine (ophthalmologic gtts)
Classification: anticholinergic/antiemetic
λ: 2–4.5 hrs
V_d: 1.6–1.9 L/kg
Usual dosage: 0.4–0.8 mg q 8 hrs

Source	Therapeutic/ Nontoxic	Toxic	Lethal
Blood	0.0002–0.019 mg/L	0.0009 mg/L	No data available
Urine		0.11 mg/L	

Comments

- Metabolized by CYP 3A

Selected Sources

Putcha L, Cintrón NM, Tsui J, Vanderploeg JM, and Kramer WG (1989), Pharmacokinetics and oral bioavailability of scopolamine in normal subjects, *Pharm Res* , 6(6): 481–5.

Renner UD, Oertel R, and Kirch W (2005), Pharmacokinetics and pharmacodynamics in clinical use of scopolamine, *Ther Drug Monit*, 27(5): 655–65.

Sennhauser FH and Schwarz HP (1986), Toxic psychosis from transdermal scopolamine in a child, *Lancet*, 2(8514): 1033.

Secobarbital

Brand names: Seconal
Classification: barbiturate
λ: 15–30 hrs
V_d: 1.6–1.9 L/kg
Usual dosage: 100–300 mg qd

Source	Therapeutic/ Nontoxic	Toxic	Lethal
Blood	0.48–2.2 mg/L	3.2–22 mg/L	4–40 mg/L
Vitreous			2–10 mg/L
Urine	0.7–1.8 mg/L		
Liver	3.1–3.2 mg/kg		3–213 mg/kg
Kidney	1.8–2.8 mg/kg		3–30 mg/kg
Brain	0.6–1.8 mg/kg		1–25 mg/kg

Comments

- Tolerance can develop and should be considered when interpreting drug concentrations

Selected Sources

Bexar County Medical Examiner's Office data 1996–2007.

Caplan YH, Ottinger WE, and Crooks CR (1983), Therapeutic and toxic drug concentrations in post mortem blood: A six year study in the State of Maryland, *J Anal Tox*, 7(5): 225–30.

Clifford JM, Cookson JH, and Wickham PE (1974), Absorption and clearance of secobarbital, heptabarbital, methaqualone and ethinamate, *Clin Pharm Thera*, 16(2): 376–89.

Faulkner TP, McGinity JW, Hayden JH, Martinez M, and Comstock EG (1978), Pharmacokinetic studies on tolerance to sedative-hypnotics in a poly-drug abuse population. I Secobarbital, *Clin Pharm Thera*, 23(1): 36–46.

Finkle BS (1971), Ubiquitous reds: A local perspective on secobarbital abuse, *Clin Tox*, 4(2): 253–64.

Parker KD, Elliott HW, Wright JA, Nomof H, and Hine CH (1970), Blood and urine concentrations of subjects receiving barbiturates, meprobamate, glutethimide, or diphenylhydantoin, *Clin Tox*, 3(1): 131–45.

Sunshine I and Hackett E (1957), Chemical findings in cases of fatal barbiturate intoxications, *J For Sci*, 2(2): 149–58.

Selegiline

Brand names: Eldepryl, Zelapar, Emsam, Deprenyl, Anipryl (veterinary)
Classification: anti-Parkinson's (MAOI)
λ: 1–3 hrs
V_d: 4.3–18 L/kg
Usual dosage: 2–15 mg qd

Source	Therapeutic/ Nontoxic	Toxic	Lethal
Blood	0.002–0.005 mg/L selegiline 0.04 mg/L *l*-methamphetamine 0.02–0.03 mg/L *l*-amphetamine	No data available	0.17–0.28 mg/L *l*-methamphetamine 0.07–0.08 mg/L l-amphetamine
Urine			2.4 mg/L *l*-methamphetamine 0.72 mg/L *l*-amphetamine
Liver			0.71 mg/kg *l*-methamphetamine 0.36 mg/kg *l*-amphetamine

Comments

- Active metabolites: *l*-methamphetamine, *l*-amphetamine, and *l*-desmethylselegiline

Selected Sources

Azzaro AJ, Ziemniak J, Kemper E, Campbell BJ, and Van den Berg C (2007), Pharmacokinetics and absolute bioavailability of selegiline following treatment of healthy subjects with the selegiline transdermal system (6 Mg/24 H): A comparison with oral selegiline capsules, *J Clin Pharmacol*, 47(10): 1256–67.

Meeker JE and Reynolds PC (1990), Postmortem tissue methamphetamine concentrations following selegiline administration, *J Anal Tox*, 4(5): 330–1.

Sertindole

Brand names: Serdolect, Serlect
Classification: antipsychotic
λ: 36–100 hrs
V_d: 16–28 L/kg
Usual dosage: 8–24 mg qd

Source	Therapeutic/ Nontoxic	Toxic	Lethal
Blood	0.001–0.07 mg/L	No data available	

Comments

- Metabolized by CYP 2D6 and 3A
- May prolong QT interval

Selected Sources

Wong SL, Cao G, Mack RJ, and Granneman GR (1997), Pharmacokinetics of sertindole in healthy young and elderly male and female subjects, *Clin Pharmacol Ther*, 62(2): 157–64.

Wong SL and Granneman GR (1998), Modeling of sertindole pharmacokinetic disposition in healthy volunteers in short term dose-escalation studies, *J Pharma Sci*, 87(12): 1629–31.

Sertraline

Brand names: Zoloft
Classification: antidepressant (SSRI)
λ: 13–45 hrs
V_d: 20 L/kg
Usual dosage: 50–200 mg qd

Source	Therapeutic/ Nontoxic	Toxic	Lethal
Blood	0.03–0.3 mg/L	0.99–2.9 mg/L	15 mg/L
Vitreous	0.03 mg/L		
Urine	0.03–0.63 mg/L		
Bile	2.1–10 mg/L		
Liver	17–20 mg/kg		
Kidney	2.5–8.7 mg/kg		
Skeletal muscle			8.3 mg/kg

Comments

- Active metabolite: desmethylsertraline
- Prolongs QT interval
- Metabolized by CYP 2B6, 2C9, and 2C19

Selected Sources

Bexar County Medical Examiner's Office data 1996–2007.

Brendel DH, Bodkin JA, and Yang JM (2000), Massive sertraline overdose, *Ann Emer Med*, 36(5): 524–6.

Démolis JL, Angebaud P, Grangé JD, Coates P, Funck-Brentano C, and Jaillon P (1996), Influence of liver cirrhosis on sertraline pharmacokinetics, *Br J Clin Pharmacol*, 42(3): 394–7.

Goeringer KE, Raymon L, Christian GD, and Logan BK (2000), Postmortem forensic toxicology of selective serotonin reuptake inhibitors: A review of pharmacology and report of 168 cases, *J For Sci*, 45(3): 633–48.

Gupta RN and Dziurdzy SA (1994), Therapeutic monitoring of sertraline, *Clin Chem*, 40(3): 498–9.

Kassner J and Woolf A (1993), Sertraline hydrochloride: Correlation of clinical presentation with plasma concentration, *Vet Hum Tox*, 35: 341.

Levine B, Jenkins AJ, and Smialek JE (1994), Distribution of sertraline in postmortem cases, *J Anal Tox*, 18(5): 272–4.

Pao M and Tipnis T (1997), Serotonin syndrome after sertraline overdose in a 5-year-old girl, *Arch Pediatr Adolesc Med*, 151(10): 1064–7.

Rohrig TP and Goodson LJ (2004), A sertraline-intoxicated driver, *J Anal Tox*, 28(8): 689–91.

Sevoflurane

Brand names: Ultane
Classification: inhalation anesthetic
λ: 2–4 hrs
V_d: 0.3–0.8 L/kg
Usual dosage: 1.4%–3.3% inhaled

Source	Therapeutic/ Nontoxic	Toxic	Lethal
Blood	7.2–134 mg/L	No data available	8–26 mg/L
Vitreous			87 mg/L
Urine			1.1–105 mg/L
Bile			9.9 mg/L
Liver			31–269 mg/kg
Kidney			13–29 mg/kg

Comments

- Metabolized by CYP 2E1
- Metabolized to fluoride
- Therapeutic concentrations can be fatal if drug not administered in a monitored medical setting

Selected Sources

Burrows DL, Nicolaides A, Stephens GC, and Ferslew KE (2004), The distribution of sevoflurane in a sevoflurane induced death, *J For Sci*, 49(2): 394–7.

Levine B, Cox D, Jufer-Phipps RA, Li L, Jacobs A, and Fowler D (2007), A fatality from sevoflurane abuse, *J Anal Tox*, 31(8): 534–6.

Physicians' Desk Reference 60 Edition (2006), Thomson PDR, Montvale, NJ, p. 526.

Wissing H, Kuhn I, Rietbrock S, and Fuhr U (2000), Pharmacokinetics of inhaled anaesthetics in a clinical setting: Comparison of desflurane, isoflurane and sevoflurane, *Br J Anaesth*, 84(4): 443–9.

Yasuda N, Lockhart SH, Eger EI, Weiskopf RB, Liu J, and Laster M (1991), Comparison of kinetics of sevoflurane and isoflurane in humans, *Anesth Analg*, 72(3): 316–24.

Sibutramine

Brand names: Meridia
Classification: anorexiant (SNRI)
λ: 1 hr
V_d: unknown
Usual dosage: 5–15 mg qd

Source	Therapeutic/ Nontoxic	Toxic	Lethal
Blood	0.002–0.01 mg/L	No data available	

Comments

- Active metabolites: desmethylsibutramine (λ 14 hrs) and didesmethylsibutramine (λ16–19 hrs)

Selected Sources

Abolfathi Z, Couture J, Vallée F, LeBel M, Tanguay M, and Masson E (2004), A pilot study to evaluate the pharmacokinetics of sibutramine in healthy subjects under fasting and fed conditions, *J Pharm Pharmaceut Sci*, 7(3): 345–9.

Hind ID, Mangham JE, Ghani SP, Haddock RE, Garratt CJ, and Jones RW (1999), Sibutramine pharmacokinetics in young and elderly healthy subjects, *Eur J Clin Pharmacol*, 54(11): 847–9.

Sildenafil

Brand names: Revatio, Viagra
Classification: phosphodiesterase inhibitor
λ: 3–5 hrs
V_d: 1.5–3.5 L/kg
Usual dosage: 25–100 mg qd

Source	Therapeutic/ Nontoxic	Toxic	Lethal[a]
Blood	0.05–0.9 mg/L	No data available	6.3 mg/L
Urine	9.6 mg/L		
Bile	0.99 mg/L		
Liver	5.5 mg/kg		
Kidney	4.3 mg/kg		
Brain	6.4 mg/kg		

[a] Fatalities are associated with heart disease

Comments

- Metabolized by CYP 3A4 and 2C9
- Active metabolite: N-desmethylsildenafil

Selected Sources

Al-Ghazawi M, Tutunji M, and Aburuz S (2007), Simultaneous determination of sildenafil and N-desmethyl sildenafil in human plasma by high-performance liquid chromatography method using electrochemical detection with application to a pharmacokinetic study, *J Pharma Biomed Anal*, 43(2): 613–8.

Milligan PA, Marshall SF, and Karlsson MO (2002), A population pharmacokinetic analysis of sildenafil citrate in patients with erectile dysfunction, *Br J Clin Pharmacol*, 53(Suppl 1): 45S–52S.

Tracqui A, Miras A, Tabib A, Raul JS, Ludes B, and Malicier D (2002), Fatal overdosage with sildenafil citrate (viagra): First report and review of the literature, *Hum Exp Tox*, 21(11): 623–9.

Strychnine

Brand names: component of pesticides
Classification: plant alkaloid
λ: 10–11 hrs
V_d: 13 L/kg
Usual dosage: not applicable

Source	Therapeutic/ Nontoxic	Toxic	Lethal
Blood	None detected	0.1–4.7 mg/L	0.2–25 mg/L
Vitreous			0.36 mg/L
Urine			1–3.3 mg/L
Bile			1.2–11 mg/L
Liver			0.3–99 mg/kg
Kidney			0.5–16 mg/kg
Brain			0.86–2.4 mg/kg
Skeletal muscle			2.3 mg/kg
Cardiac muscle			16 mg/kg

Comments

- From *Strychnos nux vomica*
- Is significant at any concentration
- Causes muscular convulsions

Selected Sources

Bexar County Medical Examiner's Office data 1996–2007.

Duverneuil C, de la Grandmaison GL, de Mazancourt P, and Alvarez J-C (2004), Liquid chromatography/photodiode array detection for determination of strychnine in blood: A fatal case report, *For Sci Intl,* 141(1): 17–21.

Edmunds M, Sheehan TM, and Van't Hoff W (1986), Strychnine poisoning: Clinical and toxicological observations on a non-fatal case, *J Tox Clin Tox,* 24(3): 245–55.

Heiser JM, Daya MR, Magnussen AR, Norton RL, Spyker DA, and Allen DW (1992), Massive strychnine intoxication: Serial blood levels in a fatal case, *J Tox Clin Tox,* 30(2): 269–83.

Lindsey T, O'Hara J, Irvine R, and Kerrigan S (2004), Strychnine overdose following ingestion of gopher bait, *J Anal Tox,* 28(2): 135–7.

Marques EP, Gil F, Proenca P, Monsanto P, Oliveira MF, and Castanheira A (2000), Analytical method for the determination of strychnine in tissues by gas chromatography/mass spectrometry: Two case reports, *For Sci Intl,* 110(2): 145–52.

Palatnick W, Meatherall R, Sitar D, and Tenenbein M (1997), Toxicokinetics of acute strychnine poisoning, *J Tox Clin Tox,* 35(6): 617–20.

Rosano TG, Hubbard JD, Meola JM, and Swift TA (2000), Fatal strychnine poisoning: Application of gas chromatography and tandem mass spectrometry, *J Anal Tox,* 24(7): 642–7.

Wood D, Webster E, Martinez D, Dargan P, and Jones A (2002), Case report: Survival after deliberate strychnine self-poisoning, with toxicokinetic data, *Critical Care,* 6(5): 456–9.

Succinylcholine

Brand names: Anectine, Quelicin, Sucostrin
Classification: neuromuscular blocker
λ: 25–26 sec
V_d: 0.002–0.016 L/kg
Usual dosage: 0.3–1.1 mg/kg/dose

Source	Therapeutic/ Nontoxic	Toxic	Lethal
Blood	3.3–360 mg/L	No data available	

Comments

- Difficult to find in postmortem cases due to short half-life
- Absorbs onto glassware during storage
- Rapidly hydrolyzed to succinylmonocholine and succinic acid, both of which are found endogenously
- Therapeutic concentrations can be fatal if drug not administered in a monitored medical setting

Selected Sources

Hoshi K, Hashimoto Y, and Matsukawa S (1993), Pharmacokinetics of succinylcholine in man, *Tohoku J Exp Med*, 170(4): 245–50.

Kato M, Shiratori T, Yamamuro M, Haga S, Hoshi K, and Matsukawa S (1999), Comparison between in vivo and in vitro pharmacokinetics of succinylcholine in humans, *J Anesth*, 13(4): 189–92.

Lagerwerf AJ, Vanlinthout LE, and Vree TB (1991), Rapid determination of succinylcholine in human plasma by high-performance liquid chromatography with fluorescence detection, *J Chromatogr A*, 570(2): 390–5.

LeBeau M and Quenzer C (2003), Succinylmonocholine identified in negative control tissues, *J Anal Tox*, 27(8): 600–1.

Sufentanil

Brand names: Sufenta
Classification: narcotic
λ: 1.5–5 hrs
V_d: 0.2–2.9 L/kg
Usual dosage: 1–2 μg/kg/dose

Source	Therapeutic/ Nontoxic[a]	Toxic	Lethal
Blood	0.0005–0.1 mg/L	0.0006–0.003 mg/L	0.001–0.007 mg/L

[a] Surgical anesthesia

Comments

- Therapeutic concentrations can be fatal if drug not administered in a monitored medical setting

Selected Sources

Borenstein M, Shupak R, Barnette R, Cooney G, Johnson W, and Tzeng TB (1997), Cardiovascular effects of different infusion rates of sufentanil in patients undergoing coronary surgery, *Eur J Clin Pharmacol*, 51(5): 359–66.

Bovill JG, Sebel PS, Blackburn CL, Oei-Lim V, and Heykants JJ (1984), The pharmacokinetics of sufentanil in surgical patients, *Anesthesiology*, 61(5): 502–6.

Scholz J, Steinfath M, and Schulz M (1996), Clinical pharmacokinetics of alfentanil, fentanyl and sufentanil. An update, *Clin Pharmacokinet*, 31(4): 275–92.

Wiggum DC, Cork RC, Weldon ST, Gandolfi AJ, and Perry DS (1985), Postoperative respiratory depression and elevated sufentanil levels in a patient with chronic renal failure, *Anesthesiology*, 63(6): 708–10.

Tadalafil

Brand names: Cialis
Classification: phosphodiesterase inhibitor
λ: 16–22 hrs
V_d: 0.5–1 L/kg
Usual dosage: 5–20 mg qd

Source	Therapeutic/ Nontoxic	Toxic	Lethal
Blood	0.02–0.38 mg/L	No data available	

Selected Sources

Forgue ST, Phillips DL, Bedding AW, Payne CD, Jewell H, and Patterson BE (2007), Effects of gender, age, diabetes mellitus and renal and hepatic impairment on tadalafil pharmacokinetics, *Br J Clin Pharmacol*, 63(1): 24–35.

Mehrotra N, Gupta M, Kovar A, and Meibohm B (2007), The role of pharmacokinetics and pharmacodynamics in phosphodiesterase-5 inhibitor therapy, *Int J Impot Res*, 19(3): 253–64.

Trocóniz IF, Tillmann C, Staab A, Rapado J, and Forgue ST (2007), Tadalafil population pharmacokinetics in patients with erectile dysfunction, *Eur J Clin Pharmacol*, 63(6): 583–90.

Temazepam

Brand names: Restoril
Classification: benzodiazepine
λ: 7–25 hrs
V_d: 0.5–1.2 L/kg
Usual dosage: 7.5–30 mg qHS

Source	Therapeutic/ Nontoxic	Toxic	Lethal
Blood	0.1–0.8 mg/L	1 mg/L	2.9–9 mg/L
Urine			2.3 mg/L
Liver			39–107 mg/kg
Skeletal muscle	0.5–0.6 mg/kg		3.0–8.8 mg/kg

Comments

- Active metabolite: oxazepam
- Metabolite of nordiazepam
- Tolerance can develop and should be considered when interpreting drug concentrations

Selected Sources

Bexar County Medical Examiner's Office data 1996–2007.

Bittencourt P, Richens A, Toseland PA, Wicks JF, and Latham AN (1979), Pharmacokinetics of the hypnotic benzodiazepine, temazepam, *Br J Clin Pharmacol*, 8(1): 37S–38S.

Forrest AR, Marsh I, Bradshaw C, and Braich SK (1986), Fatal temazepam overdoses, *Lancet*, 2: 226.

Langford AM, Taylor KK, and Pounder DJ (1998), Drug concentration in selected skeletal muscles, *J For Sci*, 43(1): 22–7.

Martin CD and Chan SC (1986), Distribution of temazepam in body fluids and tissues in lethal overdose, *J Anal Tox*, 10(2): 77–8.

Williams KR and Pounder DJ (1997), Site-to-site variability of drug concentrations in skeletal muscle, *Am J For Med Path*, 18(3): 246–50.

Terbutaline

Brand names: Brethine
Classification: β-agonist
λ: 2.5–4.5 hrs
V_d: 0.6–1.1 L/kg
Usual dosage: 2.5–5 mg tid

Source	Therapeutic/ Nontoxic	Toxic	Lethal
Blood	0.002–0.009 mg/L	0.2 mg/L	0.04 mg/L
Liver	0.009–0.05 mg/kg		
Kidney	0.05 mg/kg		
Skeletal muscle	0.06 mg/kg		
Cardiac muscle	0.004–0.04 mg/kg		

Selected Sources

Heath A and Hultén BA (1987), Terbutaline concentrations in self-poisoning: A case report, *Hum Tox*, 6(6): 525–6.

Leferink JG, van den Berg W, Wagemaker-Engels I, Kreukniet J, and Maes RA (1982), Pharmacokinetics of terbutaline, a beta 2-sympathomimetic, in healthy volunteers and asthmatic patients, *Drug Res/Arzneimittel-Forschung*, 32(2): 159–64.

Leferink JG, Wagemaker-Engels I, Maes RA, and Van der Straeten M (1979), Determination of terbutaline in post mortem human tissues by gas chromatography-mass spectrometry, *Vet Hum Tox*, 21 Suppl: 164–7.

Lyrenäs S, Grahnén A, Lindberg B, Lindström B, and Lönnerholm G (1986), Pharmacokinetics of terbutaline during pregnancy, *Eur J Clin Pharmacol*, 29(5): 619–23.

Tetrahydrocannabinol

Brand names: Marinol (dronabinol, synthetic THC)
Alternate names: Δ^9THC, THC
Street names: Pot, Weed, Grass, Mary Jane, Dope, Doobie, Hashish, Hash
Classification: cannabinoid/psychoactive
λ: 2–57 hrs
V_d: 1–10 L/kg
Usual dosage: 10–30 mg/dose

Source	Therapeutic/Nontoxic	Toxic	Lethal
Blood	0.05–0.27 mg/L THC 0.02–0.1 mg/L 11-OH-THC	0.18 mg/L THC	
Urine	0.003–0.05 mg/L THC 0.02–0.08 mg/L 11-OH-THC 0.04–0.18 mg/L THC COOH		
Liver			37 mg/kg THC
Kidney			42 mg/kg THC

Comments

- Active ingredient in *Cannabis*
- Metabolized to active 11-OH-THC (hydroxy-THC; λ 12–36 hrs) and inactive THC-COOH (carboxy-THC; λ 1–6 dys)
- Metabolized by CYP 2C9
- May be associated with sudden cardiac death and coronary artery disease

Selected Sources

André C, Jaber-Filho JA, Bento RMQ, Damasceno LMP, and Aquino-Neto FR (2006), Delirium following ingestion of marijuana present in chocolate cookies, *CNS Spectrums*, 11(4): 262–4.

Garrett CP, Braithwaite RA, and Teale JD (1977), Unusual case of tetrahydrocannabinol intoxication confirmed by radioimmunoassay, *Br Med J*, 2: 166.

Gaziano JM (2008), Marijuana use among those at risk for cardiovascular events, *Am Heart J*, 155: 395–396.

Grotenhermen F (2003), Pharmacokinetics and pharmacodynamics of cannabinoids, *Clin Pharmacokinet*, 42(4): 327–60.

Hunt CA and Jones RT (1980), Tolerance and disposition of tetrahydrocannabinol in man, *J Pharmacol Exp Ther*, 215(1): 35–44.

Kauert GF, Ramaekers JG, Schneider E, Moeller MR, and Toennes SW (2007), Pharmacokinetic properties of delta9-tetrahydrocannabinol in serum and oral fluid, *J Anal Tox*, 31(5): 288–93.

Law B (1981), Cases of cannabis abuse detected by analysis of body fluids, *For Sci Soc J*, 21(1): 31–9.

Tewari SN and Sharma JD (1980), Detection of delta-9-tetrahydrocannabinol in the organs of a suspected case of cannabis poisoning, *Tox Letters*, 5(3–4): 279–81.

Thallium

Brand names: component of some pesticides/insecticides
Classification: metal
λ: 3–30 dys
V_d: 3.6 L/kg
Usual dosage: not applicable

Source	Therapeutic/ Nontoxic	Toxic	Lethal
Blood	0.002–0.08 mg/L	0.1–2.4 mg/L	0.5–11 mg/L
Urine	0.15–0.2 mg/L	0.2–26 mg/L	1.7–245 mg/L
Bile			11 mg/L
Liver	0.001–0.19 mg/kg		3.1–54 mg/kg
Kidney	0.001–0.08 mg/kg		2.9–37 mg/kg
Brain	0.001–0.02 mg/kg		5.2–55 mg/kg
Skeletal muscle			5.9–13 mg/kg
Cardiac muscle			3.7–13 mg/kg

Selected Sources

Berman E (1980), *Toxic Metals and Their Analysis*, Heyden, Philadelphia.

de Groot G, van Leusen R, and van Heijst AN (1985), Thallium concentrations in body fluids and tissues in a fatal case of thallium poisoning, *Vet Hum Tox*, 27(2): 115–9.

Desenclos JC, Wilder MH, Coppenger GW, Sherin K, Tiller R, and VanHook RM (1992), Thallium poisoning: An outbreak in Florida, 1988, *South Med J*, 85(12): 1203–6.

Grunfeld O and Hinostroza O (1964), Thallium poisoning, *Arch Int Med*, 114: 132–8.

Heath A, Ahlmén J, Branegård B, Lindstedt S, Wickström I, and Andersen O (1983), Thallium poisoning—Toxin elimination and therapy in three cases, *J Tox Clin Tox*, 20(5): 451–63.

Herrero F, Fernandez E, Gomez J, Pretel L, Canizares F, and Frias J (1995), Thallium poisoning presenting with abdominal colic, paresthesia, and irritability, *J Tox Clin Tox*, 33(3): 261–4.

Hologgitas J, Ullucci P, Driscoll J, Grauerholz J, and Martin H (1980), Thallium elimination kinetics in acute thallotoxicosis, *J Anal Tox*, 4(2): 68–75.

Knight B (1991), *Forensic Pathology*, Oxford University Press, New York, p. 532.

Malbrain ML, Lambrecht GL, Zandijk E, Demedts PA, Neels HM, and Lambert W (1997), Treatment of severe thallium intoxication, *J Tox Clin Tox*, 35(1): 97–100.

Meggs WJ, Hoffman RS, Shih RD, Weisman RS, and Goldfrank LR (1994), Thallium poisoning from maliciously contaminated food, *J Tox Clin Tox*, 32(6): 723–30.

Richelmi P, Bono F, Guardia L, Ferrini B, and Manzo L (1980), Salivary levels of thallium in acute human poisoning, *Arch Tox*, 43(4): 321–5.

Singh NP, Bogden JD, and Joselow MM (1975), Distribution of thallium and lead in children's blood, *Arch Environ Health*, 30(11): 557–8.

Smith DH and Doherty RA (1964), Thallitoxicosis: Report of three cases in Massachusetts, *Pediatrics*, 34: 480–90.

Vrij AA, Cremers HM, and Lustermans FA (1995), Successful recovery of a patient with thallium poisoning, *Netherlands J Med*, 47(3): 121–6.

Theophylline

Brand names: Quibron-T, Slo-phyllin, Senophylline, Theo-24, Theo-Dur, Slo-bid
Classification: bronchodilator
λ: 3–13 hrs
V_d: 0.3–0.7 L/kg
Usual dosage: 100–300 mg q 6–8 hrs

Source	Therapeutic/ Nontoxic	Toxic	Lethal
Blood	1–20 mg/L	31–170 mg/L	80–290 mg/L
Urine		320–498 mg/L	
Bile			275 mg/L
Liver			108–200 mg/kg
Kidney			212 mg/kg
Brain			231 mg/kg
Stomach contents			704 mg

Comments

- Metabolized by CYP 1A2 and 2E1

Selected Sources

Anderson JR, Poklis A, and Slavin RG (1983), A fatal case of theophylline intoxication, *Arch Int Med*, 143(3): 559–60.

Baltassat P, Hartmann E, Bory C, and Frederich A (1979), Theophylline acute poisoning in a child: Evidence for biotransformation of theophylline into caffeine, *Vet Hum Tox*, 21 Suppl: 211–3.

Bexar County Medical Examiner's Office data 1996–2007.

Burgan TH, Gupta I, and Bate CM (1982), Fatal overdose of theophylline simulating acute pancreatitis, *Br Med J (Clin Res Ed)*, 284: 939.

Druid H and Holmgren P (1997), A compilation of fatal and control concentrations of drugs in postmortem femoral blood, *J For Sci*, 42(1): 79–87.

Ehlers SM, Zaske DE, and Sawchuk RJ (1978), Massive theophylline overdose: Rapid elimination by charcoal hemoperfusion, *JAMA*, 240(5): 474–5.

Gitomer JJ, Khan AM, and Ferris ME (2001), Treatment of severe theophylline toxicity with hemodialysis in a preterm neonate, *Pediatr Nephrol*, 16(10): 784–6.

Korsheed S, Selby NM, and Fluck RJ (2007), Treatment of severe theophylline poisoning with the molecular adsorbent recirculating system (MARS), *Nephrol Dial Transplant*, 22(3): 969–70.

Physicians' Desk Reference 60 Edition (2006), Thomson PDR, Montvale, NJ, pp. 2708–14.

Rose C (1979), Theophylline toxicity, *Western J Med*, 130(5): 466–7.
Rutten J, van den Berg B, van Gelder T, and van Saase J (2005), Severe theophylline intoxication: A delay in charcoal haemoperfusion solved by oral activated charcoal, *Nephrol Dial Transplant*, 20(12): 2868–9.
Tsokos M and Sperhake JP (2002), Coma blisters in a case of fatal theophylline intoxication, *Am J For Med Path*, 23(3): 292–4.
Winek CL, Bricker JD, Collom WD, and Fochtman FW (1980), Theophylline fatalities, *For Sci Int*, 15(3): 233–6.

Thiopental

Brand names: Pentothal
Classification: barbiturate
λ: 3–11 hrs
V_d: 0.4–4 L/kg
Usual dosage: 25–250 mg/dose

Source	Therapeutic/ Nontoxic	Toxic	Lethal
Blood	3–50 mg/L[a]	8–10 mg/L	11–279 mg/L
Urine			13 mg/L
Liver			32–114 mg/kg
Kidney			16–41 mg/kg
Brain			3.3–22 mg/kg
Skeletal muscle			5.4–55 mg/kg
Cardiac muscle			5–64 mg/kg

[a] Therapeutic concentrations during surgical anesthesia

Comments

- Active metabolite: pentobarbital
- Therapeutic concentrations can be fatal if drug not administered in a monitored medical setting

Selected Sources

Backer RC (1975), Thiopental suicide—Case report, *J Tox Clin Tox*, 8(3): 283–7.
Bruce AM, Oliver JS, and Smith H (1977), A suicide by thiopentone injection, *For Sci*, 9(3): 205–7.
Campbell JE (1960), Deaths associated with anesthesia, *J For Sci*, 5: 501–49.
Christensen JH, Andreasen F, and Jansen JA (1981), Influence of age and sex on the pharmacokinetics of thiopentone, *Br J Anaesth*, 53(11): 1189–95.
Druid H and Holmgren P (1997), A compilation of fatal and control concentrations of drugs in postmortem femoral blood, *J For Sci*, 42(1): 79–87.
Fernando GC (1990), A suicide by thiopentone infusion, *Am J For Med Path*, 11(4): 309–11.
Winek CL, Collom WD, and Davis ER (1969), Death from rectal thiopental, *J Tox Clin Tox*, 2: 75–9.

Thioridazine

Brand names: Mellaril
Classification: antipsychotic
λ: 7–36 hrs
V_d: 18 L/kg
Usual dosage: 20–200 mg bid/tid/qid

Source	Therapeutic/ Nontoxic	Toxic	Lethal
Blood	0.1–0.73 mg/L	2.4–12 mg/L	1.8–28 mg/L
Urine			5–236 mg/L
Liver	3–7 mg/kg		25–513 mg/kg
Kidney			18–135 mg/kg
Brain			6.4 mg/kg
Skeletal muscle	0.3–1.4 mg/kg		

Comments

- Active metabolite: mesoridazine
- Metabolized by CYP 2D6
- Prolongs QT interval
- Causes agranulocytosis and hepatitis

Selected Sources

Baselt RC, Wright JA, and Gross EM (1978), Human tissue distribution of thioridazine during therapy and after poisoning, *J Anal Tox*, 2: 41–43.

Bexar County Medical Examiner's Office data 1996–2007.

Bonnichsen R, Geertinger P, and Maehly AC (1970), Toxicological data on phenothiazine drugs in autopsy cases, *Zeitschrift für Rechtsmedizin*, 67(3): 158–69.

Burgess KR, Jefferis RW, and Stevenson IF (1979), Fatal thioridazine cardiotoxicity, *Med J Australia*, 2(4): 177–8.

Caplan YH, Ottinger WE, and Crooks CR (1983), Therapeutic and toxic drug concentrations in post mortem blood: A six year study in the State of Maryland, *J Anal Tox*, 7(5): 225–30.

Donlon PT and Tupin JP (1977), Successful suicides with thioridazine and mesoridazine: A result of probable cardiotoxicity, *Arch Gen Psychiatry*, 34(8): 955–7.

Druid H and Holmgren P (1997), A compilation of fatal and control concentrations of drugs in postmortem femoral blood, *J For Sci*, 42(1):7 9–87.

Joubert PH, Olivier JA (1974), Fatal suicidal ingestion of thioridazine, *Clin Tox*, 7(2): 133–8.

Langford AM, Taylor KK, and Pounder DJ (1998), Drug concentration in selected skeletal muscles, *J For Sci*, 43(1): 22–7.

Murray LM, Hackett LP, and Hett KF (2001),Delayed absorption and peak cardiotoxicity following massive thioridazine overdose, *Clin Tox*, 39(5): 493–4.

Poklis A, Wells CE, and Juenge EC (1982), Thioridazine and its metabolites in post-mortem blood, including two stereoisomeric ring sulfoxides, *J Anal Tox*, 6(5): 250–2.
Tompsett SL (1968), The spectrofluorimetric determination of phenothiazine drugs in blood serum, *Acta Pharmacologica et Toxicologica*, 26(4): 298–302.
Weiden PL and Buckner CD (1973), Thioridazine toxicity: Agranulocytosis and hepatitis with encephalopathy, *JAMA*, 224(4): 518–20.

Thiothixene

Brand names: Navane
Classification: antipsychotic
λ: 16–35 hrs
V_d: unknown
Usual dosage: 2–20 mg tid/bid/qd

Source	Therapeutic/ Nontoxic	Toxic	Lethal
Blood	0.003–0.06 mg/L	0.05–0.5 mg/L	0.09 mg/L
Urine		9 mg/L	

Selected Sources

Hobbs DC, Welch WM, Short MJ, Moody WA, and Van der Velde CD (1974), Pharmacokinetics of thiothixene in man, *Clin Pharm Ther*, 16(3): 473–8.
Kemal M and Imami RH (1985), Acute thiothixene overdose, *J Anal Tox*, 9(2): 94–5.
Yesavage JA, Becker J, Werner PD, Mills MJ, Holman CA, and Cohn R (1982), Serum level monitoring of thiothixene in schizophrenia: Acute single-dose levels at fixed doses, *Am J Psychiatry*, 139(2): 174–8.

Tiagabine

Brand names: Gabitril
Classification: anticonvulsant
λ: 5–8 hrs
V_d: 0.5–1.8 L/kg
Usual dosage: 2–24 mg bid

Source	Therapeutic/ Nontoxic	Toxic	Lethal
Blood	0.04–0.5 mg/L	0.4–4.6 mg/L	7–9 mg/L

Comments

- Metabolized by CYP 3A

Selected Sources

Forbes RA, Kalra H, Hackett LP, and Daly FFS (2007), Deliberate self-poisoning with tiagabine: An unusual toxidrome, *Emer Med Australasia*, 19(6): 556–8.

Fulton JA, Hoffman RS, and Nelson LS (2005), Tiagabine overdose: A case of status epilepticus in a non-epileptic patient, *Clin Tox*, 43(7): 869–71.

Gustavson LE and Mengel HB (1995), Pharmacokinetics of tiagabine, a γ-aminobutyric acid-uptake inhibitor, in healthy subjects after single and multiple doses, *Epilepsia*, 36(6): 605–11.

Kazzi ZN, Jones CC, and Morgan BW (2006), Seizures in a pediatric patient with a tiagabine overdose, *J Med Tox*, 2(4): 160–2.

Leach JP, Stolarek I, and Brodie MJ (1995), Deliberate overdose with the novel anticonvulsant tiagabine, *Seizure*, 4(2): 155–7.

Ostrovskiy D, Spanaki MV, and Morris GL (2002), Tiagabine overdose can induce convulsive status epilepticus, *Epilepsia*, 43(7): 773–4.

Viner,K, Clifton JC, and Hryhorczuk DO (1999), Status epilepticus following acute tiagabine overdose, *Clin Tox*, 37(5): 638.

Toluene

Brand names: component of paints, adhesives, solvents
Alternate names: methylbenzene, phenylmethane
Classification: volatile (aromatic hydrocarbon)
λ: 1–18 hrs
V_d: 7–72 L/kg
Usual dosage: not applicable

Source	Therapeutic/ Nontoxic	Toxic	Lethal
Blood	0.00001–1 mg/L	0.2–74 mg/L	1–114 mg/L
Urine		0.01–22 mg/L	0.15 mg/L
Liver			3.6–433 mg/kg
Kidney			39 mg/kg
Brain			19–740 mg/kg
Lung			6.6–100 mg/kg
Cardiac muscle			63 mg/kg
Adipose tissue			12 mg/kg

Comments

- Cardiotoxic: intoxication associated with arrhythmias
- Metabolized to benzoic acid

Selected Sources

Ameno K, Fuke C, Ameno S, Kiriu T, Sogo K, and Ijiri I (1989), A fatal case of oral ingestion of toluene, *For Sci Intl*, 41(3): 255–60.

Bexar County Medical Examiner's Office data 1996–2007.

Brugnone F, Perbellini L, Apostoli P, Locatelli M, and Mariotto P (1983), Decline of blood and alveolar toluene concentration following two accidental human poisonings, *Intl Arch Occup Environ Health*, 53(2): 157–65.

Collom WD and Winek CL (1970), Detection of glue constitutents in fatalities due toglue sniffing, *Clin Tox*, 3(1): 125–30.

Hobara T, Okuda M, Gotoh M, Oki K, Segawa H, and Kunitsugu I (2000), Estimation of the lethal toluene concentration from the accidental death of painting workers, *Ind Health*, 38(2): 228–31.

Knight B (1991), Chapter 34, Deaths for organic solvents, in *Forensic Pathology*, Oxford University Press. New York, pp. 533–6.

Musshoff F, Padosch SA, Kroener LA, and Madea B (2006), Accidental autoerotic death by volatile substance abuse or nonsexually motivated accidents?, *Am J For Med Path*, 27(2): 188–92.

Park SW, Kim N, Yang Y, Seo B, and Paeng KJ (1998), Toluene distribution of glue sniffers' biological fluid samples in Korea, *J For Sci*, 43(4): 888–90.

Sato A, Nakajima T, Fujiwara Y, and Hirosawa K (1974), Pharmacokinetics of benzene and toluene, *Intl Arch Occup Health*, 33(3): 169–82.

Stephens BG (2004), Chapter XXII, Investigation of deaths from drug abuse, in *Spitz and Fisher's Medicolegal Investigation of Death Fourth Edition*, Spitz WU (Ed.), Charles C Thomas, Springfield, IL, pp. 1166–217.

Takeichi S, Yamada T, and Shikata I (1986), Acute toluene poisoning during painting, *For Sci Intl*, 32(2): 109–15.

Topiramate

Brand names: Topamax
Classification: anticonvulsant
λ: 19–25 hrs
V_d: 0.6–0.8 L/kg
Usual dosage: 50–400 mg bid

Source	Therapeutic/ Nontoxic	Toxic	Lethal
Blood	1.7–5 mg/L	4.2–10 mg/L	36–170 mg/L
Vitreous			65 mg/L
Liver			140 mg/kg
Stomach contents			>300 mg

Selected Sources

Easterling DE, Zakzewski T, and Moyer MD (1988), Plasma pharmacokinetics of topiramate, a new anticonvulsant in humans, *Epilepsia*, 29: 662.

Langman LJ, Kaliciak HA, and Boone SA (2003), Fatal acute topiramate toxicity, *J Anal Tox*, 27(5): 323–4.

Lin G and Lawrence R (2006), Pediatric case report of topiramate toxicity, *J Tox Clin Tox*, 44(1): 67–9.

Perucca E (1996), Pharmacokinetic profile of topiramate in comparison with other new antiepileptic drugs, *Epilepsia*, 37(Suppl. 2): S8–S13.

Sachdeo RC, Sachdeo SK, Walker SA, Kramer LD, Nayak RK, and Doose DR (1996), Steady-state pharmacokinetics of topiramate and carbamazepine in patients with epilepsy during monotherapy and concomitant therapy, *Epilepsia*, 37(8): 774–80.

Tomson T and Johannessen SI (2000), Therapeutic monitoring of the new antiepileptic drugs, *Eur J Clin Pharm*, 55(10): 697–705.

Traub SJ, Howland MA, Hoffman RS, and Nelson LS (2003), Acute topiramate toxicity, *J Tox Clin Tox*, 41(7): 987–90.

Tramadol

Brand names: Ultram, Ultracet (w/ aceta)
Classification: narcotic
λ: 4.5–7.5 hrs
V_d: 2.3–3.9 L/kg
Usual dosage: 50–100 mg q 4–6 hrs

Source	Therapeutic/ Nontoxic	Toxic	Lethal
Blood	0.1–0.8 mg/L	1–24 mg/L	1.3–20 mg/L
Urine	30 mg/L		46–110 mg/L
Bile	0.31 mg/L		46 mg/L
Liver	0.3 mg/kg		6.2–69 mg/kg
Kidney	0.4 mg/kg		3.1–37 mg/kg

Comments

- Active metabolites: *O*-desmethyltramadol and *N*-desmethyltramadol
- Metabolized by CYP 2D6
- Tolerance may develop and should be considered when interpreting drug concentrations

Selected Sources

Bexar County Medical Examiner's Office data 1996–2007.

Daubin C, Quentin C, Goullé JP, Guillotin D, Lehoux P, and Lepage O (2007), Refractory shock and asystole related to tramadol overdose, *Clin Tox*, 45(8): 961–4.

De Decker K, Cordonnier J, Jacobs W, Coucke V, Schepens P, and Jorens PG (2008), Fatal intoxication due to tramadol alone: Case report and review of the literature, *For Sci Intl*, 175(1): 79–82.

Goeringer KE, Logan BK, and Christian GD (1997), Identification of tramadol and its metabolites in blood from drug-related deaths and drug-impaired drivers, *J Anal Tox*, 21(7): 529–37.

Levine B, Ramcharitar V, and Smialek JE (1997), Tramadol distribution in four postmortem cases, *For Sci Intl*, 86(1–2): 43–8.

Loughrey MB, Loughrey CM, Johnston S, and O'Rourke D (2003), Fatal hepatic failure following accidental tramadol overdose, *For Sci Intl*, 134(2–3): 232–3.

Lusthof KJ and Zweipfenning PG (1998), Suicide by tramadol overdose, *J Anal Tox*, 22(3): 260.

Moore KA, Cina SJ, Jones R, Selby DM, Levine B, and Smith ML (1999), Tissue distribution of tramadol and metabolites in an overdose fatality, *Am J For Med Path*, 20(1): 98–100.

Musshoff F and Madea B (2001), Fatality due to ingestion of tramadol alone, *For Sci Intl*, 116(2–3): 197–9.

Sindrup SH, Madsen C, Brøsen K, and Jensen TS (1999), The effect of tramadol in painful polyneuropathy in relation to serum drug and metabolite levels, *Clin Pharm Ther*, 66(6): 636–41.

Trazodone

Brand names: Desyrel
Classification: antidepressant
λ: 3–9 hrs
V_d: 0.9–1.5 L/kg
Usual dosage: 50–300 mg bid

Source	Therapeutic/ Nontoxic	Toxic	Lethal
Blood	0.5–1.6 mg/L	1.5–26 mg/L	5–25 mg/L
Liver			26–82 mg/kg
Kidney			40 mg/kg
Brain			21 mg/kg
Skeletal muscle			6.6–9 mg/kg

Comments

- Active metabolite: m-chlorophenylpiperazine
- Metabolized by CYP 3A4
- May prolong QT interval

Selected Sources

Ankier SI, Martin BK, Rogers MS, Carpenter PK, and Graham C (1981), Trazodone—A new assay procedure and some pharmacokinetic parameters, *Br J Clin Pharmacol*, 11(5): 505–9.

Bexar County Medical Examiner's Office data 1996–2007.

de Meester A, Carbutti G, Gabriel L, and Jacques JM (2001), Fatal overdose with trazodone: Case report and literature review, *Acta Clinica Belgica*, 56(4): 258–61.

Flanagan RJ (1998), Guidelines for the interpretation of analytical toxicology results and unit of measurement conversion factors, *Ann Clin Biochem*, 35: 261–7.

Greenblatt DJ, Friedman H, Burstein ES, Scavone JM, Blyden GT, and Ochs HR (1987), Trazodone kinetics: Effect of age, gender, and obesity, *Clin Pharm Ther*, 42(2): 193–200.

Henry JA, Ali CJ, Caldwell R, and Flanagan RJ (1984), Acute trazodone poisoning: Clinical signs and plasma concentrations, *Psychopathology*, 17(Suppl. 2): 77–81.

Lesar T, Kingston R, Dahms R, and Saxena K (1983), Trazodone overdose, *Ann Emer Med*, 12(4): 221–3.

Martin A and Pounder DJ (1992), Post-mortem toxico-kinetics of trazodone, *For Sci Intl*, 56(2): 201–7.

Martínez MA, Ballesteros S, de la Torre CS, and Almarza E (2005), Investigation of a fatality due to trazodone poisoning: Case report and literature review, *J Anal Tox*, 29(4): 262–8.

Root I and Ohlson GB (1984), Trazodone overdose: Report of two cases, *J Anal Tox*, 8(2): 91–4.

Triazolam

Brand names: Halcion
Classification: benzodiazepine
λ: 1.1–4.4 hrs
V_d: 1.1–2.7 L/kg
Usual dosage: 0.125–0.25 mg qHS

Source	Therapeutic/ Nontoxic	Toxic	Lethal
Blood	0.002–0.02 mg/L	0.004–0.04 mg/L	0.01–0.4 mg/L
Urine			0.24 mg/L
Bile			1.1 mg/L
Liver			0.09–0.4 mg/kg
Kidney			0.07–0.25 mg/kg

Comments

- Active metabolites: 1-methyl-hydroxy-triazolam and 4-hydroxy-triazolam
- Metabolized by CYP 3A
- Tolerance can develop and should be considered when interpreting drug concentrations

Selected Sources

Bexar County Medical Examiner's Office data 1996–2007.

Friedman H, Greenblatt DJ, Burstein ES, Harmatz JS, and Shader RI (1986), Population study of triazolam pharmacokinetics, *Br J Clin Pharmacol*, 22(6): 639–42.

Joynt BP (1993), Triazolam blood concentrations in forensic cases in Canada, *J Anal Tox*, 17(3): 171–7.

Levine B, Grieshaber A, Pestaner J, Moore KA, and Smialek JE (2002), Distribution of triazolam and alpha-hydroxytriazolam in a fatal intoxication case, *J Anal Tox*, 26(1): 52–4.

Moriya F and Hashimoto Y (2003), A case of fatal triazolam overdose, *Legal Med*, 5(Suppl. 1): S91–5.

Olson KR, Yin L, Osterloh J, and Tani A (1985), Coma caused by trivial triazolam overdose, *Am J Emer Med*, 3(3): 210–1.

Steentoft A and Worm K (1993), Cases of fatal triazolam poisoning, *For Sci Soc J*, 33(1): 45–8.

Sunter JP, Bal TS, and Cowan WK (1988), Three cases of fatal triazolam poisoning, *Br Med J*, 297: 719.

Trichloroethane

Brand names: component of correction fluid
Alternate names: methylchloroform
Classification: volatile (halogenated hydrocarbon)
λ: unknown
V_d: unknown
Usual dosage: not applicable

Source	Therapeutic/ Nontoxic	Toxic	Lethal
Blood	0.0001–0.02 mg/L	No data available	0.1–720 mg/L
Urine			1 mg/L
Bile			10 mg/L
Liver			4.9–220 mg/kg
Kidney			2.6–120 mg/kg
Brain			3.2–1230 mg/kg
Lung			1.8–22 mg/kg
Skeletal muscle			2.6–49 mg/kg

Comments

- Cardiotoxic: intoxication associated with arrhythmias

Selected Sources

Caplan YH, Backer RC, and Whitaker JQ (1976), 1,1,1-Trichloroethane: Report of a fatal intoxication, *Clin Tox*, 9(1): 69–74.

Hajimiragha H, Ewers U, Jansen-Rosseck R, and Brockhaus A (1986), Human exposure to volatile halogenated hydrocarbons from the general environment, *Intl Arch Occup Environ Health* 58(2): 141–50.

Hall FB and Hine CH (1966), Trichloroethane intoxication: A report of two cases, *J For Sci*, 11(3): 404–13.

Johns DO, Daniell WE, Shen DD, Kalman DA, Dills RL, and Morgan MS (2006), Ethanol-induced increase in the metabolic clearance of 1,1,1-trichloroethane in human volunteers, *Toxicol Sci*, 92(1): 61–70.

Jones RD and Winter DP (1983), Two case reports of deaths on industrial premises attributed to 1,1,1-trichloroethane, *Arch Environ Health*, 38(1): 59–61.

Knight B (1991), Chapter 34, Deaths for organic solvents, in *Forensic Pathology*, Oxford University Press, New York, pp. 533–6.

Stahl CJ, Fatteh AV, and Dominguez AM (1969), Trichloroethane poisoning: Observations on the pathology and toxicology in six fatal cases, *J For Sci*, 14(3): 393–7.

Stephens BG (2004), Chapter XXII, Investigation of deaths from drug abuse, in *Spitz and Fisher's Medicolegal Investigation of Death Fourth Edition*, Spitz WU (Ed.), Charles C Thomas, Springfield, IL, pp. 1166–217.

Trichloroethylene

Brand names: component of dry cleaning chemicals, solvents
Alternate names: trichloroethene, TCE
Classification: volatile (halogenated hydrocarbon)
λ: 22–50 hrs
V_d: unknown
Usual dosage: not applicable

Source	Therapeutic/ Nontoxic	Toxic	Lethal
Blood	0.0001–2.2 mg/L	31 mg/L	1.1–210 mg/L
Urine			<5 mg/L
Bile			4.5–104 mg/L
Liver			2.5–747 mg/kg
Kidney			12–78 mg/kg
Brain			32–809 mg/kg
Lung			9.3–21 mg/kg

Comments

- Can cause arrhythmias and seizures

Selected Sources

Brüning T, Vamvakas S, Makropoulos V, and Birner G (1998), Acute intoxication with trichloroethene: Clinical symptoms, toxicokinetics, metabolism, and development of biochemical parameters for renal damage, *Toxicol Sci*, 41(2): 157–65.
Coopman VAE, Cordonnier JACM, De Letter EA, and Piette MHA (2003), Tissue distribution of trichloroethylene in a case of accidental acute intoxication by inhalation, *For Sci Intl*, 134(2–3): 115–9.
De Baere S, Meyer E, Dirinck I, Lambert W, Piette M, and Van Peteghem C (1997), Tissue distribution of trichloroethylene and its metabolites in a forensic case, *J Anal Tox*, 21(3): 223–7.
Ford ES, Rhodes S, McDiarmid M, Schwartz SL, and Brown J (1995), Deaths from acute exposure to trichloroethylene, *J Occup Environ Med*, 37(6): 749–54.
Ikeda M (1977), Metabolism of trichloroethylene and tetrachloroethylene in human subjects, *Environ Health Perspect*, 21: 239–45.
Jones GR and Singer PP (2008), An unusual trichloroethanol fatality attributed to sniffing trichloroethylene, *J Anal Tox*, 32(2): 183–6.
Kleinfeld M (1954), Trichloroethylene toxicity, *Arch Ind Hyg Occup Med*, 10:134.
Pleil JD, Fisher JW, and Lindstrom AB (1998), Trichloroethene levels in human blood and exhaled breath from controlled inhalation exposure, *Environ Health Perspect*, 106(9): 573–80.

Stephens BG (2004), Chapter XXII, Investigation of deaths from drug abuse, in *Spitz and Fisher's Medicolegal Investigation of Death Fourth Edition*, Spitz WU (Ed.), Charles C Thomas, Springfield, IL, pp. 1166–217.

Yoshida M, Fukabori S, Hara K, Yuasa H, Nakaaki K, and Yamamura Y (1996), Concentrations of trichloroethylene and its metabolites in blood and urine after acute poisoning by ingestion, *Hum Exp Tox*, 15(3): 254–8.

Trifluoperazine

Brand names: Stelazine
Classification: antipsychotic
λ: 7–18 hrs
V_d: unknown
Usual dosage: 2–20 mg bid/qd

Source	Therapeutic/ Nontoxic	Toxic	Lethal
Blood	0.0003–0.05 mg/L	0.3–2.1 mg/L	0.4 mg/L
Liver			198 mg/kg
Kidney			83 mg/kg

Comments

- May prolong the QT interval

Selected Sources

Midha KK, Hawes EM, Hubbard JW, Korchinski ED, and McKay G (1988), A pharmacokinetic study of trifluoperazine in two ethnic populations, *Psychopharmacology*, 95(3): 333–8.
Qual I, Fagarasan M, and Fagarasan E (1985), A fatal case of trifluoperazine poisoning, *J Anal Tox*, 9(1): 43–4.
Tompsett SL (1968), The spectrofluorimetric determination of phenothiazine drugs in blood serum, *Acta Pharmacologica et Toxicologica*, 26(4): 298–302.

Trimeprazine

Brand names: Panectyl, Vellergan, Alimezine, Temaril-P (w/ prednisolone, veterinary)
Classification: antihistamine
λ: 4–18 hrs
V_d: unknown
Usual dosage: 5–40 mg qd

Source	Therapeutic/ Nontoxic	Toxic	Lethal
Blood	0.0008–0.4 mg/L	No data available	0.5–6.5 mg/L
Urine			6.2 mg/L
Bile			4.4 mg/L
Liver			19 mg/kg
Kidney			19 mg/kg
Brain			20 mg/kg
Skeletal muscle			1.4 mg/kg
Cardiac muscle			17 mg/kg
Stomach contents			80 mg/L

Selected Sources

Glover WJ, Hatch DJ, and Sumner E (1992), Trimeprazine premedication in children, *Anaesthesia*, 47(5): 441–2.

Hu OY, Gfeller E, Perrin JH, and Curry SH (1986), Relative bioavailability of trimeprazine tablets investigated in man using HPLC with electrochemical detection, *J Pharm Pharmacol*, 38(3): 172–6.

Kintz P, Berthault F, Tracqui A, and Mangin P (1995), A fatal case of alimemazine poisoning, *J Anal Tox*, 19(7): 591–4.

Sponheim S, Aune H, Gulliksen M, and Mørland J (1990), Pharmacokinetics of trimeprazine in children, *Pharm Tox*, 67(3): 243–5.

Trimipramine

Brand names: Surmontil
Classification: antidepressant (TCA)
λ: 16–39 hrs
V_d: 17–48 L/kg
Usual dosage: 50–100 mg qHS

Source	Therapeutic/ Nontoxic	Toxic	Lethal
Blood	0.01–0.3 mg/L	0.5–1 mg/L	1.8–9.6 mg/L
Urine			0.6 mg/L
Liver			51 mg/kg

Comments

- Active metabolite: desmethyl-trimipramine
- May prolong QT interval

Selected Sources

Abernathy DR, Greenblatt DJ, and Shader RI (1984), Trimipramine kinetics and absolute bioavailability: Use of gas-liquid chromatography with nitrogen-phosphorus detection, *Clin Pharm Ther*, 35(3): 348–53.
Bexar County Medical Examiner's Office data 1996–2007.
Druid H and Holmgren P (1997), A compilation of fatal and control concentrations of drugs in postmortem femoral blood, *J For Sci*, 42(1):79–87.
Druid H and Holmgren P (1991), Fatal seizures associated with trimipramine poisoning, *For Sci Intl*, 49(1): 75–9.
Fraser AD, Isner AF, and Perry RA (1987), Distribution of trimipramine and its major metabolites in a fatal overdose case, *J Anal Tox*, 11(4): 168–70.

Tripelennamine

Brand names: Pyribenzamine
Classification: antihistamine
λ: 3–8 hrs
V_d: 9–12 L/kg
Usual dosage: 25–100 mg q 4–6 hrs

Source	Therapeutic/ Nontoxic	Toxic	Lethal
Blood	0.005–0.2 mg/L	No data available	10 mg/L
Urine			287 mg/L
Liver			83 mg/kg
Kidney			35 mg/kg
Brain			43 mg/kg
Stomach contents			1070 mg/L

Selected Sources

Bayley M, Walsh FM, and Valske MJ (1975), Report of a fatal, acute tripelennamine intoxication, *J For Sci*, 20(3): 539–43.

Yeh SY, Todd GD, Johnson RE, Gorodetzky CW, and Lange WR (1986), The pharmacokinetics of pentozocine and tripelennamine, *Clin Pharmacol Ther*, 39(6): 669–675.

Triprolidine

Brand names: Zymine, Actifed (w/ pseudoephedrine)
Classification: antihistamine
λ: 2–6 hrs
V_d: 6–9 L/kg
Usual dosage: 1.25–2.5 mg q 4–6 hrs

Source	Therapeutic/ Nontoxic	Toxic	Lethal
Blood	0.002–0.05 mg/L	No data available	

Selected Sources

DeAngelis RL, Kearney MF, and Welch RM (1977), Determination of triprolidine in human plasma by quantitative TLC, *J Pharm Sci*, 66(6): 841–3.

Miles MV, Balasubramanian R, Pittman AW, Grossman SH, Pappa KA, and Smith MF (1990), Pharmacokinetics of oral and transdermal triprolidine, *J Clin Pharmacol*, 30(6): 572–5.

Williams BO, Liao SH, Lai AA, Arnold JD, Perkins JG, and Blum MR (1984), Bioavailability of pseudoephedrine and triprolidine from combination and single-ingredient products, *Clin Pharm*, 3(6): 638–43.

Tubocurarine

Brand names: Delacurarine, Jexin, Tubarine
Classification: neuromuscular blocker
λ: 89–174 min
V_d: 0.3–0.7 L/kg
Usual dosage: 0.025–1 mg/kg/dose

Source	Therapeutic/ Nontoxic	Toxic	Lethal
Blood	0.18–1.2 mg/L	No data available	0.8 mg/L

Comments

- Therapeutic concentrations can be fatal if drug not administered in a monitored medical setting

Selected Sources

Fisher DM, O'Keeffe C, Stanski DR, Cronnelly R, Miller RD, and Gregory GA (1982), Pharmacokinetics and pharmacodynamics of d-tubocurarine in infants, children, and adults, *Anesthesiology*, 57(3): 203–8.

Stevens HM and Fox RH (1971), A method for detecting tubocurarine in tissues, *J For Sci Soc*, 11: 177–82.

Valproic Acid

Brand names: Depakene, Depacon, Depakote
Alternate names: valproate, divalproex, dipropylacetic acid
Classification: anticonvulsant
λ: 5–20 hrs
V_d: 0.1–0.4 L/kg
Usual dosage: 250–500 mg tid

Source	Therapeutic/ Nontoxic	Toxic	Lethal
Blood	50–100 mg/L	200–1440 mg/L	720–2204 mg/L
Vitreous			516–821 mg/L
Urine			150 mg/L
Bile			713–1360 mg/L
Liver			450–985 mg/kg
Kidney			1580 mg/kg
Brain			510–545 mg/kg
Skeletal muscle			482 mg/kg
Cardiac muscle			670 mg/kg
Stomach contents			15 g

Comments

- Metabolized by CYP 2C9 and 2C19

Selected Sources

Andersen GO and Ritland S (1995), Life threatening intoxication with sodium valproate, *J Tox Clin Tox*, 33(3): 279–84.
Bexar County Medical Examiner's Office data 1996–2007.
Christianson GS, Mowry JB, and Furbee RB (2001), Death associated with massive valproic acid ingestion, *J Tox Clin Tox*, 39: 498.
Flanagan RJ (1998), Guidelines for the interpretation of analytical toxicology results and unit of measurement conversion factors, *Ann Clin Biochem*, 35: 261–7.
Garnier R, Boudignat O, and Fournier PE (1982), Valproate poisoning, *Lancet*, 2: 97.
Graudins A and Aaron CK (1996), Delayed peak serum valproic acid in massive divalproex overdose—Treatment with charcoal hemoperfusion, *J Tox Clin Tox*, 34(3): 335–41.
Lee WL, Yang CC, Deng JF, Chen YF, Lin HD, and Wang PH (1998), A case of severe hyperammonemia and unconsciousness following sodium valproate intoxication, *Vet Hum Tox*, 40(6): 346–8.
Lokan RJ and Dinan AC (1988), An apparent fatal valproic acid poisoning, *J Anal Tox*, 12(1): 35–7.

Poklis A, Poklis JL, Trautman D, Treece C, Backer R, and Harvey CM (1998), Disposition of valproic acid in a case of fatal intoxication, *J Anal Tox*, 22(6): 537–40.

Sikma MA, Mier JC, and Meulenbelt J (2008), Massive valproic acid overdose, a misleading case, *Am J Emer Med*, 26(1): 110e3–6.

Wasserman GS, Aldridge SC, Kelly JC, and Abdel-Rahman SM (2001), A unique valproic acid ingestion, *J Tox Clin Tox*, 39(4): 419–22.

Vardenafil

Brand names: Levitra
Classification: phosphodiesterase inhibitor
λ: 4–5 hrs
V_d: 2–3 L/kg
Usual dosage: 2.5–20 mg qd

Source	Therapeutic/ Nontoxic	Toxic	Lethal
Blood	0.003–0.07 mg/L	No data available	
Bile	1.7 mg/L		
Liver	0.09 mg/kg		
Kidney	0.02 mg/kg		
Skeletal muscle	0.008 mg/kg		
Cardiac muscle	0.03 mg/kg		

Selected Sources

Johnson RD, Lewis RJ, and Angier MK (2007), The postmortem distribution of vardenafil (Levitra) in an aviation accident victim with an unusually high blood concentration, *J Anal Tox*, 31(6): 328–33.

Klotz T, Sachse R, Heidrich A, Jockenhövel F, Rohde G, and Wensing G (2001), Vardenafil increases penile rigidity and tumescence in erectile dysfunction patients: A rigiscan and pharmacokinetic study, *World J Urol*, 19(1): 32–9.

Mehrotra N, Gupta M, Kovar A, and Meibohm B (2007), The role of pharmacokinetics and pharmacodynamics in phosphodiesterase-5 inhibitor therapy, *Int J Impot Res*, 19(3): 253–64.

Vecuronium

Brand names: Norcuron
Classification: neuromuscular blocker
λ: 0.6–3 hrs
V_d: 0.1–0.7 L/kg
Usual dosage: 0.01–0.015 mg/kg/dose

Source	Therapeutic/ Nontoxic	Toxic	Lethal
Blood	0.06–1.1 mg/L	0.04–0.08 mg/L	0.2–0.7 mg/L

Comments

- Active metabolite: 3-desmethylvecuronium
- Therapeutic concentrations can be fatal if drug not administered in a monitored medical setting

Selected Sources

Segredo V, Caldwell JE, Matthay MA, Sharma ML, Gruenke LD, and Miller RD (1992), Persistent paralysis in critically ill patients after long-term administration of vecuronium, *NEJM*, 327(8): 524–8.

Segredo V, Matthay MA, Sharma ML, Gruenke LD, Caldwell JE, and Miller RD (1990), Prolonged neuromuscular blockade after long-term administration of vecuronium in two critically Ill patients, *Anesthesiology*, 72(3): 566–70.

Sohn YJ, Bencini AF, Scaf AH, Kersten UW, and Agoston S (1986), Comparative pharmacokinetics and dynamics of vecuronium and pancuronium in anesthetized patients, *Anesth Analg*, 65(3): 233–9.

Venlafaxine

Brand names: Effexor
Classification: antidepressant (SNRI)
λ: 2.5–15 hrs
V_d: 4–12 L/kg
Usual dosage: 25–100 mg bid/tid

Source	Therapeutic/ Nontoxic	Toxic	Lethal
Blood	0.05–0.2 mg/L	1.8–15 mg/L	6.5–90 mg/L
Vitreous			6.7–58 mg/L
Urine			9–143 mg/L
Bile			90–229 mg/L
Liver			81–425 mg/kg
Kidney			420 mg/kg
Brain			543 mg/kg
Stomach contents			10–800 mg

Comments

- Active metabolite: *O*-desmethylvenlafaxine
- Metabolized by CYP 2D6
- Prolongs QT interval

Selected Sources

Banham ND (1998), Fatal venlafaxine overdose, *Med J Australia*, 169(8): 445, 448.

Blythe D and Hackett LP (1999), Cardiovascular and neurological toxicity of venlafaxine, *Hum Exp Tox*, 18(5): 309–13.

Dahl B, Crouch BI, and Rollins D (1996), Death from venlafaxine overdose (Effexor), *Clin Tox*, 34: 557.

Fantaskey A and Burkhart KK (1995), A case report of venlafaxine toxicity, *J Tox Clin Tox*, 33(4): 359–61.

Jaffe PD, Batziris HP, van der Hoeven P, DeSilva D, and McIntyre IM (1999), A study involving venlafaxine overdoses: Comparison of fatal and therapeutic concentrations in postmortem specimens, *J For Sci*, 44(1): 193–6.

Koken L and Dart RC (1996), Life-threatening hypotension from venlafaxine overdose, *J Tox Clin Tox*, 34: 559.

Levine B, Jenkins AJ, Queen M, Jufer R, and Smialek JE (1996), Distribution of venlafaxine in three postmortem cases, *J Anal Tox*, 20(6): 502–5.

Long C, Crifasi J, Maginn D, Graham M, and Teas S (1997), Comparison of analytical methods in the determination of two venlafaxine fatalities, *J Anal Tox*, 21(2): 166–9.

Mazur JE, Doty JD, and Krygiel AS (2003), Fatality related to a 30-G venlafaxine overdose, *Pharmacotherapy*, 23(12): 1668–72.

Parsons AT, Anthony RM, and Meeker JE (1996), Two fatal cases of venlafaxine poisoning, *J Anal Tox*, 20(4): 266–8.

Troy SM, Parker VD, Fruncillo RJ, and Chiang ST (1995), The pharmacokinetics of venlafaxine when given in a twice-daily regimen, *J Clin Pharm*, 35(4): 404–9.

Woo OF, Vredenburg M, Freitas P, and Olson KR (1995), Seizures after venlafaxine overdose: A case report, *Clin Tox*, 33: 549–50.

Verapamil

Brand names: Calan
Classification: calcium channel blocker
λ: 2–14 hrs
V_d: 4.5–7 L/kg
Usual dosage: 40–120 mg tid/qid

Source	Therapeutic/ Nontoxic	Toxic	Lethal
Blood	0.03–0.4 mg/L	1.5–4 mg/L	1.5–85 mg/L
Urine			1.4 mg/L
Liver			2.4–258 mg/kg
Kidney			1.5–33 mg/kg
Stomach contents			1.2–1148 mg

Comments

- Active metabolite: norverapamil
- Metabolized by CYP 1A2 and 3A

Selected Sources

Batalis Nick I, Harley RA, and Schandl CA (2007), Verapamil toxicity: An unusual case report and review of the literature, *Am J For Med Path*, 28(2): 137–40.

Chan LF, Chiluy LH, and Crowley RJ (1987), Verapamil tissue concentrations in fatal cases, *J Anal Tox*, 11(4): 171–4.

Crouch DJ, Crompton C, Rollins DE, Peat MA, and Francom P (1986), Toxicological findings in a fatal overdose of verapamil, *J For Sci*, 31(4): 1505–8.

Gelbke HP, Schlicht HJ, and Schmidt G (1977), Fatal poisoning with verapamil, *Arch Tox*, 37(2): 89–94.

Kivistö KT, Neuvonen PJ, and Tarssanen L (1997), Pharmacokinetics of verapamil in overdose, *Hum Exp Tox*, 16(1): 35–7.

Koepke JF and McBay AJ (1987), Fatal verapamil poisoning, *J For Sci*, 32(5): 1431–4.

Oe H, Taniura T, and Ohgitani N (1998), A case of severe verapamil overdose, *Japanese Circ J*, 62(1): 72–6.

Perkins CM (1978), Serious verapamil poisoning: Treatment with intravenous calcium gluconate, *Br Med J*, 2: 1127.

Szekely LA, Thompson BT, and Woolf A (1999), Use of partial liquid ventilation to manage pulmonary complications of acute verapamil-sustained release poisoning, *J Tox Clin Tox*, 37(4): 475–9.

Thomson BM and Pannell LK (1981), The analysis of verapamil in postmortem specimens by HPLC and GC, *J Anal Tox*, 5(3): 105–9.

Wilimowska J, Piekoszewski W, Krzyanowska-Kierepka E, and Florek E (2006), Monitoring of verapamil enantiomers concentration in overdose, *Clin Tox*, 44(2): 169–71.

Woodcock BG, Hopf R, and Kaltenbach M (1980), Verapamil and norverapamil plasma concentrations during long-term therapy in patients with hypertrophic obstructive cardiomyopathy, *J Cardiovasc Pharmacol*, 2(1): 17–23.

Woodcock BG, Kraemer N, and Rietbrock N (1986), Effect of a high protein meal on the bioavailability of verapamil, *Br J Clin Pharmacol*, 21(3): 337–8.

Vigabatrin

Brand names: Sabril, Sabrilex
Classification: anticonvulsant
λ: 5–8 hrs
V_d: 0.8 L/kg
Usual dosage: 1–4 g/d

Source	Therapeutic/ Nontoxic	Toxic	Lethal[a]
Blood	15–43 mg/L	No data available	40–49 mg/L

[a] Fatality was due to hepatotoxicity

Selected Sources

Kellermann K, Soditt V, Rambeck B, and Klinge O (1996), Fatal hepatotoxicity in a child treated with vigabatrin, *Acta Neurologica Scandinavica*, 93(5): 380–1.

Rey E, Pons G, and Olive G (1992), Vigabatrin: Clinical pharmacokinetics, *Clin Pharmacokinet*, 23(4): 267–78.

Wafarin

Brand names: Coumadin
Classification: anticoagulant
λ: 20–70 hrs
V_d: 0.1–0.2 L/kg
Usual dosage: 1–10 mg qd

Source	Therapeutic/ Nontoxic	Toxic	Lethal[a]
Blood	0.72–2.35 mg/L	> 10 mg/L[a]	

[a] Toxicity/lethality results from bleeding diatheses

Comments

- Metabolized by CYP 2C9, 2C19, 2C8, 2C18, 1A2, and 3A4
- Toxicity can be diagnosed by prothrombin time

Selected Sources

Midha KK, McGilveray IJ, and Cooper JK (1974), GLC determination of plasma levels of warfarin, *J Pharm Sci*, 63(11): 1725–9.
Orme M, Breckenridge A, and Brooks RV (1972), Interactions of benzodiazepines with warfarin, *Br Med J*, 3(5827): 611–4.

Xylene

Brand names: component of paints, pesticides, gasoline, cleaning chemicals
Alternate names: dimethylbenzene
Classification: volatile
λ: 14–55 hrs
V_d: 5.3–28 L/kg
Usual dosage: not applicable

Source	Therapeutic/ Nontoxic	Toxic	Lethal
Blood	0.0001–1.4 mg/L	3.2–12 mg/L	4.9–110 mg/L
Liver			3.6–29 mg/kg
Brain			6.1–19 mg/kg
Cardiac muscle			12 mg/kg
Adipose tissue			7.1 mg/kg
Stomach contents			495–8800 mg/kg

Comments

- Cardiotoxic: intoxication associated with arrhythmias
- Composed of three isomers: ortho-xylene, meta-xylene, and para-xylene
- Metabolized to methylhippuric acid (MHA)

Selected Sources

Abu Al Ragheb S, Salhab AS, and Amr SS (1986), Suicide by xylene ingestion: A case report and review of literature, *Am J For Med Path*, 7(4): 327–9.
Adams JC, Dills RL, Morgan MS, Kalman DA, and Pierce CH (2005), A physiologically based toxicokinetic model of inhalation exposure to xylenes in Caucasian men, *Regulatory Toxicol Pharmacol*, 43(2): 203–14.
Hajimiragha H, Ewers U, Brockhaus A, and Boettger A (1989), Levels of benzene and other volatile aromatic compounds in the blood of non-smokers and smokers, *Int Arch Occup Environ Health*, 62(1): 513–6.
Harada K, Ichiyama T, Ikeda H, and Yoshida K (1999), A fatal case of oral ingestion of benzene, *Am J For Med Path*, 20(1): 84–9.
Krämer A, Linnert M, Wrbitzky R, and Angerer J (1999), Occupational chronic exposure to organic solvents XVII. Ambient and biological monitoring of workers exposed to xylenes, *Int Arch Occup Environ Health*, 72(1): 52–5.

Musshoff F, Padosch SA, Kroener LA, and Madea B (2006), Accidental autoerotic death by volatile substance abuse or nonsexually motivated accidents? *Am J For Med Path*, 27(2): 188–92.

Savolainen K, Riihimäki V, Seppäläinen AM, and Linnoila M (1980), Effects of short-term m-xylene exposure and physical exercise on the central nervous system, *Intl Arch Occup Environ Health*, 45(2): 105–21.

Stephens BG (2004), Chapter XXII, Investigation of deaths from drug abuse, in *Spitz and Fisher's Medicolegal Investigation of Death Fourth Edition*, Spitz WU (Ed.), Charles C Thomas, Springfield, IL, pp. 1166–217.

Yohimbine

Brand names: Aphrodyne, Yocon, Viritab, Yohimex
Classification: α-adrenergic blocker
λ: 0.7–3 hrs
V_d: 0.3–1.8 L/kg
Usual dosage: 5.4 mg tid

Source	Therapeutic/ Nontoxic	Toxic	Lethal
Blood	0.003–0.27 mg/L	No data available	

Comments

- Active metabolite: 11-OH-yohimbine

Selected Sources

Le Corre P, Dollo G, Chevanne F, and Le Verge R (1999), Biopharmaceutics and metabolism of yohimbine in humans, *Eur J Pharma Sci*, 9(1): 79–84.
Varkey S (1992), Overdose of yohimbine, *Br Med J*, 304(6826): 548.

Zaleplon

Brand names: Sonata
Classification: sedative/hypnotic
λ: 0.9–1.3 hrs
V_d: 1–1.5 hrs
Usual dosage: 5–20 mg qHS

Source	Therapeutic/ Nontoxic	Toxic	Lethal[a]
Blood	0.01–0.08 mg/L	No data available	2.2 mg/L
Urine			1.4 mg/L
Bile			8.6 mg/L

[a] Co-intoxicants promethazine (0.8 mg/L) and butalbital (9.9 mg/L)

Comments

- Metabolized by CYP 3A

Selected Sources

Drover D, Lemmens H, Naidu S, Cevallos W, Darwish M, and Stanski D (2000), Pharmacokinetics, pharmacodynamics, and relative pharmacokinetic/pharmacodynamic profiles of zaleplon and zolpidem, *Clin Ther*, 22(12): 1443–61.

Moore KA, Zemrus TL, Ramcharitar V, Levine B, and Fowler DR (2003), Mixed drug intoxication involving zaleplon ("Sonata"), *For Sci Intl*, 134(2–3): 120–2.

Rosen AS, Fournié P, Darwish M, Danjou P, and Troy SM (1999), Zaleplon pharmacokinetics and absolute bioavailability, *Biopharm Drug Dispos*, 20(3): 171–5.

Zipeprol

Brand names: Respilene, Santus, Mirsol, Bronx
Classification: cough suppressant
λ: 4.5–5.5 hrs
V_d: unknown
Usual dosage: 50–350 mg/dose

Source	Therapeutic/ Nontoxic	Toxic	Lethal
Blood	0.1–0.76 mg/L	No data available	2.3–31 mg/L
Vitreous			6.1 mg/L
Urine			16–628 mg/L
Bile			9.5–56 mg/L
Liver			4.6–122 mg/kg
Kidney			3.2–44 mg/kg
Brain			2.5–53 mg/kg
Cardiac muscle			4.8–48 mg/kg
Stomach contents			60–126 mg/kg

Selected Sources

Beckett AH and Achari R (1977), Plasma concentrations and excretion of zipeprol in man under acidic urine conditions, *J Pharm Pharmacol*, 29(10): 589–92.
Crippa O, Polettini A, and Avato FM (1990), Lethal poisoning by zipeprol in drug addicts, *J For Sci*, 35(4): 992–9.
Kintz P, Cirimele V, Tracqui A, and Mangin P (1995), Fatal zipeprol intoxication, *Int J Legal Med*, 107(5): 267–8.
Kintz P, Flesch F, Jaeger A, and Mangin P (1993), GC-MS procedure for the analysis of zipeprol, *J Pharm Biomed Anal*, 11(4–5): 335–8.
Kintz P, Tracqui A, Potard D, Petit G, and Mangin P (1994), An unusual death by zipeprol overdose, *For Sci Intl*, 64(2–3): 159–63.
Yoo Y, Chung H, Kim E, and Kim M (1994), Postmortem distribution of zipeprol, *J Anal Tox*, 18(4): 213–6.

Ziprasidone

Brand names: Geodon
Classification: antipsychotic
λ: 3.1–7 hrs
V_d: 1.1–1.5 L/kg
Usual dosage: 20–80 mg bid

Source	Therapeutic/ Nontoxic	Toxic	Lethal[a]
Blood	0.02–0.1 mg/L	No data available	5.7 mg/L[a]

[a] Co-intoxicants (BAC 0.16%, venlafaxine 120 mg/L, zolpidem 0.08 mg/L)

Comments

- Prolongs QT interval

Selected Sources

Roman M, Kronstrand R, Lindstedt D, and Josefsson M (2008), Quantitation of seven low-dosage antipsychotic drugs in human postmortem blood using LC-MS-MS, *J Anal Tox*, 32(2): 147–55.

Wilner KD, Tensfeldt TG, Baris B, Smolarek TA, Turncliff RZ, and Colburn WA (2000), Single- and multiple-dose pharmacokinetics of ziprasidone in healthy young and elderly volunteers, *Br J Clin Pharmacol*, 49(Suppl. 1): 15S–20S.

Zolpidem

Brand names: Ambien
Classification: sedative/hypnotic
λ: 1.5–5 hrs
V_d: 0.6–1.0 L/kg
Usual dosage: 5–10 mg qHS

Source	Therapeutic/ Nontoxic	Toxic	Lethal
Blood	0.08–0.2 mg/L	0.12–0.7 mg/L	1.6–7.7 mg/L
Vitreous			0.5–1.6 mg/L
Urine			1.2 mg/L
Bile			2.6–8.9 mg/L
Liver			12–23 mg/kg
Stomach contents			0.9–42 mg

Comments

- Metabolized by CYP 3A4

Selected Sources

Drover D, Lemmens H, Naidu S, Cevallos W, Darwish M, and Stanski D (2000), Pharmacokinetics, pharmacodynamics, and relative pharmacokinetic/pharmacodynamic profiles of zaleplon and zolpidem, *Clin Ther*, 22(12): 1443–61

Druid H and Holmgren P (1997), A compilation of fatal and control concentrations of drugs in postmortem femoral blood, *J For Sci*, 42(1):79–87.

Gock SB, Wong SH, Nuwayhid N, Venuti SE, Kelley PD, and Teggatz JR (1999), Acute zolpidem overdose—Report of two cases, *J Anal Tox*, 23(6): 559–62.

Jönsson A, Holmgren P, and Ahlner J (2004), Fatal intoxications in a Swedish forensic autopsy material during 1992–2002, *For Sci Intl*, 143(1): 53–9.

Keller T, Schneider A, and Tutsch-Bauer E (1999), GC/MS determination of zolpidem in postmortem specimens in a voluntary intoxication, *For Sci Intl*, 106(2): 103–8.

Lheureux P, Debailleul G, De Witte O, and Askenasi R (1990), Zolpidem intoxication mimicking narcotic overdose: Response to flumazenil, *Hum Exp Tox*, 9(2): 105–7.

Winek CL, Wahba WW, Janssen JK, Rozin L, Rafizadeh V (1996), Acute overdose of zolpidem, *For Sci Intl*, 78(3): 165–8.

Zonisamide

Brand names: Zonegran
Classification: anticonvulsant
λ: 49–77 hrs
V_d: 0.9–1.8 L/kg
Usual dosage: 25–200 mg bid/qd

Source	Therapeutic/ Nontoxic	Toxic	Lethal
Blood	2.3–30 mg/L	40–100 mg/L	44 mg/L

Comments

- Metabolized by CYP 3A4

Selected Sources

Frampton JE and Scott LJ (2005), Zonisamide: A review of its use in the management of partial seizures in epilepsy, *CNS Drugs*, 19(4): 347–67.

Kochak GM, Page JG, Buchanan RA, Peters R, and Padgett CS (1998), Steady-state pharmacokinetics of zonisamide, an antiepileptic agent for treatment of refractory complex partial seizures, *J Clin Pharm*, 38(2): 166–71.

Physicians' Desk Reference 60 Edition (2006), Thomson PDR, Montvale, NJ, pp. 1089–92.

Sztajnkrycer MD, Huang EE, and Bond GR (2003), Acute zonisamide overdose: A death revisited, *Vet Hum Tox*, 45(3): 154–6.

Zopiclone

Brand names: Imovane, Zimovane, Lunesta (eszopiclone)
Classification: sedative/hypnotic
λ: 3.5–8 hrs
V_d: 1.3–1.9 L/kg
Usual dosage: 3.75–7.5 mg qHS

Source	Therapeutic/ Nontoxic	Toxic	Lethal
Blood	0.02–0.05 mg/L	0.07–1.6 mg/L	0.6–4.1 mg/L
Vitreous			94 mg/L
Urine			7.3–10 mg/L
Bile			14–115 mg/L
Liver			0.5–8.7 mg/kg
Kidney			1.7 mg/kg
Brain			2.8 mg/kg
Skeletal muscle			1.9–3.3 mg/kg
Cardiac muscle			1.6 mg/kg
Stomach contents			13–133 mg

Comments

- Most laboratories cannot differentiate between zopiclone and eszopiclone

Selected Sources

Boniface PJ and Russell SG (1996), Two cases of fatal zopiclone overdose, *J Anal Tox*, 20(2): 131–3.

Bramness JG, Arnestad M, Karinen R, and Hilberg T (2001), Fatal overdose of zopiclone in an elderly woman with bronchogenic carcinoma, *J For Sci*, 46(5): 1247–9.

Cienki JJ, Burkhart KK, and Donovan JW (2005), Zopiclone overdose responsive to flumazenil, *Clin Tox*, 43(5): 385–6.

Drover DR (2004), Comparative pharmacokinetics and pharmacodynamics of short-acting hypnosedatives: Zaleplon, zolpidem and zopiclone, *Clin Pharmacokinet*, 43(4): 227–38.

Druid H and Holmgren P (1997), A compilation of fatal and control concentrations of drugs in postmortem femoral blood, *J For Sci*, 42(1): 79–87.

Fernandez C, Martin C, Gimenez F, and Farinotti R (1995), Clinical pharmacokinetics of zopiclone, *Clin Pharmacokinet*, 29(6): 431–41.

Meatherall RC (1997), Zopiclone fatality in a hospitalized patient, *J For Sci*, 42(2): 340–3.

Pounder DJ and Davies JI (1994), Zopiclone poisoning: Tissue distribution and potential for postmortem diffusion, *For Sci Intl*, 65(3): 177–83.

Royer-Morrot MJ, Rambourg M, Jacob I, Bauer P, and Royer RJ (1992), Determination of zopiclone in plasma using column liquid chromatography with ultraviolet detection, *J Chromatogr A*, 581(2): 297–9.

Zuclopenthixol

Brand names: Clopixol, Cisordinol, Ciatyl-Z
Classification: antipsychotic
λ: 12–30 hrs
V_d: 15–20 L/kg
Usual dosage: 10–20 mg bid

Source	Therapeutic/ Nontoxic	Toxic	Lethal
Blood	0.005–0.1 mg/L	0.15–0.3 mg/L	0.4–0.9 mg/L
Urine			0.96 mg/L
Liver			0.75 mg/kg
Kidney			1.4 mg/kg
Brain			0.12 mg/kg
Stomach contents			105 mg/L

Comments

- Metabolized by CYP 2D6

Selected Sources

Jerling M, Dahl ML, Aberg-Wistedt A, Liljenberg B, Landell NE, and Bertilsson L (1996), The CYP2D6 genotype predicts the oral clearance of the neuroleptic agents perphenazine and zuclopenthixol, *Clin Pharmacol Ther*, 59(4): 423–8.

Kollroser M, Henning G, Gatternig R, and Schober C (2001), HPLC-ESI-MS/MS determination of zuclopenthixol in a fatal intoxication during psychiatric therapy, *For Sci Intl*, 123(2–3): 243–7.

Kratzsch C, Peters FT, Kraemer T, Weber AA, and Maurer HH (2003), Screening, library-assisted identification and validated quantification of fifteen neuroleptics and three of their metabolites in plasma by liquid chromatography/mass spectrometry with atmospheric pressure chemical ionization, *J Mass Spectrum*, 38(3): 283–95.

Linnet K (1997), An evaluation of linearity of kinetics for the neuroleptics perphenazine and zuclopenthixol, *Eur J Clin Pharm*, 52(4): 317–8.

Schulz M and Schmoldt A (2003), Therapeutic and toxic blood concentrations of more than 800 drugs and other xenobiotics, *Pharmazie*, 58(7): 447–74.

Tracqui A, Kintz P, Cirimele V, Berthault F, P Mangin P, and Ludes B (1997), HPLC-DAD and HPLC-MS findings in fatality involving (Z)-Cis-clopenthixol (zuclopenthixol), *J Anal Tox*, 21(4): 314–8.

Appendix A

Common Acetylcholinesterase Inhibitors

- Can be used to treat Alzheimer's disease and myasthenia gravis
- Commonly used as pesticides/herbicides
- Toxicity measured by percentage of acetylcholinesterase (ACh) activity
    - Testing utilizes RBC ACh as it better reflects neural ACh activity
    - Toxicity begins at 20% below the level of normal activity (80% activity level), pronounced by 50%
    - Severe toxicity/death occurs at 90% suppression (10% of normal activity)

Drugs

Alzheimer's Disease	Myasthenia Gravis	Glaucoma
Donezepil (Aricept)	Physostigmine (Antilirium)	Demarcarium (Humorsol)
Tacrine (Cognez)	Neostigmine (Prostigmin)	Echothiophate (Phopholine Iodide)
Metrifonate	Pyridostigmine (Mestinon, Regonol)	
Rivastigmine (Elexon)	Ambenonium (Mytelase)	
Huperzine A	Edrophonium (Tensilon, Enlon, Reversol)	
Galantamine (Razadyne, Reminyl, Nivalin)		

Nerve Agents

Cyclosarin	Soman	VX	VG
Sarin	Tabun	VE	VM

Insecticides/Pesticides

Acephate (Orthene)	Dimethoate (Cygon, De-Fend)	Methomyl (Lannate, Nudrin)
Aldicarb (Temik)	Dioxathion (Delnav)	Methylparathiomevinphos (Phosdrin)
Azinphos-methyl (Guthion)	Disulfoton (Di-Syston)	Monocrotophos naled (Dibrom)
Bendiocarb (Ficam)	Ethiofencarb	Oxamyl (Vydate)
Bufencarb	Ethion	Oxydemeton-methyl
Carbaryl (Sevin)	Ethoprop (Mocap)	Parathion (Niran, Phoskil)
Carbofuran (Furadan)	Famphur	Phorate (Thimet)
Carbophenothion (Trithion)	Fenamiphos (Nemacur)	Phosalone (Zolonc)
Chlorfenvinphos (Birlane)	Fenitrothion (Sumithion)	Phosmet (Irnidan, Prolate)
Chlorpyrifos (Dursban, Lorsban)	Fensulfothion (Dasanit)	Phosphamidon (Dimecron)
Coumaphos (Co-Ral)	Fenthion (Baytex, Tiguvon)	Pinmicarb (Pirimor)
Crotoxyphos (Ciodrin, Ciovap)	Fonofos (Dyfonate)	Propoxur (Baygon)
Crufomate (Ruelene)	Formetanate (Carzol)	Temephos (Abate)
Demeton (Systox)	Isofenfos (Oftanol, Amaze)	Terbufos (Counter)
Diazinon (Spectracide)	Malathion (Cythion)	Tetrachlorvinphos (Rabon)
Dichlorvos (DDVP, Vapona)	Methamidophos (Monitor)	Trichlorfon (Dylox, Neguvon)
Dicrotophos (Bidrin)	Methidathion (Supracide)	
Diisopropyl fluorophosphate (Dyflos)	Methiocarb (Mesurol)	

Selected Sources

Worek F, Koller M, Thiermann H, and Szinicz L (2005), Diagnostic aspects of organophosphate poisoning, *Toxicology*, 214(3): 182–9.

EXTOXNET (Extension Toxicology Network), Cholinesterase inhibition, accessed at http://extoxnet.orst.edu/tibs/cholines.htm on June 1, 2008.

Appendix B

Drugs That Prolong the QT Interval

The QT interval is defined as the time it takes for the ventricular conduction system to depolarize then repolarize. Using the electrocardiogram, the QT interval is defined as the duration from the beginning of the QRS complex to the end of the t-wave. Normally, this interval is approximately 420 msec. The definition of a prolonged QT interval ranges from an absolute interval of 450 to 500 msec, or an increase of 30 to 60 msec over the baseline.

If the QT interval is prolonged, as can occur in several genetic conditions or with certain medications, an environment ripe for cardiac arrhythmias is created. Usually, the abnormal rhythm is *torsades de pointes*, although a prolonged QT interval can also lead to ventricular tachycardia and/or ventricular fibrillation or flutter. Symptoms can include syncope, dizziness, seizures, and even sudden death.

Certain prescription drugs may prolong the QT interval. In the setting of a normal individual, this prolongation may not cause symptoms or rhythm disturbances; however, in the presence of an inherited prolongation or additional stress or physical exertion, this prolongation may cause rhythm disturbances creating symptoms or even death. Thus, it is important know which drugs are associated with a prolongation of the QT interval when evaluating the circumstances and cause of death. Many of the drugs which affect the QT interval are cardiac medications designed to cause or correct rhythm abnormalities, while others are commonly prescribed antibiotics and pain medications.

Category	Drugs	Category	Drugs
Cardiac	Amiodarone Bepridil Bretylium Disopyramide Dofetilide Flecainide Ibutilide Isradipine Mexiletine Moexipril Nicarpine Procainamide Propafenone Quinidine Sotalol	Antibiotic/ antimalarial/ antifungal	Amantadine Azithromycin Chloroquine Ciprofloxacin Clarithromycin Erythromycin Fluconazole Foscarnet Gatifloxacin Halofantrine Ketoconazole Levofloxacin Moxifloxacin Ofloxacin Pentamidine Quinine Sparfloxacin Trimethopromsulfa Voriconazole
Antihistamine	Azelastine Desloratadine Diphenhydramine Hydroxyzine	Migraine serotonin agonists	Naratriptan Sumatriptan Zolmitriptan
Cancer	Arsenic trioxide Tacrolimus Tamoxifen	Gastro-intestinal	Cisapride Domperidone Droperidol Ondansetron
Anticonvulsant	Felbamate Fosphenytoin	Analgesics/muscle relaxants	Levomethadyl Methadone Tizanidine

Category	Drugs	Category	Drugs
Psychiatric (antidepressants, antipsychotics)	Amitriptyline Amoxapine Atomoxetine Chlorpromazine Citalopram Clomipramine Clozapine Desipramine Doxepin Escitalopram Fluoxetine Fluphenazine Haloperidol Imipramine Maprotiline Mesoridazine Mianserin Nortriptyline Paroxetine Pimozide Prochlorperazine Quetiapine Risperidone Sertindole Sertraline Thioridazine Trazodone Trifluoperazine Trimipramine Venlafaxine Ziprasidone	Other	Indapamide (diuretic) Octreotide (endocrine) Salmeterol (asthma) Vasopressin

Appendix C

Pharmacogenetics

In the late 1950s, it was discovered that individuals with an inherited deficiency of glucose-6-phosphate dehydrogenase would develop severe hemolysis when administered certain drugs, most notably the antimalarial drug primiquine. This observation led to the realization that besides environmental and physiological differences, people may respond differently to drugs based on their own genetic profile. Genetics plays a role in how an individual absorbs, distributes and metabolizes a drug. It is estimated that genetic differences may account for 15%–30%, or even 95% depending upon the drug, of the differences in how individuals metabolize/respond to drugs. In fact, drug concentrations can vary by a factor of 600 between two physically similar individuals given the same dosage.

The majority of these genetic differences seem to affect the drug metabolizing enzymes, although some can affect drug transport or result in receptor polymorphism affecting drug response. A mutation in a drug metabolizing enzyme can lead to accumulation of a drug and toxicity, which may have forensic implications. Approximately 30% of all drugs are affected by a drug-metabolizing enzyme, the majority of which enzymes are part of the CYP450 system.

The CYP450 system refers to cytochrome enzymes (CY), which are pigmented (P) at 450 nm. They are each labeled with a number (denoting gene family) followed by a letter (denoting subfamily) and a second number that indicates the individual gene (i.e., CYP2D6). An asterisk followed by a numeral denotes a specific allele (i.e., CYP2D6*8). More than 50 CYP isoenzymes have been identified. Four CYP enzymes account for the majority of the drugs metabolized by the CYP system: CYP2C9, CYP2C19, CYP2D6, and CYP3A4.

A mutation of an enzyme in the CYP450 system, or any drug metabolizing enzyme, can lead to variation in how an individual metabolizes a drug. The interindividual differences have been denoted as EM (extensive metabolizers), UM (ultra-extensive metabolizers), PM (poor metabolizers), and IM (intermediate metabolizers). The "wild-type" or "normal" metabolizers are denoted by EM. UM individuals have increased enzyme activity, leading to the decreased drug concentrations at standard doses, while IM individuals have decreased enzyme activity, leading to the increased drug concentrations at standard doses. PM individuals have little to no enzyme activity, leading to an inability to breakdown certain drugs and allowing for the possibility of toxicity.

Drug classes that are known to be metabolized by the CYP system include opioids, antidepressants, anxiolytics, antipsychotics, and anticonvulsants, encompassing a great many drugs seen in the forensic setting. Since genetic factors and metabolizer status may have forensic implications, the following chart was created listing those drugs that are known to be metabolized by a certain enzyme and those that are known to inhibit the same enzyme. The chart is by no means complete but encompasses most of the drugs reviewed within these pages.

Enzyme	Drugs Metabolized by Enzyme	Drugs that Inhibit Enzyme	Enzyme	Drugs Metabolized by Enzyme	Drugs that Inhibit Enzyme
CYP 1A2	Acetaminophen Amitriptyline Caffeine Clomipramine Clozapine Cyclobenzaprine Duloxetine Fluvoxamine Haloperidol Imipramine Lidocaine Methadone Mirtazapine Moclobemide Naproxen Olanzapine Ondansetron Propanolol Theophylline Verapamil Warfarin	Amiodarone Ciprofloxacin Cimetidine Echinacea Enoxacin Estradiol Floro-quinolones Furafylline Interferon Isoniazid Methoxsalen Mibefradil Zileuton	CYP 2C19	Amitryptyline Carisoprodol Citalopram Clomipramine Diazepam Doxepin Fluoxetine Imipramine Phenobarbital Phenytoin Propranolol Quinine Sertraline Valproic acid Warfarin	Cimetidine Estradiol Felbamate Fluvoxamine Indomethacin Ketoconazole Lansoprazole Miconazole Modafinil Omeprazole Oral contraceptives Oxcarbazepine Probenecid Ritonavir Ticlopidine Topiramate
CYP 2B6	Bupropion Meperidine Methadone Nicotine Sertraline	Paroxetine Fluoxetine Fluvoxamine Estradiol Ritonavir Ticlopidine	CYP 2C8	Ibuprofen Phenytoin Warfarin	Isoniazid Itraconazole Ketoconazole
CYP 2C9	Fluoxetine Ibuprofen Naproxen Phenobarbital Phenytoin Sertraline Sildenafil Tetrahydro-cannabinol Valproic acid Warfarin		CYP 2E1	Amiodarone Cimetidine Fenfibrate Fluconazole Fluvoxamine Fluvastatin Isoniazid Lansoprazole Lovastatin Miconazole Phentlbutzone Ritonavir Sulfamethazole Sulfaphenzole Teniposide Trimethoprim Voriconazole	Isoniazid Disulfiram

Enzyme	Drugs Metabolized by Enzyme	Drugs that Inhibit Enzyme
CYP 2D6	Amitriptyline	Amiodarone
	Amphetamine	Bupropion
	Aripiprazole	Celecoxib
	Atomoxetine	Chlorpheniramine
	Benztropine	Cimetidine
	Chlorpromazine	Chloroquine
	Citalopram	Cocaine
	Clomipramine	Doxorubicin
	Clozapine	Fluoxetine
	Codeine	Levomepromazine
	Desipramine	Paroxetine
	Dexfenfluramine	Pimozide
	Dextromethorphan	Quinidine
	Diphenhydramine	Ranitidine
	Donepezil	Ritonavir
	Doxepin	Terbinafine
	Duloxetine	
	Fluvoxamine	
	Haloperidol	
	Hydrocodone	
	Hydroxyzine	
	Ibogaine	
	Imipramine	
	Loratadine	
	MDMA	
	Methadone	
	Metoprolol	
	Mirtazapine	
	Moclobemide	
	Nortriptyline	
	Ondansetron	
	Perphenazine	
	Propranolol	
	Risperidone	
	Sertindole	
	Thioridazine	
	Tramadol	
	Venlafaxine	
	Zuclopenthixol	
CYP 3A	Alprazolam	Cimetidine
	Amitryptyline	Ciprofloxacin
	Aripiprazole	Clarithromycin
	Buprenorphine	Delavirdine
	Carbamazepine	Doxycycline
	Citalopram	Echinacea
	Clomipramine	Enoxacin
	Clozapine	Ethinyl estradiol
	Cocaine	Fluvoxamine
	Desloratadine	Grapefruit juice
	Diazepam	Indinavir
	Diltiazem	Isoniazid
	Donepezil	Itraconazole
	Estazolam	Ketoconazole
	Felbamate	Nelfinavir
	Fentanyl	Prednisone
	Fluoxetine	Ritonavir
	Haloperidol	Saquinavir
	Ketamine	
	Lidocaine	
	Loratadine	
	Methadone	
	Midazolam	
	Nefazodone	
	Nifedipine	
	Ondansetron	
	Quetiapine	
	Quinidine	
	Quinine	
	Risperidone	
	Scopolamine	
	Sertindole	
	Sildenafil	
	Tiagabine	
	Trazodone	
	Triazolam	
	Verapamil	
	Warfarin	
	Zaleplon	
	Zolpidem	
	Zonisamide	

Selected Sources

Eichelbaum M, Ingelman-Sundberg M, and Evans WE (2006), Pharmacogenomics and individualized drug therapy, *Annu Rev Med*, 57: 119–37.

Kupiec T and Raj V (2007), Pharmacogenomics—Basics and Applications, presented at the 59th Annual American Academy of Forensic Sciences Meeting, San Antonio, TX, February 19, 2007.

Appendix D

Normal Laboratory Values

Blood

Cell counts	
WBC	$4.1–10.9 \times 10^3/\mu L$
Hb	13.2–17.2 g/dL male; 12.0–15.2 g/dL female
Hct	40%–52% male; 37%–48% female
Plt	$140–450 \times 10^3/\mu L$
PT/pTT	12–14 sec/18–28 sec
Electrolytes	
Ca	8.5–10.5 mg/dL
Cl	98–108 mEq/L
K	3.5–5 mEq/L
Na	135–145 mEq/L
Liver	
NH_4	12–55 μmol/L
Bilirubin (total)	0.2–1.3 mg/dL
AST/ALT	5–35 U/L/7–56 U/L
GGT	8–78 U/L
Renal	
BUN	7–21 mg/dL
Cr	0.6–1.5 mg/dL
Glucose	65–110 mg/dL
Blood Gases	
pH	7.35–7.45
pCO2	35–45 mmHg
pO2	75–100 mmHg

Cardiac	
CPK (total)	38–120 ng/mL
Troponin	<0.4 ng/mL

Enzymes	
Amylase	30–110 U/L
Lipase	7–60 U/L
Alk Phos	38–126 U/L

Vitreous

K	3.5–10 mEq/L (levels >15 mEq/L indicate decomposition)
Na	130–155 mEq/L
Cl	105–135 mEq/L
Ca	6–8.4 mg/dL
Urea	7–30 mg/dL
Cr	<1.5 μg/L
Glucose	<60 mg/mL (or ½ serum level)

Note: After death, potassium levels increase, while sodium and chloride levels decrease.

Appendix E

Conversion Chart

Metric Units

m = milli = 10^{-3}
μ = micro = 10^{-6}
n = nano = 10^{-9}
p = pico = 10^{-12}
k = kilo = 10^{3}
d = deci = 10^{-1}

Conversions

Volume

1 L = 1000 mL = 1000 cc
30 mL = 1 fluid ounce

Weight

65 mg = 1 grain
28.35 grain = 1 oz
1 kg = 2.2 lbs

Length

1 mm = 0.04 inch
1 cm = 0.4 inch
2.54 cm = 1 inch
1 meter = 39.37 inches

Temperature

°F = (°C = –32) x 0.555
°C = °F × 1.8 + 32

Concentration

μg/mL = mg/L
μg/g = mg/kg
μg/L = ng/mL

Index

A

B

C

D

I

J

K

L

M

N

O

T

U

V

W

X

Y

Z